Cardinal Mazarin smiled, holding out his hands, as if to convey the expectation that such things would happen only on the correct meridian.

—Umberto Eco
The Island of the Day Before

THE CHACO MERIDIAN

CENTERS OF POLITICAL POWER IN THE ANCIENT SOUTHWEST

Stephen H. Lekson

ALTAMIRA
PRESS

A Division of Sage Publications, Inc.
Walnut Creek • London • New Delhi

For information address:

AltaMira Press
A Division of Sage Publications, Inc.
1630 North Main Street, Suite 367
Walnut Creek, California 94596
explore@altamira.sagepub.com
www.altamirapress.com

SAGE Publications, Ltd.   SAGE Publications India Pvt. Ltd.
6 Bonhill Street   M-32 Market
London EC2A 4PU   Greater Kailash 1
United Kingdom   New Delhi 110 048 India

PRINTED IN THE UNITED STATES OF AMERICA

99 00 01 02 03 04 05 06 07   8 7 6 5 4 3 2 1

Library of Congress Cataloging-in-Publication Data

Lekson, Stephen H.
   The Chaco meridian : centers of political power in the ancient
Southwest / Stephen H. Lekson.
     p. cm.
  Includes bibliographical references and index.
   ISBN 0-7619-9180-8 (cloth)
   ISBN 0-7619-9181-6 (pbk.)
   1. Pueblo Indians—Antiquities. 2. Pueblo Indians—Politics and government. 3. Pueblo
roads. 4. Mimbres culture. 5. Chaco Culture National Historical Park (N.M.) 6. Aztec
Ruins National Monument (N.M.) 7. Casas Grandes Site (Mex.) I. Title.
   E99.P9 L44 1998
   320.9789'82--dc21   98-40239
                                             CIP

Production and Editorial Services: Pattie Rechtman
Cover Design: Joanna Ebenstein
Cover Photo: Val Brinkerhof

For Alden C. Hayes,
who noticed the meridian years ago,
and for J. Charles Kelley, who warned me about Culiacán.

Contents

FIGURES

Acknowledgments, Apologies

When the thought first came to him, Farmer Hoggett dismissed it as mere whimsey. . . but, like most of his hare-brained ideas, it wouldn't go away.

—*Babe*

This book is a rip-off: it's other peoples' work. Charles Di Peso advanced the idea of Paquime-Chaco connections twenty years ago; John Stein, Jim Judge, and others nominated Aztec as Chaco's successor; Mike Marshall, Anna Sofaer, and others recorded the North Road; Peter McKenna and Tom Windes got hundreds of new dates (and new data) from Aztec; Jeff Dean and John Ravesloot put Paquime in its chronological place; Pueblo people passed their histories down through the generations; God made north. I just put it all together.

Illumination came while I was defacing a page of the *National Atlas,* adding Paquime's location to the margin of the "Arizona and New Mexico" sheet. The margin was, of course, blank white; I needed Paquime's coordinates to plot my dot. When I scaled out the latitude and longitude, I noticed some alarming geography: the plotted dot was hot, potentially important, and (mildly) dangerous, professionally. After several months of cold feet, I decided to plunge in: just another dent, after all, in my junkyard reputation.

Something this dicey—for let me be frank: This argument skates the thin ice of a globally warm and fuzzy New Age—needed special treatment. There is the *Science* strategy: Keep it close to the vest until the truth is revealed (presto!) like a new car at an auto show. But this argument, unlike a shiny new Dodge, is not immediately compelling. It's complicated, it grows on you—or, at least, it grew on me. So I decided on Plan B: market saturation. I presented innumerable papers and posters; preached to meetings and chapters; invited myself to universities and museums; published in newspapers and magazines; corrupted graduate students. I sent out early drafts to a select list of Southwestern archaeologists. Most, understandably, did not respond; but two-pound manuscripts are impossible to ignore. I spent a small fortune in photocopies and postage, not so much fishing for converts as beating the bushes.

Like Holmes's giant rat of Sumatra, this was a story for which the world is not yet prepared. I tried to prime my audience, to dull the sharp edge of reaction and yet whet the appetite. There's more than one way to make a case. *Science* works for quantitative hard-science blockbusters; complicated semi-historical semi-anthropological diatribes require a different approach.

My arguments received polite interest at professional meetings (actually, a poster version won the "best of show" award at an SAA meeting, a fact of which I am inordinately proud). I sensed a reaction among my colleagues much like that which greeted Edward Ferdon's argument, at an early Pecos Conference, linking the Southwest and Mexico: "He called across the table and congratulated me for having put some life into the session, and then added, 'of course I knew you didn't believe a word you were saying'" (Ferdon 1995:10). Well, Ferdon did, and so do I. I'm not just stirring up the waters to see what floats and what sinks: I think the Chaco-Aztec-Paquime business is/was real. This might have been easier had I simply demonstrated the remarkable material similarities and sequential chronology of Chaco, Aztec, and Paquime, and then footnoted the alignment as a possible subject for future research. Where's the fun in that? I admit that one of the appeals of this work was seeing how far I can push the boundaries of polite research before I'm on the outside looking in. Life's too short to play safe.

Time to name a few names. For services real and imagined, I would like to thank: Doug Bamforth, Bruce Bradley, Dave Brugge, Jim Byrkit, Linda Cordell, Darrell Creel, Bill Davis, Jeff Dean, Joey Donahue, Chris Downum, David Doyel, Andrew Duff, Patucche Gilbert, George Gumerman, Lou Hacker, Al Hayes, Alice Kehoe, Klara Kelley, David Kelley, Jane Kelley, Ed Ladd, Fred Lange, Bob Leonard, Brad Lepper, Bill Lipe, Kim Malville, Joan Mathien, Randy McGuire, Barbara Mills, Paul Minnis, Ben Nelson, Ben Patrusky, Lori Pendleton, David Phillips, Stella Pino, Rene Reitsma, Carroll Riley, John Rinaldo, Dean Saitta, Curt Schaafsma, Jason Shapiro, Payson Sheets, Rolf Sinclair, Anna Sofaer, John Speth, John Stein, Steven Swanson, John Taylor, Wolky Toll, Sharon Urban, Mark Varien, Gwinn Vivian, Barbara Voorhies, Michael Whalen, David Wilcox, Chip Wills, Tom Windes, Norman Yoffee, and the participants at the 1996, 1997, and 1998 CU Field Schools, the 1996 Oxford V meetings, the 1995 Southwest Symposium, the 1996 34th Annual New Horizons in Science Briefing, various Pecos and Mogollon and Anasazi conferences, colloquia audiences at ASU, UNM, UA, NAU, CU, Colorado Archaeological Society, Edge-of-the-Cedars Museum, the CU Center at Cortez Colorado, and CU classes who got guest-lectured. My particular thanks to Roger Kennedy and Peter Pino—scholars and gentlemen—who offered encouraging counsel when most needed. None of these people, institutions, or convocations are responsible or liable, but they all had a role in shaping the argument. Thanks!

I thought (and read) about these matters while flying back and forth to Chicago, Washington, New York, and other pots-of-gold in the service of Crow Canyon Archaeological Center. Thanks for the bonus miles and airline meals! The final summer of 1998 was supported by a JFDA grant from the University of Colorado; when not fleeing from militiamen or digging Great Houses, I spent that summer trying to tame this beast.

I fear that I am losing patience with some longstanding southwestern "debates"—in particular, Chaco's singular complexity and Mimbres' place in the larger Pueblo world (themes of chapter 2). The new stuff in this book (chapters 3, 4, and 5) builds on common understandings of Chaco and Mimbres—understandings not shared by a number of important Southwesternists. We cannot, apparently, resolve those arguments with the data at hand, but we should not let entrenched debates impede new and, perhaps, interesting developments. This book presents my views on these matters, sometimes phrased as an argument (alas!) with a half-dozen esteemed colleagues. I beg your pardon for my occasional exasperations in Chapters 1 and 2. I guess I'm getting cranky in my old age.

Several people slogged through this manuscript near the end, when it was getting really ripe: reviewers Mitch Allen, Brian Fagan, Keith Kintigh, Bill Lipe, and Dean Saitta; and several volunteers: Chris Pierce, Dan Falt, and Chris Ward. The reviewers improved things for both author and reader by insisting on compressions, truncations, and digestions (this is a lot shorter than it used to be) and asking for more pictures. Mitch Allen was a great publisher, Patricia Rechtman an excellent editor, and Marjorie Leggitt an outstanding illustrator.

My wife and colleague, Cathy Cameron, has been wonderfully patient with my fads and enthusiasms. She is blameless, not culpable for this book; I couldn't have written it without her support and kindness—but these sins are my own.

Who haven't I thanked? Probably lots of people; if you actually want to see your name here, associated with these heretical ideas, but I missed you, let me know. I may be forgetful but I'm not an ingrate. Happy trails to you until we meet again.

—S. H. L.
November 1998

1

POURPARLERS

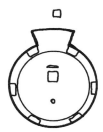

> Anyone who knows what they are doing can find the
> crumbs—the *wheres, whats,* and *whos.* . . . The art is in the
> *whys:* the ability to read between the crumbs.
>
> —Daryl Zero, *Zero Effect*

This book is not for the faint of heart, or for neophytes. If you are a practicing Southwestern archaeologist with hypertension problems, stop. Read something safe. If you are healthy, but new to the region, I highly recommend starting with Linda Cordell's (1994) *Ancient Pueblo People.* Fill up, because we're diving into the deep end and not coming up for air.

THE ARGUMENT IN BRIEF

In Pueblo prehistory, there were three "capitals"—small ceremonial cities where low-grade political complexity encompassed and organized surrounding regions: Chaco Canyon, Aztec Ruins, and Paquime (also called Casas Grandes) (fig. 1.1). These centers were sequential, and historically related. Each was by far the most important settlement of its time and place, and each controlled the distribution of exotic materials—parrots, copper bells, shells, and so forth. Chaco, Aztec, and Paquime spanned in sequence five centuries, from about A.D. 900 to A.D. 1450. (All dates are A.D. or C.E. and hereafter I dispense with those abbreviations.) A variety of symbols and architectural forms were used to signify historical continuity from each successor capital back to its predecessor. Among these symbols

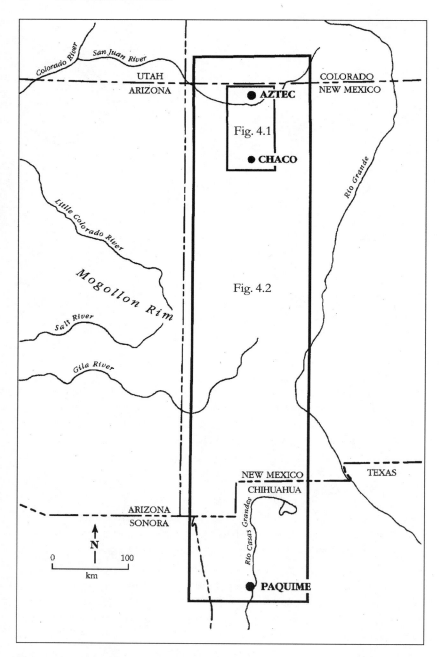

Figure 1.1. The Southwest, along the Great Divide.

was an interesting (but not unique) use of positional alignment: The capitals were all built on the same meridian. Pueblo traditional histories allude to places and events that may refer to these sites and their sequence. That's all simple enough, I think.

PLAN OF THE BOOK

The story behind that story is not so simple, or so neat. It emerged piecemeal over the last five years, and continued to change and evolve during the writing of this book. My own work, over two decades in the San Juan Basin, in the Mesa Verde region, and in southwestern New Mexico, prepared the ground, hoed the long row. Other people's research—Charles Di Peso, John Fritz, Earl Morris, Peter McKenna, John Stein, and dozens of others—fell into line, like seeds in a furrow. Ideas germinated on airplanes, at meetings, at ruins, during tribal consultations. One idea crowded out another; pruning was as much a problem as weeding. And the result is still a tangle, a thick spiny hedge of concepts and facts.

The presentation in this book reflects that unruly growth—as much a research program as an argument. It is, in fact, a very personal research program (no one crowds my bandwagon), so I insert my own experiences to illustrate particular points or quandaries. As discussed later, most of the data and many of the interpretations are not mine: They are others', but I do not expect the original researchers (dead or alive) to be thrilled by my use. There are many side arguments and tangents, explaining reuse of old data and reworkings of old interpretations, and begging forgiveness. Be warned: It's messy in here.

Still, there are beginnings, middles, ends. I begin with descriptions of Chaco and Mimbres (chap. 2). Chaco was the *fons et origo*. Mimbres was its brilliant neighbor to the south. Chapter 3 looks at Chaco and Paquime—the even more brilliant successor, even further south. Chaco and Paquime frame an archaeological problem first posed by Charles Di Peso, Paquime's excavator. Di Peso suggested Chaco and Paquime were, somehow, similar: too similar for chance or coincidence. In chapter 3, I also introduce Aztec Ruins, excavated by Earl Morris but fully described, much later, by Peter McKenna, John Stein, and their several colleagues. Aztec forms a bridge between Chaco and Paquime, but it surfaced in my thinking long after I had concluded that Di Peso was probably right: Chaco and Paquime meant more together than apart. Thus, chapter 3 emphasizes Chaco and Paquime, but brings in Aztec as a key— even critical—afterthought. Chapter 4 focuses sharply on the meridian alignment of Chaco, Aztec, and Paquime: The long thin line, linking the capitals. People have many problems with that part of my argument, and a few of those problems are real and merit consideration. Chapter 4 presents the evidence and anticipates a few challenges. Chapter 5 serves as a narrative recapitulation and offers a few conclusions about emergent order, cognitive evolution, and archaeological methods.

COMPLEXITY IN THE PUEBLO SOUTHWEST

"Complexity in the Pueblo Southwest"—an idea whose time has come . . . and gone, and come and gone, and come and gone. We've danced too many rounds with the beast, the devil-hound that drives otherwise pleasant, sober scholars to apoplectic sputtering. Something about "complexity"—the idea of Pueblo political hierarchy—brings out our worst. Through cycles of heated argument and frustrated truce, it's the topic we love to hate.

Archaeologists of a certain age will remember the Grasshopper-Chavez Pass "debates," which rivaled Ali-Frazier and Hatfield-McCoy for endless blood-letting. (Archaeologists of uncertain age might want to review that "debate"; see Cordell 1984:346–351 and 1997:421–423). At issue: Was there or was there not "complexity" at two 14th-century pueblos in central Arizona? A simple question, with dire and dreadful results. Single combat pitted professor against professor; platoons of students rushed in; surrounding regions were engulfed; battle became general. Journals filled with invective essays. Meetings crackled with jabs and insults. Those of us not caught in the mangle looked on, appalled. We hoped the combatants would wear themselves out before something awful happened. "Can't we all just get along?" more-or-less summed it up.

You have to choose your battles. Why quibble over complexity at PIV pueblos when there's Chaco Canyon? Chaco is not a cause worth dying for, exactly, but if any Pueblo place was a capital, it was Chaco. And there's a fight to be had. The literature weighs heavily in favor of Chacoan complexity (e.g., Sebastian 1992)— heavily, but not entirely: even at Chaco, there are advocates of something simpler (Vivian 1990; Johnson 1989). I'm a peaceful sort, and I don't want to fight or even to argue; I will take *as given* the development of complexity at Chaco Canyon by the mid-11th century. This book is about what political hierarchies did, during Chaco's run and after.

Political hierarchy is a constant question. In general, because most farmers we know about had it; and in the Southwest, because the Pueblos are so famous for avoiding it—at least in our stereotypes. (I decline here to review the literature on complexity, in general or in Pueblos.) Diagnosing complexity is a technical issue for archaeologists of every stripe; we need to know how to find it, and the Grasshopper-Chavez Pass debate sharpened our tools, to be sure. But, beyond writing more accurate local histories ("Chaco: Was She or Wasn't She?"), why should we care?

Most of this book is local history—the political history of the ancient Pueblo world—but you will also find themes of hopefully larger interest: archaeological method, cognitive evolution, and emergent order. Methodology needs no apology (except to the lay reader, who may as well abandon all hope). Archaeology is as much about how we know as about what we know, and I will devote some space to our methods. Cognitive evolution, considered at more length in chapter 5, is an old interest (Lekson 1981) long suppressed, now decloseted. It's OK, in this brave new postmodern world, to think about thinking. I suspect that much of our current cognitive apparatus evolved, culturally, in Neolithic contexts; so Chaco is a good place to consider thinking. Emergent order is trickier: "Complexity" in its narrower-yet-broader Santa Fe Institute sense seeks to restore cosmological consonance to Darwinian chaos through emergent order, "order for free." As discussed in chapter 5, emergent order might explain archaeologically primal complexity—in the sense of political hierarchy; like government at Chaco Canyon. It's undeniably interesting to know where governments come from, even if that interest is slightly morbid.

Those broader issues are a tease. The title is honest: This book is about political power in the ancient Southwest. But regional stories must have wider implications, spark broader interests. If Southwestern archaeologists don't ask big questions, we will slide back into feeble provincialism—endlessly fine-tuning the record of a region where archaeology is easy and research overfunded. It's time to take some chances: Live dangerously, turn the page.

2

MONDO CHACO

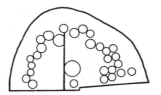

It all starts with Chaco. Chaco was the first stable, strong pattern in the Pueblo Southwest. For centuries before, Pueblo developments had been impressive but evanescent: Villages, prior to Chaco, were grown and gone in a generation, popping up again in the next valley, a pattern repeated over and over. At Chaco, traditions took root (Lekson 1989b). Chaco transformed Pueblo life and set the trajectory for all that followed.

In this chapter, I present my view of Chaco: what it was, where it came from, how it worked. The question of "where it went" occupies succeeding chapters; but the answer to *that* question involves Mimbres (Chaco's brilliant contemporary), so I devote the last sections of this chapter to Chaco and Mimbres—an uneasy relationship.

Chaco Canyon contains a dozen "Great Houses"—large sandstone masonry buildings, remarkable for both their scale and their formality (fig. 2.1). Building began by 900, and perhaps as early as 850 (Windes and Ford 1996) Construction peaked in the 11th and early 12th centuries, and at its height—about 1020 to 1125—Chaco was unique in the Pueblo Southwest (Lekson, Stein, Windes, and Judge 1988). Most 11th-century Pueblo people lived in single family homes: five or six stone masonry rooms and a "kiva" (fig. 2.2). The walls and layouts of those homes (often called "unit pueblos") were irregular and informal, compared with the massive masonry and rigid geometries of Chaco Great Houses.

The Great Houses are the principal "fact" of Chaco (Lekson 1984a). They were architecture, by any standard, designed by one (or a few) to be seen by many. Some of the canons and geometries governing Chacoan building have been discovered (Fritz 1978; Sofaer 1997; Stein, Suiter, and Ford 1997); the control and organization of construction has been described (Lekson 1986a); the larger architectonics of the Chaco Canyon built environment are currently unfolding. Each building was a separate composition, with multistoried room blocks around an open plaza. Many, and perhaps most, of the rooms were not residential; rather, they were nondomestic storage, transient lodging, or simple massing—but not homes.

A small number of people—hundreds, at most—lived in each Chaco Canyon Great House, and those people were of high status. They were elites, who lived (and were buried) differently and more expensively than their contemporaries. The total population of Chaco was probably about 2,500 to 3,000 (Lekson 1986a, 1988c), of which about half lived in Great Houses; the other half lived in unit pueblos. The total population of the San Juan Basin was probably in the several tens of thousands, and the population of the northern Southwest was probably about one hundred thousand. (I offer these estimates simply to indicate the approximate scales of Chaco and its region that frame my argument.)

Great House residents probably did not build their own homes; at least, the disparity between the labor required (Lekson 1986a) and the probable number of residents at each Great House (Windes 1984) strongly suggests that architect, builder, and user were three very distinct social roles (Lekson 1981; Stein and Lekson 1992). Great House residents probably did not make their own pottery: Over 50 percent of the pottery at Pueblo Alto was made 80 km away, in the Chuska Valley and elsewhere (Toll 1991). They may not even have cooked their own meals: Archaeologists search in vain for domestic cooking hearths, our customary index of the household (Windes 1984; Lekson 1986a). But there were elaborate, bathtub-sized cooking pits in plazas of every Great House—for example, the kitchen excavated in the plaza of Pueblo Alto (Plaza Feature 1 in Windes 1987b:410–445)—which suggest centralized cooking and cooks (fig. 2.3).

These, and other evidence, make a strong case for sizable elites at Chaco (among others: Schelberg 1984; Sebastian 1992). The people who lived in Chacoan Great Houses were not like the people who lived at Cliff Palace, or Alkali Ridge, or any of the thousands of hamlets, homes, and unit pueblos that housed the vast majority of ancient Pueblo people.

Chaco was so unlike ordinary Pueblo villages that archaeologists in the early 1970s thought that its inspiration must have come from the high civilizations of Mexico (Hayes 1981; Di Peso 1974). The Chaco Project—a National Park

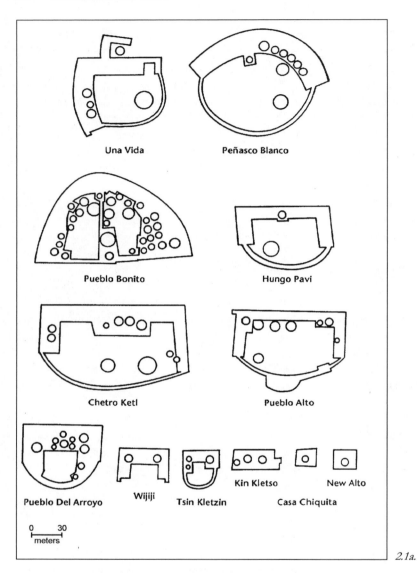

Una Vida

Peñasco Blanco

Pueblo Bonito

Hungo Pavi

Chetro Ketl

Pueblo Alto

Pueblo Del Arroyo

Wijiji

Tsin Kletzin

Kin Kletso

New Alto

Casa Chiquita

0   30
meters

2.1a.

Figure 2.1. Chaco Great House, a; and outliers, b (reproduced from Stephen H. Lekson, "Settlement Pattern and the Chacoan Region," 1991; courtesy School of American Research Press). Ground plans of Chaco Canyon and San Juan Basin great houses demonstrate the differences in scale between most "outliers" and large Chaco Canyon buildings. Note, however, that the largest "outliers" are comparable to the more diminutive Chaco Canyon buildings, such as the aptly named Casa Chiquita. The diagrammetric representation emphasized similarities by compressing detail. North varies.

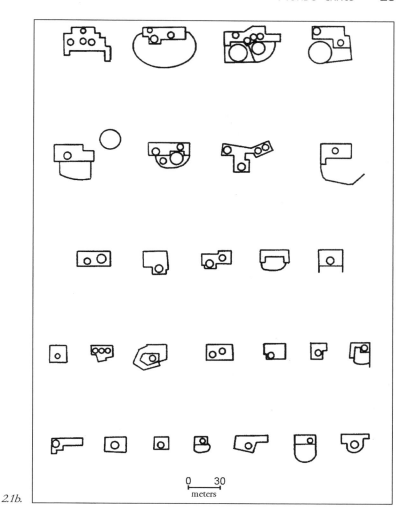

2.1b.

Service research program of the New Archaeology 1970s and '80s—reclaimed Chaco for the Southwest, denying significant Mexican involvement and deriving Chaco from an adaptation to local ecological conditions (Judge 1979, 1989). The pendulum swings, and in the 1990s we are groping toward a new understanding of Chaco that incorporates both historicity and environment.

Mimbres is an archaeological region in southwestern New Mexico, famed for its black-on-white pottery (fig. 2.4). Most pots were decorated with intricate geometric designs, but a considerable number show images and scenes of great artistic merit and compelling intrinsic interest: quotidian affairs and esoteric rituals, people of this world and spiritual beings of another (e.g., Brody 1977).

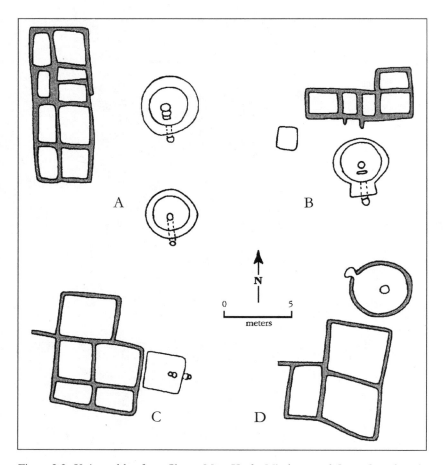

Figure 2.2. Unit pueblos from Chaco, Mesa Verde, Mimbres, and Casas Grandes. A, Three C site at Chaco Canyon (ca. 1050); B, 5MT-3 at Yellow Jacket, in the Mesa Verde district of southwestern Colorado (ca. 1250); C, Dinwiddie site, in the Cliff Valley in the Mimbres region of southwestern New Mexico (ca. 1100); and D, an intriguing room block at the Convento site (ca. 1150)—the only major excavated pre-Paquimé site in the Rio Casas Grandes valley.

These "six-rooms-and-a-kiva" modules mark, architecturally, the greatest extent of the 10th and 11th-century Pueblo world. The "kivas" were probably not ceremonial structures, but rather the last manifestation of the long tradition of pit houses. A few archaeologists seem unpleasantly surprised by "Anasazi-style" unit pueblos appearing prominently in the Mimbres sequence; a separate-but-equal Mimbres has become an *idée fixe*. But unit-pueblo sites appear almost everywhere we today see pinyon and juniper, almost certainly including the Mimbres Valley. The Casas Grandes example, from the Convento site, is my interpretation of a very small sample: one site. The Convento "unit pueblo" may prove aberrant or even wrong, when other pre-Paquimé sites are excavated.

Figure 2.3. Alto's kitchen (Plaza Feature 1, Room 3; courtesy National Park Service, Neg. #15814). Bathtub-sized ovens, like these in a small outbuilding in Pueblo Alto's plaza, were also found in the plazas of Pueblo Bonito and Chetro Ketl. This partially answers the Chaco Question: "where are the hearths?" Chaco people were not cooking like other Pueblo people. Chaco people had kitchens and, presumably, cooks. The putative hearth-dearth is fully resolved by Chacoan "kivas," each of which sports a fine, square fire pit. There, sirs and madams, are your hearths.

Mimbres architecture did not equal its ceramic art. Villages of considerable size were constructed of crude masonry in haphazard arrangements. Kivas—a key element of Anasazi villages—were present (fig. 2.2), generally one to each roomblock (Anyon and LeBlanc 1980). The stone masonry, kivas, and black-on-white pottery suggested to early researchers that Mimbres was, in essence, Anasazi (e.g., Haury 1986). New Archaeologists of the 1970s changed all that, asserting local origins, (again) in a local adaptive setting (e.g., LeBlanc 1983; Shafer 1995). The pendulum swings: Mimbres may rejoin the larger Pueblo world—a theme of this chapter.

LORDS OF THE GREAT HOUSE

I think it was Robert Euler (but it may have been George Gumerman) who, sometime in the early 1970s, declared Chaco "both *bête noir* and *deus ex machina* of Anasazi archaeology." We didn't know what Chaco was, but we were pretty sure that it was important.

Chaco: then and now, the 800-pound gorilla of Anasazi archaeology. Most archaeologists agree that Chaco was an elemental event in Southwestern prehistory; certainly the principal phenomenon of the 11th century, perhaps the major matter of Pueblo prehistory (e.g., Cordell 1994, 1997; Schelberg 1984; Sebastian 1992; Wilcox 1993). (Other archaeologists think Chaco is just so much hype, but let us ignore those provincial naysayers.)

But, what *was* Chaco? For twenty years I've weaseled out of a direct answer to that question. There are some evident facts: Chaco was big. It was showy. It was expensive. It had clearly differentiated housing: "Great Houses" with high-status buildings on one side of the canyon, and small, modest, "unit pueblos" on the other. Not many people lived in the Great Houses, and several of those who did were buried with pomp, circumstance and, probably, retainers (Akins and Schelberg 1984; Neitzel 1989b:536–537). Chaco was a magnet for costly baubles (of which, more below).

Chaco was several orders of magnitude larger than any contemporary settlements in its region. The dense architectural core of Chaco Canyon was monumental, built to scales far larger than other 11th- and early 12th-century Pueblo homes and villages. The place was built to impress, even awe. A vast network of roads and "outliers" surrounded the center and radiated out into a heavily populated hinterland—the Chacoan "regional system."

Does all this sound anthropologically familiar? If I were describing a neolithic center in Turkistan or Shansi or Wessex or Bolivia or Illinois, what would we think? Chaco was socially and politically "complex"—that is, a hierarchy, with definite haves and definite have-nots. Hierarchy, not heterarchy: A few people at Chaco regularly and customarily directed the actions of many other people, and those few lived in more expensive houses and had more baubles (at least in death) than the many. Were they chiefs, priests, kings, queens, duly-elected representatives? Who knows? And, for now, who cares? They were elite leaders, Major Dudes; that much seems clear. If ever anyone in the Pueblo Southwest were elite, it was those two guys buried in the famous log crypts of Old Bontio (Akins and Schelberg 1984). Those boys had power.

We can invent alternate scenarios for Chaco that project, backwards, the Pueblo present. Or rather, a stereotype of an egalitarian Pueblo society that probably never existed. There remains intractable, deeply rooted opposition to anything untoward or unegalitarian at Chaco. The shadows of Hewett's democratic city-states and Benedict's Apollonians are long indeed. Despite the clear evidence of archaeology and the conclusions of ethnology (e.g., Brandt 1994; Reyman 1987; Upham 1982; Whiteley 1988), some archaeologists cling

Figure 2.4. Some famous pottery types, clockwise from top left: Gallup Black-on-white, UCM 9501; Ramos Polychrome, UCM 36526; Mimbres Black-on-white, UCM 3180; Smudged-Polished Interior bowl, UCM 36759; Mesa Verde Black-on-white, UCM 9422. Courtesy of the University of Colorado Museum.

Regional entities may or may not have had ceramic "signatures," but these types are touted as typical. Gallup Black-on-white and similar types are generally associated with 11th-century Chaco; Mesa Verde Black-on-white characterizes its eponymous park, and most of the northern Southwest in the 13th century, including Aztec Ruins; Ramos Polychrome was most frequent of 14th-century Paquime polychromes; Mimbres Black-on-white—the most famous Southwestern pottery—was contemporary with (but of little evident interest to) Chaco; after 1130, unpainted smudged-polished interior bowls (not really famous) completely replace the remarkable Mimbres painted pottery, suggesting a dramatic repudiation of Mimbres ideology.

to a model of ancient Pueblo society that projects Gilded Age hopes and Flower Power fantasies on the ancient past. Egalitarian processes did not create this starter-kit kingdom. Bonito was no barnraising.

There are so many competing scenarios for how Chaco was governed that I will finesse the issue by jumping back to one of the very earliest Pueblo ethnographies: Frank Hamilton Cushing's reconstruction of ancient Zuni government, summarized here by Jesse Green (editor of Cushing's journals):

> The body which "governed, protected and cared for" the people of the pueblo was a council composed of the chief *A:shiwani* of the six cardinal directions. . . . In Cushing's phrase, these august figures were the

"Masters of the Great House"— "house" in this context meaning literally their place of meeting (thought to be located over the direct center of the world). . . . Themselves removed from the world of secular work, warfare, and day-to-day government (hence the need for "the good share"), it was they who named the officers who took practical charge of such affairs. (Green 1990:373)

The importance of the "Masters of the Great House" was manifested *a rchitecturally,* by a building at the exact center of the world. The masters did not work. Their needs were met by "the good share"—taxes regularly paid by the Zuni people. They did not rule directly, but formed policy and then chose and instructed managing officials—a proto-bureaucracy. Directional and positional symbolism structured the ideology of power, but the political hierarchy was anything but symbolic: The council was the highest order of authority in Zuni, with legitimate use of institutional force. A century of scholarship has critiqued Cushing's reconstruction (e.g., Watts 1997), and some have suggested that this highly centralized, highly hierarchical body was in some way a response to colonial contingencies (Ladd 1979).[1] No matter; to borrow a Tilleyism, Chaco was *something like that.* At Zuni, it was a council living in a Great House, directing the cities of Cibola; eight centuries earlier at Chaco, it was a ceremonial city housing an elite community, ruling a vaster region.

THE (SOCIAL) DYNAMICS OF CHACO PREHISTORY

Chaco was not a happy, hippy-dippy commune. It was larger, less pleasant, more ominous. Back when my twig was bent,[2] the Southwest was fairly flooded with triple-distilled Chaco moonshine—not so much in the literature as in conference papers and Pecos Conference conversations. Asking the question "was Chaco a state?" was exciting, if silly. It made the archaeological elders writhe like egg whisks.

Chaco was big, but it was not Tikal or Tula or Cahokia. The Chaco Project "normalized" Chaco, deflated the state. It was more than a valley of pueblos, but less than Rome. The Chaco Project at least offered a Chaco reality check.

Others would just like Chaco to go away. In the early days of the Chaco Project and "outliers" (see below), when Chaco was getting a lot of ink and media attention, the University of Colorado crowd produced a bumper sticker that announced, in big red letters, "Chaco is a Dairy Queen Outlier." It must have seemed funnier around a Mesa Verde campfire. Even out of context, it has a pleasant dada spin. (I mailed a half-dozen out to Chaco with a bogus Park Service memo on park privatization.) Chaco knocked Mesa Verde off the charts, and scores of other underpublicized Southwestern districts faded that much further into obscurity. It must have been annoying for someone working on a really neat Rio Grande site to open the morning paper and read Chaco-this, Chaco-that. The extravagant claims made for the canyon (the Chaco state!) were bad enough, but "outliers" really drove the Southwest wild. "Outliers"—Chaco-like sites at considerable distances from the canyon—unleashed Chaco, and delivered it right to everyone else's front door.

I snuck up on Chaco from Salmon Ruins (fig. 2.5), where Cynthia Irwin-Williams (1972) coined the term "Chaco Phenomenon." Coming from Salmon, I was keen on outliers, of which Salmon was a spectacular example. "Outliers" were . . . well, we didn't know exactly what outliers were. They seemed to be Chaco-style buildings built at impossible distances from Chaco Canyon. There were precedents excavated in the early days of Southwestern archaeology: odd places like Lowry, Village of the Great Kivas, and a few other far-flung sites corrupted by bad Chacoan "influences." In the mid-1970s, we suspected there might be more out in the great wide open, waiting to be discovered.

Figure 2.5. Salmon Ruins. Built between about 1088 and 1100, Salmon Ruins was the original terminus of the North Road. It may have been an attempt to establish a New Chaco on the San Juan River; that river was too large and violent for 11th and 12th century irrigation technology. The New Chaco was built due north of Salmon, at Aztec Ruins on the smaller Rio Animas. Throughout the northern Pueblo region, the largest villages and towns were never located along the largest river—the San Juan or the Colorado River—but along major tributaries: the Animas, La Plata, Mancos, McElmo, and Montezuma creeks.

Cynthia thought so. She told a story on herself: When she first visited
Salmon Ruins, her guides led her up a steep hill and then stopped. She asked,
"Where's the ruin?" She was standing on it. Salmon Ruins was so big you
couldn't even see it. I thought that there might be more Salmon Ruins out
there—huge buildings, *pueblos muy grandes, muy bonitos!* (In odd corners of the
Southwest, there still are huge sites, obscure to science; I've found a few myself,
and it's a blast.) Maybe we could find big Chacoan outliers. That was heady
stuff: fun, cheap, non-destructive, and a potentially big return for the money.

I approached Jim Judge, my new boss at the Chaco Project, with an
idea about an outlier survey. Bob Powers, a Chaco Project colleague and a
student of Gwinn Vivian's, had that idea first. He beat me to the boss by
hours (well, maybe by days). Bob, Bill Gillespie, and I were given time and
a truck, and we rocketed around the San Juan Basin looking for great big
ruins. We had a great time—but we didn't find great big ruins. There *are* a
few more Salmon-sized behemoths (in the Aztec area, as we shall see), but
the "outliers" we found were all rather small—at least, compared with Pueblo
Bonito. And we found these little fellows everywhere: a few right next to
the highway and many more in places known but to goats.

While we loosened bolts and dented fenders on an ill-fated string of government Suburbans, another project was busy depreciating vehicles purchased
by New Mexico rate-payers. The Public Service Company of New Mexico, in
the electricity business, lived up to its name and sponsored an outlier survey
with an all-star crew: Rich Loose, Mike Marshall, and John Stein. They found
what we found, but more (Marshall, Stein, Loose, and Novotny 1979). The
Public Service gang really covered the ground, and the San Juan Basin map
began to look measled: Red-dotted "outliers" were popping up faster than weeds.
Then the Bureau of Land Management joined in, fielding crews to study roads
that crossed potential coal fields. Some of the names changed (Kincaid 1983;
Nials, Stein, and Roney 1987), but the story stayed the same: lots of little outliers, in likely and unlikely places. Scholars began "collecting" outliers, keeping lists and dotting maps (e.g., LeBlanc 1986b; Wilcox 1993). It became
competitive: Great Houses were traded like baseball cards, and outlier lists
were compared, contrasted, and even coveted. Thou shalt not covet thy
neighbor's Great House, so I've let my list lapse. There's plenty of other
people questing after outliers. I'm not even sure of the current score: probably
more than 150 (e.g., Stein and Fowler 1996).

THE REGIONAL SYSTEM

The "regional system" is, perhaps, the single most difficult aspect of Chacoan
archaeology (Lekson 1991, 1996a). It's hard to ignore the ruins in the Chaco

Culture National Historical Park, but Chacoan regional archaeology—its "outliers" and its unprecedented size—challenges and exceeds our methods. We aren't used to archaeological entities that large in the Southwest, and denial is a common reaction. The regional archaeology of Chaco sets the stage for subsequent prehistory and for the rest of this book: Chaco is the ground floor of my house-of-cards. So it is important the reader understand my take on Chaco, even if we agree to disagree.

What were all these little "outliers"? Take Peach Springs, for example (fig. 2.6). Peach Springs was one of the first outliers the Park Service crew mapped. It was nothing more, and nothing less, than a rounded mound about 40 m long and 25 m wide and 4 m tall. In a couple of places, some sad fool had dug for treasure and found only rubble. A few courses of Chaco-like masonry were visible in those melancholy potholes. An archaeologist, of course, could tell it was a building, but I've taken the interested laity to Peach Springs, and they had the Cynthia reaction: Where's the site?

If we cleaned it out and cleaned it up, landscaped it, and trailed it, Peach Springs would be a nice little ruin. Nothing special, mind you: 25 rooms and a kiva, tops. Every cowtown in east-central Arizona has a ruin that big (plus catacombs and talking pottery!). Mesa Verde is littered with 25-room pueblos. What's the big deal? Peach Springs, thus described, sounds like a big little site—and it was, sort of.

Figure 2.6. Peach Springs. Mountain or molehill? Peach Springs, an outlying Great House that stands as an example of the class. Nine centuries of wind and rain might have left a more visible ruins, but fifty years of sheep and cattle reduced these buildings to rounded mounds or "big bumps."

My old friend and erstwhile colleague John Stein described outlier discovery as an "ah-ha experience." When you're on an outlier, things tingle. Scramble up the masonry talus of a steep-sloped mound, and reach the top: Look down on a Great Kiva and a plain dotted with dozens of conspicuously smaller rubble mounds and odd earthen berms, all looking back up at you; and you will realize that archaeology's current observational language is insufficient to record, describe, communicate, and analyze what you've just seen. That's Peach Springs, and 150 other "big little sites."

I am neither portraying nor advocating a mystical, transcendent New Age experience, or a "phenomenological" epiphany. All the concrete knowable elements of "Chaconess" are open to Southwestern archaeology, but we are unaccustomed to recording, presenting, and understanding them *en bloc*. It is the combination of "usual suspects" architectural traits (massive masonry, multiple stories, elevated kivas, etc.), commanding height, nearby Great Kivas, berms, roads, and—more than any other measure—the relative mass of the Great House contrasted to unit pueblos that cause the well-tempered antennae to hum (fig. 2.7). Start with varying mixes of architectural elements A, B, and C; observe siting D; add associated public structures E and F; G through Y could be the little pueblos in a surrounding community; Z is for the consistent patterning of all these features. Each individual lettered element can be described and understood, A to Z. Put them all together and they spell . . . trouble. For Chacoan outliers, the unit of observation cannot be the Great House outlier itself, but the landscape of which it is the principal visual focus (Fowler and Stein 1992; Lekson 1991; Stein and Lekson 1992).

Landscapes are difficult to communicate. Historically, we don't do it well. We can read old reports and site files and see variations on this theme: "One of the pueblos in the cluster, at the upper end of the terrace, was somewhat bigger, perhaps of two stories. Nearby was a large circular reservoir." Hey, mister: that's not a metastasized unit pueblo, that's a Great House. But you'd never know it from the observational language used in old articles or more recent site survey forms.

Of course, few of us have had much opportunity to practice, to hone our skills. There are over 150 outliers out there (fig. 2.8), which seems like a lot until you realize that those outliers are sprinkled over a huge area among many tens of thousands of 11th- and 12th-century pueblo sites. Outliers are actually rare birds. Assume 150 Great Houses evenly sprinkled over 40,000 square miles; that's one outlier per 267 square miles. At the industry standard of 20 acres a day, it would take an inquiring-minded archaeologist three decades just to find one of these things. How many would you have to see before a pattern began to emerge? Three? Five? Twenty?

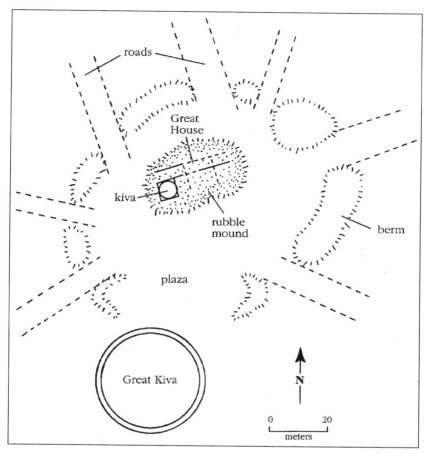

Figure 2.7. Outlier landscape (after Kintigh, Howell, and Duff 1996). The various non-masonry elements of Great Houses and outlier architecture were mostly recognized within the last decade. It was hard to miss the Great House and Great Kiva, but berms and other earthworks were generally either ignored or dismissed as "middens." John Stein and Andrew Fowler were among the first to recognize and publicize Anasazi earthen architecture, and many others have since confirmed the ubiquity of mounds and berms on the Colorado Plateau. Most of our knowledge of these features comes from surface observations, and excavations will probably alter both the terminology and understanding of these features.

It's no wonder people have problems with outliers. Those of us who, through happy opportunity or alarming obsession, have seen many outliers still lack the language to effectively describe the pattern. Most of our

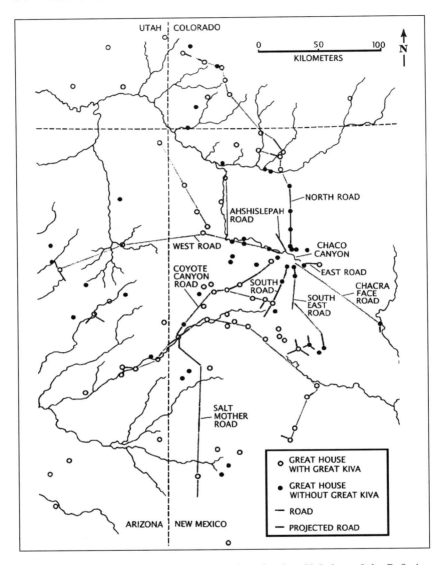

Figure 2.8. The Chaco World (Reproduced from Stephen H. Lekson, John R. Stein, Thomas Windes, and W. James Judge, "The Chaco Canyon Community," 1988; courtesy of Scientific American). This map, based on a draft by John Stein, presented the Chaco World as it was understood in the mid-1980s. A cartographic error transformed the Mogollon Rim into a river, sometimes interpreted as the Salt River—putting "outliers" in the Tonto Basin. Despite that gaffe, the empirical pattern of Great Houses should no longer be in doubt; roads, however, are open to debate. Several of the "projected roads" on this map have not survived subsequent field work. There is no sustained program to find or evaluate Chacoan roads, a glaring gap in Southwestern archaeology.

colleagues have only seen a few, usually the excavated, spruced-up, set-piece exhibits such as Lowry Ruin or Farview House. Small samples do not forge strong patterns, and it's hard to connect Farview House to an undistinguished lump like Peach Springs. You can't, until you see a whole series of Peach Springs-like lumps, in a wide range of settings and states—"states" of both condition and constitution.

How did some of us see so many of these things, and thereby become believers? Most of the 150 outliers were not discovered, they were revisited. Word-of-mouth, records of unusually large unit pueblos, remembrances of sites past, and show-me-yours-I'll-show-you-mine field trips accumulated a critical mass of personal experiences. Those experiences surmounted the limitations of the observational language. We could speak in elliptical metaphors and coded parallels: "just like Morris 41," "one of those enclosed doo-dads like Skunk Springs," "Las Ventanas, but stretched a bit." We didn't need to invent a new observational language because we shared overlapping experiences. Somebody out there may have counted coup on all 150 outliers, but not me. I've seen fifty or sixty and, because I have that set of experiences, I can understand my colleagues' descriptions of the rest.[3]

Not everyone has had those opportunities, but life's too short for outlier-angst. Take it or leave it: Outliers are an empirical pattern, no less (and no more) valid than Dogozhi Black-on-white or tchamahias or trough metates. Chacoan outliers are (almost) everywhere. Claims to the contrary are special pleading, stylite pillarism, selectionist sophistry, or—in a very few cases—*really* interesting exceptions to the rule.

Given that the pattern is real, what *were* outliers? In the past, when outliers were largely limited to the San Juan Basin, I would have dodged that question by responding, "Well, what was Chaco?" The center should define the periphery, so the meaning of "outlier" depended entirely on the nature of Chaco Canyon. Then I would hint at the staggering range of conflicting views of Chaco Canyon, and change the subject.

That evasion nearly cost me my faith. The explosive expansion of outliers out-distanced our abilities to render them believable, understandable. Our first schemata for outliers posited a system of subsistence redistribution among San Juan Basin, mediated by Chaco (see below). Redistribution imploded under the density of far-distant outliers, well beyond the economic radius of Chacoan food transport. Outliers at Hopi, outliers at Tularosa, and finally outliers in the Mimbres(!) violated the laws of time and space or, at least, conventions of time and space for our archaeological world. I began to think of outliers as "Great Houses," ubiquitous elements of ancient Pueblo life, like "kivas." Much as Great Kivas formed community foci long before and long after Chaco, perhaps

Great Houses were a temporally restricted but near-universal element of 11th-century Pueblo villages. A village without a Great House was like a western town without a liquor store: not a town. So, perhaps, Great Houses were effectively background noise: a constant pattern within which Chaco developed, possibly an unhealthy aberration. Those timid, retro ideas emerged mainly in conversations and conference presentations, but they were shared by others. Outliers outlay nothing; each Great House was entire of itself but common to some grand shared Weltanschauung—like black-on-white pottery. "The community structure, identified here as Chacoan, could instead have been a nonspecific, pan-Anasazi pattern" (Lekson 1991:48). Outliers? Outliars!

Those doubts have passed. I've seen the light and returned to the fold. The alert reader will have noted that I have revived the antique term "outlier" over the less charged "Chacoan structure" or neutral "Great House." I want to reestablish the strong connection of those many outlying Great Houses with their "prime object": the city in Chaco Canyon.

I reconsidered the consequences of my actions when the increasing specificity of outlier attributes (berms, roads, and the like; Fowler and Stein 1992) collided with the deep implausibility of a pan-Anasazi model. How would things as elaborate and standardized as Great Houses become pan-Anasazi? Great Houses stand out against a variegated Anasazi background. Archaeologists subdivide Anasazi into a dozen local traditions or districts, but Great Houses—while not identical—are sufficiently similar to form an identifiable class. If Great House weren't imposed or inspired by a central source, then they must be independent inventions or developments or adaptations. As Great House after Great House was explained (in forgettable conference papers, unsung and uncited) as local evolutionary developments, I was struck by the miracle of 150 cases of simultaneous equifinality. Miraculous? Ridiculous!

It was, of course, ridiculous: Taken to its logical conclusion, a pan-Anasazi model required a mystical faith in the powers of parallel evolution or, failing that, a near-complete ignorance of the empirical record. One hundred and fifty local evolutions might make sense one at a time, valley by valley, but together they defy belief. There must have been central control, or a central idea.

And there's Chaco itself: a prime object, in George Kubler's (1962) terms. Chaco was the center of the 11th-century Pueblo world. That is not an assertion: It's as close to a fact as archaeology can hope to produce. After a century of work, we know Chaco and we know the Southwest. There may be a few more big sites lurking out in the bush yet to be discovered, but—in the 11th century—there was no other Chaco. The mere fact of Chaco returns the question "what were outliers?" to "what was Chaco?" We're back where we began. If Chaco was real (it was) and outliers are real (they are), then the problem is not empirical but conceptual. Our models are insufficient. Repudiating redistribution or subsistence economy or adaptation as an explanation of all the outliers does not make all the outliers go away. Those tumbled Great Houses are still there, waiting for new thinking.

Chaco was a political and economic center, unique in its time and place. I call it a ceremonial city (chap. 3), where monumental buildings housed (among other things) a sizable elite. Outliers, I think, varied with distance from Chaco. Inlying outliers—those within the San Juan or Chaco Basin—probably participated in some form of the old redistribution game (Judge 1979), and this may explain Chaco's rise. Outliers beyond the practical limits of bulk food transportation (roughly equivalent to the margins of the Basin) presumably did not play that game; yet they are identical to intra-Basin outliers. Bulk food redistribution was not the primary design factor in outlier form. New models are required.

OUT ON THE EDGES

We've been digging up Chaco Canyon for one hundred years. In 1996, a formal ceremony marked the centennial of archaeology at Pueblo Bonito. Should we celebrate or weep? Poor Bonito: We've picked, probed, plumbed, and propped the old building for ten decades, and we still can't agree on what Bonito might have been. I think it was palace; others still insist that it was a pueblo. Pueblo or palace? Warehouse or temple? Village or barracks? After 100 years, we can't agree.

If Chaco is the *bête noire* of the Southwest, Bonito is the black hole. It sucks in astonishing amounts of interest, energy, and resources, like some giant space vortex. It emits almost nothing: only the faint clipped signal of Pepper's field notes ("Rooms 116 to 190: nothing of special interest was developed in these excavations"; Pepper 1920:339) or Judd's decaying reminiscences ("Admittedly, the present volume appears a long while after conclusions of field work"; Judd 1964:iv). Archaeological reporting of Pueblo Bonito was weak.

Bonito ate archaeology like a black hole eats matter, and returned only a diffuse band of information. In the process, it generated some real space oddities. Cylinder vessels, turquoise, macaws, staffs, wands, mosaic mirrors, copper bells, jet frogs, bifurcated baskets—you name it, Bonito's got it. A cornucopia of exotica: We may not know what Bonito was, but we know it was *different.*

To escape the light-bending gravity of Bonito and the canyon, we can seek answers out at the edge, the final frontiers of the Chaco world. The periphery may help us define the center. The east and north boundaries seem sharply defined; the west is fuzzier, and the south is entirely problematic.

This is archaeology, after all; let us go counterclockwise, beginning in the east. East-southeast, actually: The site of Guadalupe (fig. 2.9) sits atop the second-most spectacular setting of any outlier, a narrow high mesa overlooking the Puerco River, about 100 km from Chaco (Pippin 1987). There are a few candidate Great Kivas but no Great Houses beyond Guadalupe: The Rio Grande has been declared a Chaco-free zone. (The only possible exception is a small "mining camp" at the Cerrillos turquoise mines, south of Santa Fe; Wiseman and Darling 1986.) Guadalupe typifies the outlier quandary; in a range of criteria, it stands out from the local Pueblo homes but the archaeologist who excavated Guadalupe thinks that it was a basically local phenomenon (Pippin 1987).

Due north of Guadalupe and 140 km from Chaco, at the extreme northeast corner of the Chaco World, Chimney Rock sits in splendid isolation, atop the most spectacular setting of any Chacoan site (fig. 2.10; Eddy 1977). In the context of its local archaeology, Chimney Rock sticks out like a sore thumb. Chimney Rock is tidy and huge and very Chacoan; the community looks like somebody stepped in a unit pueblo and tracked it all over Stollsteimer Mesa (fig. 2.11). If ever there was a smoking gun outlier, it's Chimney Rock. It's the holotype of the species, and it's right out at the edge: Beyond Chimney Rock, the next stop is Cahokia.

Figure 2.9. Guadalupe. The remarkable settings of Guadalupe and Chimney Rock (fig. 2.10), atop high narrow mesas, are nearly unique in the Chacoan World. Chimney Rock marks the extreme northeast. Guadalupe is the easternmost outlier. Consider the map in fig. 1.1. Should there be a southeastern marker-outlier?—a Great House on a high ridge somewhere west of Socorro, New Mexico?

Figure 2.10. Chimney Rock (courtesy of Frank Eddy). Perched atop a tall cuesta, visibility was probably the key: Chimney Rock has an unexpected line-of-sight to Huerfano Mesa, the most prominent feature in the northern Chaco Basin. Huerfano Mesa is clearly visible from Pueblo Alto at Chaco Canyon. A high-school student, Katie Freeman, discovered these intervisibilities in a science fair project.

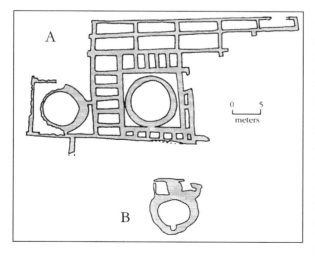

Figure 2.11. Chimney Rock, A and Parking Lot Ruin, B (after Eddy 1977). The local architecture of the Chimney Rock district, illustrated here by the Parking Lot Ruin, is even less Chacoan than these maps suggest. Beyond using the same stone, there are few similarities in the walls and forms of the Great House and its surrounding community. The outlier is Mondarian: formal, crisp, rectangular, and very Chacoan. The local architecture is more abstract, but interesting: unit pueblos more in the manner of Georges Braque. North varies.

From Chimney Rock, at the northeast, a line of outliers runs westward across southwestern Colorado, along the base of the Rocky Mountains (the San Juan and La Plata mountains, in fact), as far north as Dove Creek (about latitude 37° 30'), 200 km from Chaco. From this north pole, the frontier arcs back through southeastern Utah to approximately the area of the Bluff Great House (fig. 2.12) in the small town of that name, 200 km from Chaco (Cameron, Davis, and Lekson 1997). There are two outliers—one reported and one rumored beyond Bluff to the northwest; they would stretch the Chaco World another 40–50 km, to the very edges of the canyons of the Colorado River. We are (reasonably) certain that no outliers lie below Lake Powell, and no outliers have been identified in the Fremont country of Utah, where they should stand out like Chimney Rock.

East and north seem firmly fixed. The west is problematic in part because it is Indian country: the Navajo Nation and the Hopi reservation. The tribes are good stewards, more protective of sites and ruins than government agencies or private landowners. Understandably, they discourage digging. While many outliers have been reported on Indian lands, few have been investigated in recent times. White House, a classic Great House in Canyon de Chelly (fig. 2.13), was partially excavated by Earl Morris in the 1920s, but of the several newly discovered outliers much further west at the Hopi Mesas, we have only maps. Good maps, convincing maps but, still, maps. This dearth of work has led to

Figure 2.12. Bluff Great House. Another "big bump," on a terrace above the town of Bluff, Utah. The ruin was a local attraction, a "thing to see in Bluff," advertised on placemats at the Turquoise Diner. Everyone knew the site, but nobody recognized it as a Great House—a Chacoan outlier—until the 1980s. Bluff is 200 km from Pueblo Bonito.

Figure 2.13. White House. Not the "White House" of pueblo traditions, this building at Canyon de Chelly is one of the larger Chacoan outliers. It was partially excavated by Earl Morris, but never reported. His brief notes suggest remarkable amounts of "trade" pottery. The upper ruin is a post-Chacoan cliff-sheltered site.

draconian pronouncements that there are no outliers in the Kayenta country, which is simply wrong (Fowler and Stein 1992: fig. 9.1).

West beyond the Nations we reach the Little Colorado River and Wupatki (fig. 2.14). Wupatki has long been the subject of Chacoan speculation (Stanislawski 1963; see also Wilcox in press b), but most archaeologists rejected those claims on distance alone: Wupatki is 300 km from Chaco, and the lands of northeastern Arizona (as we have just seen) are thin for outliers. I reject that rejection: distance is no barrier. But Wupatki, as it turns out, was built between 1135 and 1195, after building ceased at Chaco; it played a role in the post-Chaco world. The Flagstaff area has not been friendly to Chaco, but wise men from the east have anointed a few candidate Chaco-era outliers (most notably, Ridge Ruin: Fowler and Stein 1992: fig. 9.1; Fowler, Stein, and Anyon 1987:213).

A conservative reading of the west would draw a line from the Bluff area south through consensus Great Houses at Hopi, on through Holbrook (with its Great Kiva; Gumerman and Olson 1968) and ending at a cluster of round Great Kivas on the Mogollon Rim (Herr 1994) (fig. 1.1). That's the "safe" western boundary, but given the case for outliers around Flagstaff and Great Kivas near Page, Arizona (Jonathan Till, personal communication 1998), that line will probably shift westward with more research.

While the west is neither as fixed nor as firm as the east and north, the south is worse—far worse, a matter central to the main argument of this book. Most maps place the south edge of the Chacoan world somewhere in the latitude of the quirky little town of Quemado, New Mexico, or about 200 km from Chaco (fig. 2.8). And that's an expansionist view. In the early days of the great outlier hunts in the 1970s, the Park Service survey cut things off well north of Quemado, indeed north of Zuni, only 125 km from Chaco (Powers, Gillespie, and Lekson 1983:fig.1). As part of that long-ago Park Service team, I proposed a hot candidate much further to the south, 250 km from Chaco—a site called "Hough's No. 111" or "Aragon" (see fig. 4.3). There was no enthusiasm for an outlier that far out

Figure 2.14. Wupatki. Various claims and counter-claims have been made for Wupatki, built about 1135–1195. It has many characteristics of a Great House, but a contemporary of Aztec. Wupatki and other nearby sites have more exotica than Aztec—for example, over fifty macaws. Wupatki may have been an independent (competing?) center. Its scale was much smaller than Aztec's, but its location was compellingly powerful: very near Sunset Crater. The volcano erupted about 1065—unprecedented in Southwestern memory. The smoking mountain and its perpetual lightning storms became a strange attractor of ideologically-charged architecture: both ballcourts and great kivas were part of Wupatki's ceremonial landscape. Intriguingly, the ballcourts are among the very last Hohokam style oval courts; later Paquime ballcourts were I-shaped. The Great Kiva, like several others of the Aztec era, was unroofed.

and, like Wupatki, the matter was dropped. In the intervening years, this southernmost outlier has independently surfaced on a few lists (e.g., Fowler and Stein 1992); I enjoy the petty satisfaction of "told you so"—and this too-far-out outlier is a textbook case of how Great Houses camouflage themselves in local descriptive conventions.

In fact, it wasn't even *my* outlier, originally. Steven LeBlanc first mentioned "Hough's No. 111" (hereafter, "Aragon") in a casual conversation, although the data were in a book with which I was quite familiar: Walter Hough's (1907) *Antiquities of the Upper Gila*. I'd thumbed that old BAE bulletin many times while working in the Upper Gila, but I never thought of it as an outlier source: The Upper Gila is Mogollon, and Chaco is Anasazi.

Hough's book contains a series of short, sketchy site descriptions, and the usual turn-of-the-century observations on pottery and stone idols. For its time, it is neither better or worse than a score of similar monographs. The descriptive language is largely formulaic: "Site X: Same as Site X − 1" or "Site Y: quite unlike Site Y + 2." Hough's descriptions were internally referenced, to compress the presentation of new but repetitive data. That's understandable, but internally-referenced descriptive languages invariably normalize the ringers. Spiky aspects of things that are, in fact, unlike anything else were smoothed to conform to the prevailing patterns and prevailing descriptive language. Aragon was described in this way:

> About one-half mile below old Fort Tularosa [today's Aragon], there is an imposing ruin situated on the ridge which extends out into the river valley. This ruin stands on top of the ridge, upon a pyramidal base which bears traces of shaping, the sides of the ridge also having been graded. The main rooms are large, and the walls well laid up with slabs of stone, some of which are sculpted on the edge. Two of the larger rooms have been excavated, and in there were found remains of the house beams. There is one large circular kiva on the platform outside the village. The ruin from its elevated position may be seen from a long distance; when viewed from the southwest, it resembles a Mexican *teocalli*. The pottery here is of good quality and the remains of shell, obsidian, chert, and beads show that the people were comparatively wealthy. (Hough 1907:74–75)

Not a hint here that the Aragon ruin is unusual, beyond its "comparative wealth" and Hough's "teocalli" throw-away. Bless Hough, however; his plate 8 shows the ruin, its walls, and its circular kiva. Now that we know better, we see that the setting is archetypically Chacoan, the walls are remarkably well coursed, and the kiva is huge, round, and masonry-walled. We don't have a ground plan and we never will: The ruin was bulldozed in the early 1980s.

To anyone in the outlier business, Aragon would be a lead-pipe cinch—if it was found on Mancos Creek, or the Rio Puerco, or Chinle Wash. With consensus outliers now pushed as far south as Quemado, I think that we are justified in proposing a further 50 km extension of the Great House pattern deep into Mogollon country, to Aragon—a distance from Chaco comparable to the Bluff area Great Houses.

The reader might note two points of interest here (beyond "told you so" which, of course, was *my* point of interest). First, Aragon is a good example of the poverty of observational language, both past and present, for Great Houses and outliers. Our descriptive frameworks are shaped and tailored to reflect, parsimoniously, the scale of our projects; as a result, unusual sites are normalized, forced into available categories like round pegs into square holes. Great Houses become "two story buildings on ridges" or "larger roomblocks" or "unusually large unit pueblos"—anything that encompasses their uniquity within the larger pattern, within two standard deviations.

Second, the boundary of the Chacoan world is sagging south. There's more argument over Chaco's south than any other compass point. The south's fuzziness results, in part, from methodological difficulties (like Aragon), exacerbated by the taxonomic turbulence where "Anasazi" meets "Mogollon."

But, more significantly, our southern conundrum reflects an archaeological circumstance of real importance. We find it hard to agree on a southern boundary, because the southern boundary of the old Chacoan world was, in fact, a very different beast than east, north, or west. To the east, the Chacoan world starkly confronts the Rio Grande and the Great Plains beyond; to the north, it butts up against the Rockies; to the west, it surely ends at the low deserts beyond Flagstaff and beneath the Mogollon Rim. But to the south? To the south lies the Plateau-like Mogollon uplands and "Anasazi"-like Mimbres. And beyond Mimbres, Mexico.

The southern border was open then, if not now. The shaky definition of the south Chaco frontier is not merely an irksome taxonomic quandary; it's a triumph of data over method. We can't establish the closure we see on the north and east, and (with reason) hope for on the west, because the south was *not closed.* Beyond the outer edge was Mimbres—Anasazi *manqué.* That south will rise again, later in this chapter.

So what does the periphery tell us about Chaco as a center? For one thing, it's real—that is, the center really was a center. There were other Chaco-style sites, but Chaco was many times larger and incomparably grander than any 11th-century outlier. Chaco alone is a simply an anomaly, a pathology, an aberration; within a region, it becomes something like a capital. With the rise and fall of roads (Lekson et al. 1988; cf. Roney 1992), outliers best define its region; but inlying outliers lack descriptive clarity and rhetorical force. Many Great Houses, surrounded by a murky sea of smaller unit pueblos, escaped detection through decades of archaeological scrutiny. Archaeologists recorded those lurker-in-the-shadows as a "big unit pueblo" and passed on. It takes a blatant ringer way out on the edge, like Chimney Rock or Bluff or Aragon, to validate all the humdrum, cookie-cutter outliers that fill our maps with dots. Stubborn advocates of local development might dig in their heels and deny some second-tier Great House in the middle of Zuni country, awash with ruins great and small, and thereby call to question the reality of all outliers. But it takes a remarkable, even perverse, obstinacy to dismiss Chimney Rock or Aragon.

Maps and reports (Eddy 1977; Lister 1993) could do the job, but better still, visit the places. Look at the Parking Lot Ruin and look at the Chimney Rock Great House. Patterns show clearest against contrasting backgrounds. The far peripheries, where backgrounds contrast most, validate the center.

REDISTRIBUTION REVISITED

OK, it's real. But how did it work? The biggest problem with the Chacoan region is that it's so very big. And at the same time, so centered: Chaco really stood alone, above the rest. There were no competing peer polities (contra Wilcox and Weigand 1993). Aztec and Paquime followed, but Chaco in the 11th and early 12th centuries was the sole figurative if not geometric center of its region. That region, in the late 1970s and early '80s, was perceived as approximately equivalent to the San Juan Basin or the Chaco drainage plus some northern San Juan territory (Marshall, Stein, Loose, and Novotny 1979; Powers, Gillespie, and Lekson 1983; Vivian 1990). More distant outliers, like Chimney Rock, were known as quirky anomalies, but that's not where we looked. We looked closer to home, nearer to Chaco, working out from the center.

Within the Chaco Basin, Jim Judge's redistribution model still makes sense (to me; and Schelberg 1992). Judge began with the fact that rainfall was uneven and unpredictable within the San Juan Basin, and argued that Chaco served as a central "food bank," routing corn surpluses, as needed, among and between its surrounding ring of outliers, with the central administration skimming a little off the top for their services (Judge 1979, 1984, 1989). Judge has since recanted, (Judge 1993) but my faith in redistribution—as an important dynamic in Chaco's early days—remains strong. That old time religion was good enough for other archaeologists (Judge et al. 1981; Schelberg 1984, 1992; Tainter 1988; Tainter and Plog 1994) and it's good enough for me.

Chiefdoms redistribute; or, at least, some do. Chaco was a chiefdom, or something like that. Over the years, Service's chiefdom (in general) and Judge's redistribution model (in particular) have been nitpicked, nickel-and-dimed, and otherwise nullified. But "chiefdom" remains a useful (almost indispensable) term, and redistribution happens; whatever their vagaries and shortcomings as universal categories, both can be used for Chaco. I decline to define either at length, since at Chaco we may be seeing things that were not available in the ethnographic record, the source of our definitions. For my purposes, a chiefdom is a society with centralized institutions of power, manifest in elites, but not a state; redistribution is the reallocation of surpluses by a central authority.

The Judge model faded not so much from compelling challenges as from a weak defense. The redistribution model was based on three sets of data: first, highly variable rainfall around the margins of the San Juan Basin; second, the vast volume of "empty" storage space at Chaco Canyon Great Houses; and third, Chaco's geographic central place, *within the Chaco Basin*. None of those data have changed: The dendroclimatic data remain valid, the empty rooms at Great Houses are still empty, and Chaco remains at the center of the San Juan Basin—in a spot of no great merit, otherwise. Claims that Chaco was a good place for agriculture (Vivian 1990), or that Chaco produced big surpluses (Sebastian 1992) seem strained. Chaco may have been better than the area immediately around it, but it was no Garden of Eden.

What has changed is the distribution of outliers; we've filled in most of the white space between the San Juan Basin and those old anomalous Chaco sites out on the far periphery. Practical people pointed out that bulk transportation of corn has energetic limits; there is a cost-benefit radius beyond which porter transport simply isn't economically feasible (Drennan 1984; Lightfoot 1979). They argue, with some force, that the Arizona, Utah, Colorado, and south-central New Mexico outliers were well beyond that limit. Redistribution models of the 1970s won't work for the inflated Chacoan region of the 1990s. But they still worked inside that limit, inside the Chaco world as we knew it, in the 1970s.

There were zones or tiers of integration around Chaco, and different models work for different zones. First, there was the canyon itself, an elaborately planned ceremonial city (fig. 2.15). Doyel and others proposed the "Chaco Halo"—a zone of high density occupation encircling the canyon, a band of about 5 km (Doyel, Breternitz, and Marshall 1984). Presumably, the Chaco Halo was intensely engaged in whatever was happening in the canyon. The San Juan Basin—or whatever we want to call the area encompassed by the 100 km radius field-of-view from the Chaco Canyon high points—represents a third zone, within which redistribution *would have worked.* "San Juan Basin" is not precisely correct, nor is "Chaco Drainage"; the area that we are considering really represents the horizon seen from the Canyon's highpoints (e.g., Pueblo Alto): Lobo Mesa on the south, the Chuska Mountains on the west, the San Juan Valley on the north, and the Nacimiento Mountains on the east. Vivian (1990) calls this area the Chaco Basin—works for me.

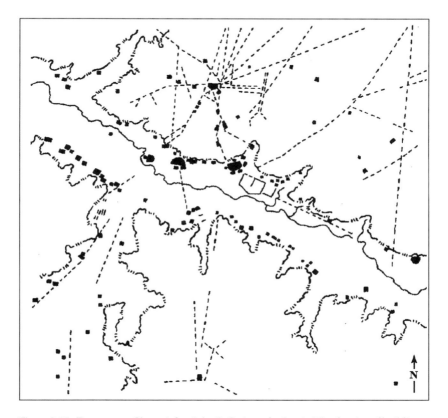

Figure 2.15. Downtown Chaco (after John R. Stein and others). The density of buildings, roads, mounds, and other constructed features at Chaco's core reflects two significant aspects of Chacoan archaeology: A remarkable amount of research energy has been expended in these ten square miles, and these ten square miles (about 25 km²) contain an unrivalled site. Neil Judd mapped many of the cliff top features and chased some of the long, low walls; Gwinn Vivian traced out the roads and mounds; Tom Windes continued the survey of non-buildings; John Stein and his colleagues have added much to the map. This map is a composite, based mainly on Stein's maps and NPS Chaco Project data. Some of these projected features will evaporate in the field and others will appear that we currently cannot see, but the density and formality of downtown Chaco is real.

So, concentrically: "Downtown Chaco," the 4–6 km² around Pueblo Bonito and Chetro Ketl (Lekson 1986a); the "Chaco Halo" in a radius of perhaps 5 km around the canyon, and the "Chaco Basin" reaching out about 100 km from the center. Chaco began with intracanyon dynamics in and around downtown (Judge 1979; Judge et al. 1981). The Halo was a zone of urban sprawl. The Basin corresponds to the area where redistribution worked, pumping up the canyon. But what was the great vast region of distant outliers beyond Chaco's horizon, beyond the Basin, beyond redistribution?

A worrisome frontier beckons, the out-there outliers that cause so much trouble. Outliers in Arizona, Utah, Colorado, and south-of-Zuni New Mexico—Bluff, White House, Aragon—poach into territories long thought beyond the reach of Chaco and really annoy the local archaeologists. Outliers that far distant outdistance Chaco-centered adaptive models. When we found outliers at Bluff and Aragon, we had to rethink redistribution; corn won't travel that far. But the empirical pattern remains.

CHACO HEGEMONY

I'd like to call this outermost ring the "Chaco Hegemony." "Hegemony" is fun to say; some people say "hegemony" a lot. Now I can say "Chacoan hegemony" at conferences and sound fashionable. I'll sidestep the multivoiced, nuanced, contextualized usages that clutter the literature, and return to the dictionary definition: "preponderant influence or authority, particularly of one state over a confederacy." Old dead white males, capitalism, latent colonialism, and all that devil's brew of hegemonic bugaboos are excused.

For me, it's either hegemony or equifinality. Either there was a source, a "prime object" that, through influence or authority, created the uniform form we call outliers, or they sprang up independently, the result of local pressures and processes. But I cannot credit equifinality; the uniform architecture of 150 outliers must *mean something*. Within the Chaco Basin, there was (I think) re-distribution. Hegemony replaces redistribution for out-there outliers. The organization of labor, the organization of space, and prestige economies of exotica all point to Chacoan political influence or authority over this huge region.

FLUFF ON THE FAR DISTANT FRINGE

Chaco was architecture or it was nothing: Outliers were buildings and the canyon itself congeries of structures. The conventional archaeological approach holds buildings as containers for action, exoskeletons of activities. Unit pueblos probably did grow and shrink with life cycles, economic boom-and-busts, relocated mothers-in-law. They were, in a word, organic. But Great Houses were not. They were designed, planned to last for years and decades. Great Houses could be modified only at great cost.

Labor is a key theme in outlier architecture: Outliers are massive, monumental labor-sinks. Outlier labor was greater and more organized than any other architectural projects. That tells us something: Outliers represent and express the organization of unusually large amounts of labor, qualitatively and quantitatively different than domestic modes of construction.

The organization of space, at and around the outlier Great House, instructed local populations. Architecture creates and commemorates authority. The earth itself was altered to reflect the rules and canons of Chacoan building (Stein and Lekson 1992). People learned from the roads, berms, buildings, and the wide range of constructed features that are being recognized at more and more distant locales (Fowler and Stein 1992). Surrounding communities learned by building, and remembered what they learned every time they saw what they had built.

We don't know what Chacoan architecture meant, but they knew. The rules presumably expressed ideas about the cosmos, about how the world worked and how society worked (most architecture does these things; Rapoport 1969, 1977, and subsequent works). Societies educate in many ways, and often through performance and ritual. Rituals have timelines; periodic, episodic, situational. Performance is transitory, but landscapes are forever. Chacoan buildings were conspicuously permanent—one generation's prodigy was the next's built environment, as real as a mesa or a mountain. Architecture shaped the Chacoan world. That investment in social training and cosmos maintenance over such a vast region suggests a very strong center indeed.

Architecture transcends feather-waving. But this is not to decry feathers. Fluff counts, too. There is nothing like good, fierce feather-waving to wake up the congregation or to drive home a point (David Wilcox and Christy Turner [quoted in Roberts 1996:98–103] suggest some *very* fierce Chacoan feather-waving). The display of exotic materials—feathers on a headdress or feathers on a spear—played a big part in the operation of low-octane hegemonies. They play an even bigger part in the archaeological study of same. Goodies are good for us to think about because they are generally well represented in older reports and museum collections, and, for many questions, they are actually important. Copper bells, turquoise, bifurcate baskets, cylinder vases, jet frogs, and all the other *significata* of ancient Chaco may not be things we understand, exactly, but they are undeniably the things we save and show: We bring them back to museums, and we picture them in plates. (Odd, that we normalize ringers in architecture and landscapes, but celebrate diversity in artifacts; archaeologists must find baubles less threatening than buildings.)

The appeal of feathers and feathered friends may be the same for us as it was for them: feathers, bells, shells, blue stones and all the rest were rare in color, texture, weight, or form (Clarke 1986). They are bright, shiny and, above all, unusual. Turquoise was rare but a macaw must have been a marvel. (Not, perhaps, to the parrot keepers of old Paquime, who could have had no fanciful notions about hundreds of squawking, biting, stinky birds—somewhere down the line, a bird is just a bird.) When macaws reached the northern Southwest, they were hotter than Hula Hoops. Pueblo histories, recounted in chapter 4, suggest that the political structure of the Greater Southwest was a case of macaws and effects.

I use macaws, here, as a loose proxy for the whole panoply of rare and exotic goodies that marked Chaco's hegemony over its region. Macaws and their company moved in what I will call a political economy, or, more specifically, a political-prestige economy. Here, as with "hegemony," I part company with the more ethereal configurations of "political economy"— another term variegated by anthropological usages (e.g., Cobb 1993; Hirth 1996). Macaw feathers were only one kind of exotica, presumably distributed from Chaco out to the edges of its hegemony, tying that huge area together in a network centered on the canyon. Turquoise was probably another (Judge 1984). Power relations cemented by exotica was a political economy in the sense of Brumfiel and Earle (1987), where "the circulation and control of luxury items were crucial for developing, defining, and expanding both regional and supraregional political networks" (Hirth 1996:208), without concomitant economies of bulk or subsistence goods. Politically directed prestige economies (or "wealth finance") were critical to emerging elite leadership: "control over the ideology of social ranking rested on control over the system of wealth finance" (Earle 1997:74). Not everyone agrees with Earle's assessment, but I do (see also, for example, Helms 1992:160).

To my simple mind, "political-prestige economy" means exchanges driven or directed by political power, in contrast to subsistence economies. The two may or may not be systemically related. The dichotomy of political-prestige economies and subsistence economies is a false one but, like so many social fictions, it is a useful convention. It works, for example, in Southwestern practice.

Southwestern archaeological writing, over its hundred-year history, has been couched in often exclusive historicist or environmental rhetorics. Gladwin (1957) spun tales of "tides of men," "the enemy at the gate," "gathering clans," and "the quick or the dead"—strong historical stuff, led by strong (but nameless) Great Men. SARG and its progeny "modeled Anasazi behavioral adaptations" correlating population aggregation with tree-ring indices or other environmental measures (Dean 1996; Gumerman 1988; Van West 1996). No one can ignore the arid limitations of the Southwestern land, but historically inclined scholars celebrate man's triumph over adversity of a marginal landscape, while environmentalists portray ancient Southwestern societies as something like a fungus, springing up when soil conditions, humidity, and solar energy converged within a specified range of values. Environmental approaches typically model subsistence economies; historical writings extol political economies.

Environmental prehistories of Chaco begin with intracanyon micro-environments: three confluences where agricultural conditions were exceptional and the first Great Houses were built. Penasco Blanco sits above the juncture of the Chaco and Escavada washes. Pueblo Bonito rose opposite South Gap, the principal side drainage of the central canyon. Una Vida looks out over the triple confluence of Chaco Wash, Gallo Canyon, and Fajada Gap. These three Great Houses were built about 900; the next Great House, Hungo Pavi, was constructed a century later, at the next largest confluence of Mockingbird Canyon.

For its first century-and-a-half, politics at Chaco were local. Three and later four Great House complexes vied for land and labor within the canyon. Perhaps Bonito won. Whatever the intracanyon story, the contagion spread, spilling out to Kin Bineola on the west and East Community, upstream (Windes and Anderson 1998). At some point in the first half of the 11th century, social and economic rivalries expanded beyond the canyon walls—perhaps signalled by the construction of Pueblo Alto, above the canyon in a setting of zero agricultural potential, about 1020. In the search for allies and confederates, Chaco discovered its centrality: It sits in the geographic center of the Chaco Basin, ringed at a 100 km radius by fertile but unpredictable farmlands. The San Juan River valley, the Chuska Valley, the north slopes of the Dutton Plateau, and the Mount Taylor foothills formed a circle or **C** of arable lands prized by contemporary Navajo peoples. As noted above, tree-ring data show us that productivity around that **C** varied wildly from year to year and place to place. This geography and paleoclimatic variability set the stage for redistribution, and redistribution allowed the accumulation of the moderate surplus needed, I think, to shift Chaco into a political hierarchy.

But beyond the Chaco Basin, a redistributive economy of bulk goods was simply impossible. Beyond the Basin, local networks presumably took care of the perennial local problem: What's for dinner? Roads cross-linking distant outliers may well define subregional redistribution, smaller copies of the Chaco Basin model. If a Chaco-centered economy operated out in the boonies, it was necessarily an economy of fluff, a political-prestige economy: rare, costly, symbolic, and above all portable. Macaws were all that. So were parrots, shells, turquoise, and copper bells.

Stunning direct evidence comes from the most impressive macaw artifact ever found in the Southwest (Borson et al. 1998). A wonderful macaw feather sash was found in 1954, in a cave in Lavender Canyon, Utah (about 270 km from Chaco and 80 km from Bluff). It was an apron or sash, with buckskin belt straps attached to a squirrel pelt, from which dangled twelve scarlet macaw feather ropes, each about 1.2 m long. A picture is worth a thousand words: look at the color images in *National Geographic* (Nov. 1982, vol. 162, no. 4:573) or *Archaeology* (Jan/Feb 1997, vol. 50, no. 1:55).

The sash was described by Hargrave (1979:5) who concluded that the sash "was manufactured outside the Southwest, probably in Mexico" in the 12th century. Recent research (Borson et al. 1998) shows that the pelt was not a Mexican species, but instead a Southwestern subspecies of the tassel-eared squirrel, *sciurus aberti*—native to New Mexico and Arizona, but *not* southeastern Utah. The workmanship of the piece is more Southwestern than Mexican.

An accelerator date on the pelt produced a date of 920 ± 35 B.P. (Borson et al. 1998), which calibrates to about 1080–1110. During the 11th century, there were only two Southwestern centers of macaw keeping: Chaco and Mimbres (of which, more below). Chaco had the plateau monopoly on macaws and the tassel-eared squirrels: Archaeological tassel-eared squirrels (*sciurus aberti*) were found at Pueblo Alto and Una Vida (Akins 1985:316).

The north frontier provides other macaw-related evidence for a Chacoan political-prestige economy. Indirect evidence comes from a group of artifacts termed "plume" or "feather holders" (fig. 2.16): small ceramic bricks with quill-sized holes, presumed to presage Hopi feather holders (Judd 1954; Sullivan and Malville 1993). Only seventeen of these remarkable artifacts have been found in the northern Southwest: two from Pueblo Bonito; two from the Wallace Ruin outlier near Cortez, Colorado; two from the Chimney Rock area; and eleven from Chimney Rock itself (Sullivan and Malville 1993:29–30). With all the digging that's gone on in the northern San Juan region, that restricted distribution is real and it tells us something.

The most spectacular macaw artifact in the Southwest was found not at Chaco, but out on the extreme northwest edge of the Chaco world. Perhaps that was an accident of preservation: Caves, like the Lavender Canyon site, have better preservation than rooms in ruins. But Bonito produced a wide range of perishable artifacts, as do most deep, dry Great Houses. Judd (1954:266) found—in addition to thirty birds—only four feathers in a single bundle (identified as macaw). The distribution points to a flow of prestige goods from the center out to the farthest periphery.

Of course, they kept a great deal of exotica at Chaco, too. Abnegation was not a conspicuous Chacoan trait. There is more turquoise at Pueblo Bonito

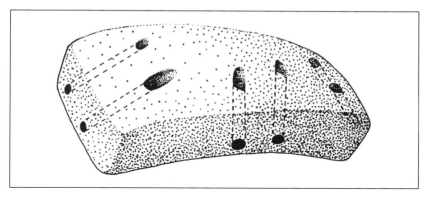

Figure 2.16. Feather holder from Chimney Rock (after Eddy 1977). These rare objects held rare feathers. Similar pieces are known from historic and modern pueblos. In the 11th century, they are known only from Chaco and its dependencies.

than all the other hundreds of excavated 11th-century sites in the Southwest. But, to some extent, they did not need the support of baubles at Chaco: They had the power of the city itself to awe the populace and to affirm power. Feathers and beads are portable, and spectacular badges of office might confirm authority better than small Great Houses, ill-built on local fabrics with local craftspeople.

PRESTIGE DEFLATED

Much ado about almost nothing: feathers boas, blue baubles, tinkler bells. Political prestige or mere frippery?

Putative southwestern prestige economies have been examined by Crown (1991) and others (Di Peso 1974; Douglas 1990; Doyel 1991; Kelley 1995; Mathien 1993; Neitzel 1989a; Nelson 1981; and Toll 1991) with varying conclusions. Some see political-prestige economies, some don't. What interests me is not so much the predictable range of interpretations as the underlying assumptions about scale and process. Exotics are typically seen as tagalongs on bulk goods.

With the obvious exception of single-class analyses (e.g., shell, R.L. Bradley 1993; copper bells, Vargas 1995), most Southwest analyses encompass bulk subsistence provisions, craft goods such as pottery, and truly rare items into single economic models, comparing and contrasting feathers and rocks, and generally giving more weight to weightier items. Pottery, in particular, was probably not a prestige item—every village could make its own, whether it did or not. Yet gallons of ink have been spilled on the relative aristocracy of redwares and the political significance of Chaco Black-on-white (does typology confer status?).

We shun the rare and embrace the ubiquitous.[4] Southwestern archaeo-logy has a strong populist penchant; and workaday pottery seems more honest than trinkets of a would-be elite. But looking for prestige economies in polychrome pots or obsidian flakes seems misguided, doomed to failure. Feathers and potsherds are apples and oranges or, rather, diamonds and dirt.

Pots, rocks, and corn were probably not part of the same economic system— or even coincident systems—as bells, birds, and baubles. At the smallest scales, a turquoise bead today might ensure a peck of corn tomorrow; but beyond the limits of local subsistence economies, gustatory quid-pro-quos were empty promises. Jumping to the very largest scales, like Mexico and the Southwest, bulk items simply dropped out. No one proposes bulk goods moving on continental scales, unless they were self-propelled, like slaves. Prestige economies probably were operationally independent of pots, rocks, and corn, on scales intermediate between district and continent—scales like the Chaco world, Chaco hegemony.

Especially the Chaco world: Consider Toll's (1991) and Mathien's (1993) minimization of exotics at Chaco. Toll (1991:86) describes exotics as "extremely small quantities," "minuscule." Mathien also minimizes, and concludes that "Chacoan control of critical goods or trade routes is unlikely" principally because of "the absence of a scarce resource" at Chaco (Mathien 1993:55, 56). This, at the epicenter of all oddities: Chaco had more weird stuff than the Santa Fe flea market.

Chaco exotics were downplayed, in part, in response to the continental claims of Charles Di Peso, who argued that Chaco was an outpost of Meso-american prestige economies. Di Peso built his model on nothing more ponderous than macaw feathers and turquoise beads—a wing and a prayer. In the rush to refute *pochteca,* bells, shells, birds and trinkets were minimized and normalized. Toll and Mathien swept them under the rug, and they were not alone. In Vivian's (1990) *Chacoan Prehistory of the San Juan Basin,* macaws and bells don't even merit index entries. "Exotics," in *Chacoan Prehistory,* refers to chipped stone and pottery; we look in vain for a macaw. "Luxury goods" (Sebastian 1992) and "exotica" (Saitta 1997), while important, are largely subordinate to agricultural surplus and surplus labor, respectively. Turquoise, ornaments, and other "long-distance imports" suffer from near-fatal "problems of differential sample size, depositional context, and differential excavation and recording techniques," but "further examination . . . would be warranted" (Sebastian 1991:117). With this faint praise, exotica are buried under other potential fruits of social and political success: labor and food.

These analyses subsume pesky exotica into an inclusive economic model that necessarily limits Chaco to its near neighborhood. As Sebastian points out, her models and others are formulated for the region conventionally termed the San Juan Basin, my Chaco Basin. "Can sites halfway across Arizona, hundreds of miles from Chaco Canyon, be considered 'Chacoan' in any meaningful sense?" (Sebastian 1992:152). Well, yes; but they could not have participated in the *subsistence* economies of Chaco, the Chaco Halo, and the Chaco Basin. Instead, those far-flung outliers appear to have been involved in the political-prestige economy of rare and wonderful things: macaws, bells, and the like. The organization of labor, the organization of space, and the prestige economy of exotica all define the larger Chaco Hegemony: "preponderant influence or authority, particularly of one state over a confederacy." I do not claim that Chaco was a state; but I propose that Chaco exerted preponderant influence or authority over a confederacy, and this authority was symbolized by things we can see in the ground: architecture and exotica.

This is relatively new territory for the Southwest. Feathers are fluff, compared to real stuff like pots, rocks, and food. Corn, beans, and squash are the meat and potatoes of Southwestern thinking. Di Peso offered bangles and birds from Mexico as evidence of Mexican control over the Southwest; we countered with redistribution, and a series of corn-fed, homegrown homilies. Somewhere along the way, we lost the goodies, beloved by museums, the engaged public, and (presumably) by their original owners. And, more important, we lost *Southwestern* political-prestige economies to pottery and obsidian. We will revisit all that good stuff in chapters 3 and 4.

CHACO AND MIMBRES

Macaws and copper and baubles bring us around, again, to the South, but not so far south as Di Peso would lead us. Beyond Aragon, 100 km beyond the old 250 km Chacoan territorial limit, was Mimbres (fig. 2.17). Mimbres and Chaco were exactly contemporary, and the Mimbres Valley was exactly south of Chaco Canyon.[5]

Famous for its pottery, Mimbres was more than just a pretty vase. Sprawling one-story masonry Mimbres settlements were, perhaps, the first real pueblos in the Southwest (Lekson 1992a, 1993). Fueled and tethered by large-scale canal irrigation systems (Herrington 1982, Lekson 1986c), Mimbres villages were truly permanent—sedentary over many generations—and they grew to remarkable size (fig. 2.18). The largest Mimbres village sites had up to 500 rooms and—unlike Pueblo Bonito and other Great Houses—most of those rooms were habitations. To cope with high densities and deep sedentism, Mimbres developed the earliest forms of kachina ceremonialism (Schaafsma 1994). These were remarkable achievements, but the florescence did not extend to architecture. Masonry and layouts were irregular and informal, compared with Four Corners ruins and, regrettably, compared with Chaco. Rough river cobble walls were the norm, and we search in vain for a right angle at Mimbres buildings.

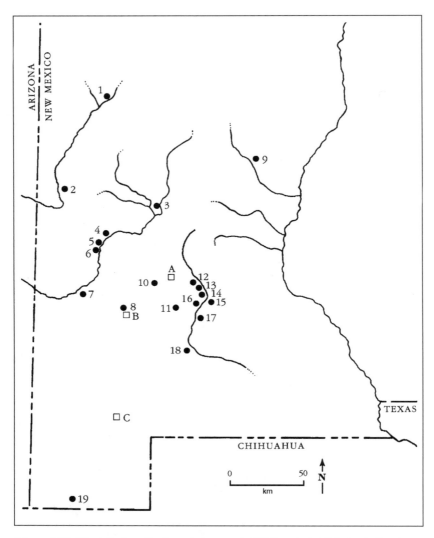

Figure 2.17. The Mimbres Region. 1, Aragon; 2, WS Ranch; 3, TJ Ruin; 4, Woodrow; 5, Saige-McFarland; 6, Dinwiddie; 7, Redrock; 8, Wind Mountain; 9, Victorio; 10, Treasure Hill; 11, Cameron Creek; 12, Mattocks; 13, Galaz; 14, Swarts; 15, NAN; 16, Baca; 17, Old Town; 18, Black Mountain; 19, Joyce Well; A, Santa Rita turquoise mines; B, White Signal turquoise mines; C, Old Hachita turquoise mines.

About a score of Mimbres sites represent large villages of up to 500 residents. Most of these were in the Mimbres Valley, but large Mimbres villages were found all along the desert-facing slopes of the Mogollon uplands from the Arizona border to the Rio Grande. Two of the very largest were on the Gila River, but the bulk of Mimbres population lived along the Mimbres River.

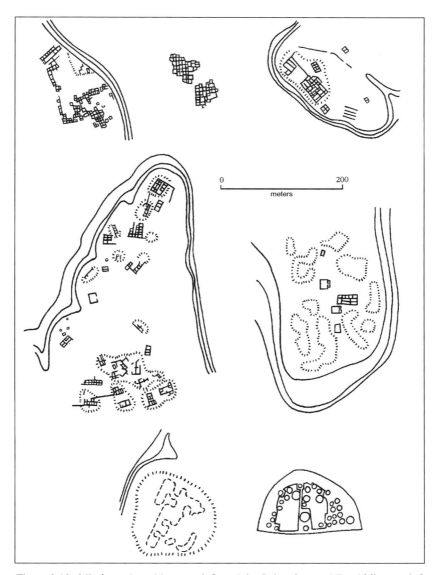

Figure 2.18. Mimbres sites. Top row, left to right Galaz, Swarts, TJ; middle row, left Redrock, right Woodrow; bottom row, left Old Town, right Pueblo Bonito, Chaco Canyon. North varies.

Some Mimbres villages were *big*. Only a few (very important) families lived in Pueblo Bonito and other Chaco Great Houses, but big Mimbres sites were towns. The evidence of village life are everywhere, as are the remains of the occupants, buried beneath the rooms. Swarts Ruin produced about 1,000 burials. Mimbres villages were the first real "pueblos": densely-packed apartment-like villages.

I once described Mimbres as a moire pattern, formed where Anasazi life-styles overlapped Hohokam economies (see fig. 4.3) (Lekson 1993). Mimbres pueblos, kivas, black-and-white and indented corrugated pottery are Anasazi; deep sedentism and canal irrigation are Hohokam. The "Anasazi-ness" of Mimbres is a long and bitterly contested research theme (contrast Haury 1986 and LeBlanc 1986a); sufficient here to note that where there's smoke, there's fire. Wiser heads than mine have looked at Mimbres and thought: Anasazi (Haury 1936, 1988). "Hohokam-ness" has often been mooted for pre-Mimbres pithouse horizons, and the discovery of Mimbres cremation cemeteries (Creel 1989; Shafer and Judkins 1996, 1997) and reports (perhaps apocryphal) of Mimbres ballcourts (Lekson in press d) suggest that my moire may be more than mere metaphor.

Hohokam exceeds the scope of this chapter (it resurfaces in chap. 5). Our principal concern here is Chaco and its world. "Anasazi-ness" in the 10th and 11th centuries—the height of Mimbres—cannot be separated from Chaco, because to a large extent Anasazi *was* Chaco. Chaco encompassed most if not all of the Anasazi region. Mimbres is taxonomically Mogollon; what did Mimbres have to do with Chaco? The answer to that question comes from two familiar classes of data: prestige goods and architecture.

I used macaws as a proxy for prestige goods in the Chaco world. Mimbres, alone in the 11th-century Pueblo region, rivalled Chaco in its aviary interests (fig. 2.19). There were lots of Mimbres macaws and parrots on pots and in the flesh (Creel and McKusick 1994). Thirty-one macaws were found at Pueblo Bonito; more than 17 have been found at Mimbres sites, and images of macaws are conspicuous on Mimbres pottery (fig. 2.19). Mimbres sites also produce copper bells in Chacoan numbers (Vargas 1995). In the 11th and early 12th century, Mimbres rivals Chaco for exotica. There may be more at Mimbres or more at Chaco; significantly, other Anasazi districts are not even in the running.[6]

Added to this are disturbing hints of architectural connections. Perhaps literal connections: Chaco-style roads are now being found in the Mimbres Valley (Creel 1998). How far north or south those roads extend is unknown; Mimbres road studies are only just beginning.[7] I have argued that the basic element of Mimbres settlement was an Anasazi-like unit pueblo (five rooms and a kiva) (fig. 2.2), jammed together in the larger Mimbres towns but scattered in Chaco-style communities where landforms allowed (Lekson 1988a, in press a; but see Shafer 1995). Most Mimbres communities centered on a Great Kiva— square, but no less Great (see fig. 3.3). In the most densely aggregated towns, the Great Kiva may have been replaced by plazas (Anyon and LeBlanc 1980) in a sequence familiar from other parts of the southern Pueblo world (Adams 1991; Haury 1950).

Figure 2.19. Mimbres macaws. (UCM 3238, courtesy of the University of Colorado Museum). Seventeen macaws and parrots have been recovered from Mimbres sites, and their images appear on numerous Mimbres bowls. This bowl shows two macaws and a tailed figure—a monkey? Monkeys flourish in the same Mexican forests as macaws. Mimbres artists favored exotic fish, fowl, and other strange fierce creatures. Their renderings were often quite accurate, and the anthropomorphized features of the monkey-man may represent an indirect sketch from travelers' tales.

All that's missing is the Great House—the outlier—and Mimbres may have had those too. If not textbook Great Houses with multiple stories, blocked-in kivas, enclosed plazas, berms and all the rest, then something very like them. A key question dogging the Chaco regional system, far to the north, concerns export versus emulation of Great Houses: Are outliers planned and built by Chaco architects ("exports"), or are they local copies by local people of the strange and wonderful buildings in that distant Emerald City ("emulation")? As long as we define outliers by a strict Chaco Canyon checklist, then outliers must necessarily *replicate* Chaco buildings in form and detail, and the argument must necessarily lean toward export. If an outlier isn't an outlier unless it duplicates a small slice of Pueblo Bonito, then outliers will appear to have been built by the same people who built Bonito. What would an emulation look like? It might lack many of the interior details, the checklist features, the Chaco-specific attributes. It might well be bigger, more massive, more formal than the surrounding houses of the people. It would *look like* a Great House, but it would be built on a local fabric—not just local materials, but local technologies and local floor plans.

There are a few such structures in the Mimbres region. I'll offer three. At the very large Woodrow Ruin, in the Mimbres Valley, a central roomblock rises conspicuously above the surrounding community of typical Mimbres roomblocks (fig. 2.20). Two huge Great Kivas are immediately adjacent. This central roomblock was excavated by a youth group in the 1960s; there's no report, but we can still see the interior walls and arrangements. Unlike other Mimbres sites, the walls are thick and straight. The roomblock is a crisp rectangle, with very large front rooms backed by pairs of smaller rear rooms. The walls, like most Mimbres walls, are river cobble set in mud. The walls are Mimbres, the form is not. This could be an emulation, a Great House, translated by Mimbres architectural habits and technologies.

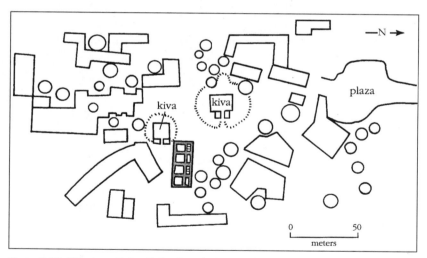

Figure 2.20. Woodrow Ruin. (After Stewart Peckham.) A site mapped first by Hattie and Burt Cosgrove about 1930, Stewart Peckham in the 1960s, and Karl Laumbach and me in the 1980s. Woodrow was very large but, for the most part, its architecture is not visibly remarkable: indistinct low ridges with a scattering of cobbles. At the center of the site rises a much more massive roomblock, with thick walls, big rooms, and (relatively) high mound height. Not a Chacoan outlier but, by Mimbres standards, a "big bump." A cabal of Mimbres archaeologists field-tripped to the site several years ago, and unanimously rejected this claim; but I think Woodrow (and some other Mimbres sites) represent local "emulations" of the Great House—for example, Baca (see fig. 2.21). North approximate.

Just behind the Visitors Center at Gila Cliff Dwellings sits one of the true archaeological jewels of the Park Service's crown and my second outlier wannabe: the TJ Ruin, the last large unbulldozed, unexcavated Mimbres site. It is also the northernmost large Mimbres site: Set in a tiny pocket of arable land amid the rugged Mogollon uplands, TJ is 300 km from Chaco (the same distance as Wupatki), but only 80 km from Aragon. The TJ Ruin has long been known among cognoscenti as the most convincing multistoried Mimbres site (McKenna and Bradford 1989). Even unexcavated, the commanding rise of its compact central roomblock dominates the site (not unlike a junior Yucca House, towering over its community—for those who know that satellite unit of Mesa Verde National Park). An imposing but compact building at an 11th-century community? Move TJ one hundred km north, and a new dot would appear on many outlier maps.

My third example is frustrating, archaeologically, but even more disturbing, formally. The Baca site, in the Mimbres Valley, was excavated by amateurs and reported by an aficionado (Evans, Ross, and Ross 1985). Baca has been bulldozed so, like Aragon, there's no looking back; the report is all we have. The maps and photos are less than we might wish, but what they show is remarkable (fig. 2.21). The tall walls of Baca were of coursed ashlar masonry, not river cobbles; the rooms are trim rectangles and the ground plan was a very Chacoan "D", with a rectangular roomblock 25–30 m long and 10–15 wide and a plaza-enclosing arc of rooms. The excavators noted a broad road-like feature running along the north edge of the building: "well-packed [and] treated like the Mimbres did their floors . . . water applied to the 'caliche' and rubbed to a smooth surface . . . it was in step-like layers

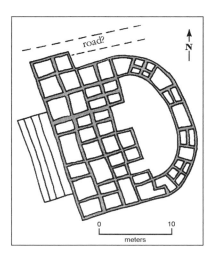

Figure 2.21. Baca site (after Evans, Ross, and Ross 1985). The Baca site map (re-drafted here) has been dismissed as the inaccurate work of amateurs. The book from which this plan was taken, *Mimbres Indian Treasure* (Evans, Ross, and Ross 1985) includes chapters on Atlantis and Barry Fell. The map is sketchy but even the general outlines—a rectangular block with a **D** arc of rooms—are unlike any Mimbres village known to me (except, perhaps, the Green-horn Arroyo site, on the Rio Grande). The discovery at Baca of a broad "road" antici-pated the confirmation of these features at the site of Old Town by Darrell Creel (1998).

that were lengthy and not very deep" (R. Evelyn Ross, personal communication, 1987). A similar road segment has recently been found at Old Town, one of the longest Mimbres Valley sites (Creel 1997).

Is Baca a Great House? Is TJ? Is Woodrow? Mimbres archaeologists deny the possibility with the same fervor Colorado archaeologists used to deny Great Houses at Mesa Verde. No Mimbres site will display the unmistakable singularity of Chimney Rock or even Bluff; geology denied access to the fine tabular sandstones that made distinctively Chacoan masonry possible. And indeed I would not suggest that Mimbres candidate Great Houses were built by Chaco masons. They are examples of what we might seek as Great House "emulations"—Great House forms on local fabrics, adapted to local social and political situations.

Mimbres was probably not submerged or encompassed politically within the Chaco regional system, but it was linked historically to that great center. Macaws and architecture show that linkage. In the 11th- and 12th-century Pueblo world, macaws and copper and other prestige items are notably concentrated only in Mimbres and Chaco.

We might object that little Mimbres pottery was found at Chaco, and only slightly more Chaco pottery was found in the Mimbres valley. As noted above, prestige economies were not about pottery. Mimbres decorated pottery was probably specific to Mimbres ritual (a cult which did not travel well) and, of course, the majority of later Chaco pottery was not actually made at Chaco. Pottery exchange between those two is not the only useful index of interaction.

It seems obvious to me, if not to others, that Chaco and Mimbres were linked by history. Specific events are lost to us, but architecture and exotica tell the story. There was no great divide between Mimbres and Chaco, only distance. Events in one were soon known in the other, travelling over the trails (road?) that carried macaws, bells, turquoise, and who knows what else. (We explore those routes in chapter 3.)

MONDO CHACO JUST SO

To review and digest those aspects of Chaco relevant to my larger argument: Chaco, like any mildly complex phenomenon, had a nonlinear history of change and transformation. Chaco Canyon had three areas of relatively high agricultural potential. By about 900, three conspicuously large buildings appeared at those hot spots: Penasco Blanco, Pueblo Bonito, and Una Vida, later joined by Hungo Pavi at a second-tier confluence. Circumscription in the isolated canyon amplified intervillage competition for labor, expressed archaeologically as competitive building. By 1020, social ferment had outgrown the canyon and allies were sought beyond the canyon's rim. Chaco, by chance, was *the* central place in the Chaco Basin, and brokered a redistribution network, within the larger Basin. It worked. Chaco took off, fueled by the surpluses skimmed from the Chaco Basin. Local power struggles were subsumed in that larger political development.

Power relations were based first on subsistence economics of the Chaco Basin, and then expanded to prestige political economies that could reach far beyond those spatial limits. By 1060, Chaco Canyon building (and everything else) transcended intracanyon rivalries of founding families and even Basin-scale redistribution. Population at the center moved past 2,500, a scalar threshold (we shall discuss in chapter 5) that almost invariably leads to hierarchy and political structure.

It wasn't altogether a bad thing. A sort of "Pax Chaco" prevailed, where families could live in small houses scattered around a Great House, without evident fear of violence or thuggery. In the century before Chaco and the century after Chaco, big villages were the rule; only during the Chacoan era was the great majority of population able to live in single-family homes. Indeed, family mobility may have been high; only monuments—Great Houses—were fixed in place. That all came to an end after 1125. Violence prevailed and single-family homes reaggregated into the big "Pueblo III" villages: safety in numbers (LeBlanc 1997).

People got power in Chaco, and liked it. People often do. Or not—it doesn't matter: Power perpetuates whether or not the boss is having fun. Power was institutionalized in something like the "Masters of the Great House," lords who lived and deliberated in a city of Great Houses, at the exact center of the world. Chaco became a node and a magnet. The Chaco Halo represents both urban sprawl and substantial in-migration, newcomers attracted to the capital. There was nothing even remotely like Chaco in the Pueblo world, no "peer polities" until Chaco reached the Hohokam frontier. Things got bigger and maybe better in that best of all possible worlds. Great things happened at Chaco, many of which are recalled in Pueblo traditional histories (to which we will return in chapter 4).

The appropriate models for archaeological understanding of Chaco shift from adaptation to politics. People from far beyond the Chaco Basin joined, or were made to join. They adopted Chacoan building canons, Chacoan world views, Chacoan hegemony and were rewarded with exotica and—more importantly—the Pax Chaco: Violence was limited and controlled by the central authority. Anasazi settlement, not coincidentally, reached its greatest geographic extent, spinning out to Las Vegas, Nevada, and nearly reaching southern Wyoming. To the south, Chaco reached Mimbres—and met something like a peer, or at least something sufficiently different to demand different dynamics. In the end, a political chain linked local groups from the Rocky Mountains on the north to the Chihuahua basins on the south.

Then, about 1125, the wheels came off. Major construction ceased at Chaco about 1125; at exactly the same time, Mimbres ends. What happened next to Chaco is the problem addressed in the remainder of this book. What happened to Mimbres?

LIFE AFTER MIMBRES

Mimbres at 1100 consisted of about twenty very large villages and scores of smaller settlements in the Mimbres Valley, the Gila Valley, and a few other creeks flowing out of the Mogollon mountains. Those villages have already been described: stone masonry pueblos and kivas. Ceramic decoration had reached an artistic peak, celebrated in museums and coffee-table books today.

At about 1125, Mimbres quit building stone masonry pueblos and quit building small kivas. They also quit painting pottery. So complete was this change that for decades, archaeologists spoke of a Mimbres "collapse," with populations vanishing or migrating out to who-knows-where (Blake, LeBlanc, and Minnis 1986; LeBlanc 1983). This, we now know, was not the case. Mimbres people did not vanish; they simply changed clothes. Villages moved slightly downstream and out into lower, desert reaches of river valleys (Lekson 1992b). Architecture shifted from stone masonry to puddled adobe—much harder to see on a survey. And the brilliant Mimbres painted pottery traditions abruptly ceased, replaced by unpainted ceramics (fig. 2.4). That ceramic change insured archaeological invisibility: In an area famed for its painted pottery, plain pottery simply disappears.

Recent survey and excavations at multicomponent sites demonstrate a substantial population in the Mimbres region long after the Mimbres "collapse" of 1125 (Creel 1997; Hegmon, Nelson, and Ruth 1998). Regionally, population may have been only slightly less than the Mimbres peak, but the region itself shifts south and east to incorporate areas beyond the old Mimbres riverine homelands (Lekson 1989d, 1990a, 1992c, in press d).

Not only was there a simple geographic shift (small, by Plateau standards; see fig. 4.4) and a change in material culture, but also a substantial watershed in ideology. Mimbres painted pottery was a primary locus for the expression of Mimbres ideology and cosmology (e.g., Brody 1977; Shafer 1995). Remarkable creative energies were invested on the interior of bowls. After 1125, the bowl-interior field of design was completely repudiated; bowls were not only *not* painted, their interiors were smudged a deep black and then highly burnished, creating a dark mirror effect.

In about a generation, bowl interiors were transformed from one of the most celebrated fields for Southwestern expressive art to a black, blank anti-design. Something big happened, something that inverted the old ideological order. People turned their backs on the old ways and built new villages with new fabrics out in the deserts of southern New Mexico and the Jornada region. These El Paso Phase and Animas-Black Mountain Phase villages (Lekson 1992b), successors to Mimbres, are the likely base population for Paquime, two centuries later. Physical anthropology links Mimbres and Paquime populations (Turner 1993).

It seems impossible that Chaco's end and Mimbres's transformation were not to some degree interrelated, even a response to a mutual cataclysm. The earlier linkages of Chaco and Mimbres, their exact contemporaneity, and—to anticipate later chapters—their positional relationships all point to profound historical connections. After 1125, all vestiges of the Chacoan system were gone from the old Mimbres region. Chaco was gone but surely not forgotten; gone, but *not* never to return.

NOTES

1. A similar institution characterized ancient Zia government (Hoebel 1979:415). A divinely appointed leader, the *tiyamunyi*, received the yields from communally cultivated fields and deer hunts, and redistributed surpluses. The *tiyamunyi* appointed secular and religious bureaucracies for adminsitration of the pueblo. No *tiyamunyi* has served since about 1900; the "acting" officer is the *tiyamunyi*'s "first assistant" or *cacique;* "he is less sacred [than the *tiyamunyi*] and, probably, less influential. Nonetheless, the cacique is the object of much reverence [and] is freed from physical labor" (Hoebel 1979:415) The situation at Acoma is not clear: members of the Antelope clan select a *cacique,* who appoints the administrative officers (Eggan 1983; Garcia-Mason 1979).

2. I'm a big Chaco fan. Many people assume that I champion Chaco simply because I once worked there. Field work happens out in the field, and it's difficult—maybe impossible—to separate site data from place sense. There's a cornfield in Tennessee I still detest, twenty years after a particular summer from hell; so don't ask me about the Cumberland Valley Archaic. I freely confess to a deep fondness (approaching bias) for the Cliff Valley of the upper Gila, vis-à-vis the Mimbres Valley (e.g., Lekson 1990c). I misspent a part of my youth around Cliff, shooting pool and having fun, so I like the place. But I'm fairly neutral about Chaco Canyon. Chaco was an entertaining place to work, but Chaco was, first and foremost, work. I do not think Chaco was important because I worked there; I worked there because I thought Chaco was important.

Working at Chaco diminished, if anything, my youthful inflated ideas about the place: Chaco was not the pyramids of Egypt nor the pyramids of Teotihuacan. Chaco was puny compared to Cahokia. My initial Park Service products were carping reality checks: no state, no *pochteca*, no American Stonehenge, no eighth Wonder of the World. But Chaco was, in fact, a big deal *in the Southwest*; there was nothing else like it in the 11th and early 12th centuries. That was clear to me before I started working for the Park Service; it remains clear today, too.

3.   Part of the difficulty in capturing and presenting outliers may well be Southwestern (and North American) archaeology's impoverished graphic faculties. Archaeology deals with objects, structures, spaces, and landscapes. Our primary data are profoundly visual, yet we worship text and tables. Our maps and diagrams are not what they could or should be. Flip through the pages of *American Antiquity*; there is little there to celebrate, visually. The maps in this book are typical, I think. The draftsperson was very good, but I provided her with rushed, skeletal originals. Part of the problem is time: more time (and emphasis) for words and numbers than for graphics. We should teach Tufte alongside Hodder. It seems likely that computer graphics will simply turn up the volume of noise—as they have done for charts and graphs. The problem transcends the technical: Data graphics constitute a whole new methodological front in near-future archaeology. But for now, a good thing we could do for Southwestern archaeology would be to hustle up some money, rent a small fleet of vans, and take the forty most skeptical, most influential Chaco critics on an outlier tour from Bug Point to Quemado, from Guadalupe to Low Mountain. Experiential education is effective education; and given the that set of experiences, it would take a deeply entrenched Chaco-phobe to deny the reality and the ubiquity of the outlier pattern. But then I think how much bother it would be to bag the money, log the trip, and cajole that particularly prickly target group.

4.   Not all archaeologists shun southwestern goodies: for example: Doyel (1991, and citations therein), Hudson (1978), Mathien (1986), Neitzel (1989a), Nelson (1986) and—of course—J. Charles Kelley (e.g., 1986), Charles Di Peso (1974), Joseph Whitecotten and Richard Pailes (e.g., 1986), and Phil Weigand (Harbottle and Weigand 1992; Weigand and Harbottle 1993). But mainstream Southwestern archaeology has, for the last three decades, consistently ignored the political implications of exotica and focused on production steps of polychrome pottery.

5.   I didn't really think about Mimbres and Chaco and all that, until I started drawing lines between Chaco and Paquime, but Chaco and Mimbres are definitely worth considering together. The contemporaneity of Chaco's Bonito phase (900–1125) and the Classic Mimbres phase (1000–1150) is a matter of public record, but curiously unremarked. The contemporaneity of Chaco and Mimbres was noted by LeBlanc (1983:158–159); but, curiously, not by Brody (1977) or LeBlanc (1986b, 1989)— remarkably wide-ranging essays—nor more pointedly by Shafer (1995).

I have an inclusive view of Mimbres (Lekson 1986b): my Mimbres ranged from west of the Arizona line to east of the Rio Grande—from about 107° to 109°. Contrary to the old saw, Mimbres was *not* Mimbres only in the Mimbres Valley. The largest Mimbres sites are in the upper Gila River valley, at Redrock and Cliff, New Mexico

(Lekson 1984b). However, when pothunters attacked the big Gila sites, those ruins did not produce the anticipated numbers of Mimbres pots: Was my valley "slightly different"? I thought there might be a hopscotch intervalley sequence (a model more fully developed by Nelson and Anyon 1996), but the surface archaeologies of the Mimbres and the Gila were nearly identical (Lekson 1992c).

But I confess: there *is* something special about the Mimbres Valley. Unquestionably, the Mimbres was the epicenter of the eponymous art-style. Better suited than the Gila or Rio Grande for small-scale canal irrigation, the Mimbres Valley could support denser occupations then those neighboring, larger river valleys. Population density is important (see chap. 5), and Mimbres Valley populations also were probably more aggregated and certainly more circumscribed than Gila and Rio Grande peoples. Those differences, together, suggest that new social and ritual organizations (i.e., kachina ceremonialism) probably developed in the Mimbres Valley—adapting elements of southern cosmologies and pantheons to purely local needs.

Which brings us back to the Mimbres Valley's longitude. Most of the Mimbres Valley—the length of the river below the confluence of its upper forks and above Deming—is due south of Chaco—the canyon from Fajada to the Escavada. Both are circumscribed, oasis-like (the Mimbes Valley was an oasis; Chaco was oasis-like), and both saw unparalleled social and architectural developments during the 11th and early 12th centuries. Both were and are the obvious major concentration of Mexican things, east of the Continental Divide. All this fits together, somehow, in some vast conspiracy theory. . .

6. Mimbres ruins produced considerable amounts of turquoise, but not Chacoan quantities (e.g., Cosgrove and Cosgrove 1932:64). An exception: Over 3,000 pieces of turquoise (mostly "residual" or "waste" fragments) were recovered from a single Mimbres context at the West Baker site (McCluney 1968). The West Baker site is located near (but not at) the turquoise mines at Old Hatchita, which rival Cerillos in scale, with twenty chambered mines (Phil Weigand personal communication 1989; Weigand and Harbottle 1993:163). "An unknown polity(s) was involved in the development of the Azure-Old Hachita areas" (Weigand and Harbottle 1993:173). Mimbres? Paquime? The Old Hachita Mines were the same distance from Paquime as the Cerillos mines were from Chaco. If Paquime politicos were responsible, turquoise did not stick to their hands. Only(!) 1.2 kg of turquoise was recovered at Casas Grandes, mostly from architectural, dedicatory deposits (Di Peso, Rinaldo, and Fenner 1974e:187).

7. And now we have roads in the Hohokam! Wilcox (Wilcox, McGuire, and Sternberg 1981) identified road-like features at the margins of Snaketown. Motsinger (1998) now traces one of these roads almost 6 km, to another site (and conspicuous landscape feature) at Gila Butte. We may soon see an explosion of Hohokam roads. I hope that Hohokam archaeologists heed the mistakes we made (and make) with Chacoan roads (presented, with diplomacy and tact, in Vivian 1997a, 1997b). There's a joke here, about reinventing wheels, which I will leave to the reader.

3

MERIDIAN
NEXUS

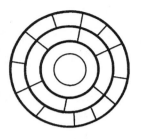

A gnomon
Our science is from the watching of shadows
Ezra Pound, *Cantos* (85)

MILLENNIAL RECAPITULATION

The 11th century set the stage for a political history of the Pueblo Southwest which ended, in 15th or early 16th century, at Paquime. This section reviews the 11th century, as the foundation for what came after, and previews the rest of the story.

Chaco emerged in the 11th century as the paramount political center of the northern Southwest. Something happened at Chaco that had not happened before in the Pueblo world: A permanent primate center organized and controlled a sizable region. ("Primate" probably in rank-size, certainly in importance.) There were large villages before Chaco, but none approached Chaco in size and regional prominence, and none lasted for more than a generation or two.[1] They were vernacular and transitory. Chaco was monumental, permanent, and very different.

So, too, was Mimbres: different, at least. New ways of living—social and ritual—developed in the 11th-century Mimbres world, which would ultimately overshadow Chaco's political heritage in the formation of modern Pueblo cultures. Large, Mimbres pueblos were both cause and effect of Mimbres canal irrigation—a Hohokam technology. Mimbres pueblos were something new under the Southwestern sun: large, permanent, high-density pueblos maintained without complex political structures. Mimbres extended Chacoan ideas far into the Chihuahuan desert; but it transformed Chacoan patterns of fluid settlement under rigid hierarchy into a new configuration of deeply sedentary pueblos with inclusive, unifying ritual.

Such was the Pueblo world by the mid-11th century. A few generations later, about 1125, large-scale construction ended at Chaco. Mimbres suddenly and completely transformed itself into something that, until recently, archaeologists couldn't even see. We have found post-Mimbres, and now it appears that the things that started at Chaco did not end at Chaco. We have found post-Chaco.

The political principles (and, perhaps, principals) that ruled Chaco were perpetuated in two subsequent, sequential centers—first Aztec and then Paquime—the latter perhaps lasting almost into colonial times. In this and the next chapter, we will trace that political history, from Chaco's beginning at 900 to Paquime's end at 1450.

This is hot stuff. Chaco alone is difficult: The Chaco hegemony of chapter 2 enrages many Southwestern archaeologists. Nothing like it appears in Pueblo ethnohistory, where we look for the proper limits of the prehistoric past. Still worse, the Chacoan regional system jumps the carefully tended taxonomic walls we have built around our research areas. It violates personal and professional space. Good fences make good neighbors, so my mega-Chaco, Chaco *uber alles*, is not a happy notion. How much worse, extending Chacoan scales not just in *space*, but in *time*, into the protohistoric period?

The political history of the Pueblo Southwest first revealed itself in a tiny bit of data: two dots on a map. It's hard for data to be more bit-like than that. The dots are Chaco and Paquime, two late prehistoric sites in the American Southwest. Chaco Canyon (900–1125) and Paquime (1250–1450) were the largest, most important sites of their respective eras and regions. They will be joined, shortly, by Aztec Ruins (1110–1275), the largest site of *its* time and place; but the archaeological historiography begins with Chaco and Paquime.

Chaco and Paquime have been the subject of sordid, tittering speculation for some years: Charles Di Peso first hinted that Chaco and Paquime were an item (Di Peso 1974). We scoffed (e.g., Lekson 1983b, 1984a), along with many others. A liaison between Chaco and Paquime seemed impossible. The two were from different worlds: 630 km apart in space and further apart in time. Chaco was too old, Paquime too young. We looked at their ages, we looked at the maps, and we knew it would never work.

However, something cartographic caught my eye. Chaco and Paquime were on the same meridian. That is, they were exactly north-south of each other. Chaco-Paquime might be May-December, but, positionally, they made a striking pair.

I initially dismissed their alignment (already, the tainted "A" word) as an unpleasant coincidence, as would most of my readers, but independent data made me reconsider. Those independent data were primarily from Aztec Ruins. Aztec, as it turns out, matches Chaco and Paquime in size and historical importance—an insight noted several years ago by John Stein and Peter McKenna (1988). Aztec was the third major center in Pueblo pre-history; it, too, was also almost exactly on the Chaco-Paquime meridian (fig. 1.1).

Two dots become three: Chaco (900–1125), Aztec (1110–1275), and Paquime (1250–1450). And that *ménage à trois*, of the three sequential centers of the Pueblo Southwest, were alarmingly aligned. Perhaps the Chaco-Paquime meridian alignment was not a fluke.

The argument is long and, I fear, complicated. There are so many side issues that every archaeologist will disagree with something. Since my con-clusions suggest major revisions of Southwestern archaeology, the argument is particularly susceptible to "false in this, false in all" rejection. Resist that temptation; suspend, for now, disbelief. Forget the decorative details and ignore the ancillary rants. The basic data of the argument are simple, straight-forward, and sound: tree-ring dating of Chaco, Aztec, and Paquime; unique architectural elements shared among only those three sites; the Great North Road; and a set of geographic coordinates.

The following section of this chapter begins with the methodological problems of unique events. The alignment of Chaco, Aztec, and Paquime, if nothing else, is unique; and archaeologists have difficulty with uniquity. After that methodological preamble, I get down to cases, briefly describing Chaco, Aztec, and Paquime and the remarkable archaeological parallels between and among those three celebrated sites. Chapter 4 presents the meridian alignment as an argument of "means, motive, and opportunity." Then, in chapter 5, I present my conclusions: substantive, methodological, cognitive, generalizing, and (finally) final.

Uniquity and Mobius Logic

In this section, I admit and lament the tactical difficulties of promoting an interpretation that many archaeologists would cross the street to avoid. The Chaco-Aztec-Paquime meridian is a mighty hard sell. There is a tale told of Leonard Woolley, when he proposed that flood deposits at Ur represented the Biblical Deluge: "'We all agree that your theory is mad,' one colleague commented. 'The problem which divides us is this: Is it sufficiently crazy to be right?'" As it turns out, Woolley *was* wrong—but he wasn't crazy.

Chaco-Aztec-Paquime is rhetorically challenging because it is unique. It cannot be shown to be part of a class, a group, or a pattern, and that makes my colleagues (and me!) uneasy. Uniquity is anathema.[2] Americanist archaeology is much more comfortable with redundancy, repetition, pattern.

The first and highest hurdle for unique past phenomena is establishing their reality. Some unique events announce themselves in the archaeological record with unmistakable clarity: the eruptions of Vesuvius, for instance, or the Ozette mudslide. Other events, less dramatically attested, are more liable to doubt. The Chaco-Aztec-Paquime alignment is surely one of the latter. This leads to a necessarily circular rhetoric: If the alignment was *not* chance, then interesting conclusions can be posited; and those conclusions support the original but tenuous assertion that the alignment was not chance. That mobius-strip circularity seems necessary, since mainstream archaeology has no developed rhetoric (or statistic!) for dealing with uniquity.

The history that I ask you to consider is this: A series of three major centers sequentially dominated their respective areas of the southwest: first, Chaco (900–1125) in northwest New Mexico; second, Aztec (1110–1275) in the Mesa Verde region; and third, Paquime (1250–1450) in northern Chihuahua. A ruling elite emerged at Chaco and perpetuated itself by moving a ceremonial city along Chaco's meridian. Position legitimized five centuries of political continuity. Local populations were variably integrated into the shifting regional systems by a political-prestige economy of West Mexican exotics—birds, bells, shells.

This abridged guide shows us where we are going, but to get there we will follow twisted paths and side roads. The following sections briefly describe Chaco, Aztec, and Paquime and present data from architecture, minor artifacts, extra-regional interactions, and regional organization. These aspects strongly suggest that the Chaco-Aztec-Paquime alignment was not a coincidence, but rather the result of something like the short historical sketch presented above.

A TALE OF TWO "NEAR-URBAN CENTERS" AND ONE WANNABE

In this section, I will briefly describe Chaco, Aztec, and Paquime; discuss parallels of scale, form, orientation, and architectural detail; and then argue for their unique preeminence in their respective places and times. Chaco and Paquime are generally recognized as the two largest regional centers in Pueblo prehistory; Aztec had the size and scale, but its role as a regional center is only beginning to be appreciated.

Introducing the Principals

I have always used the awkward but circumspect construction "near-urban" for Chaco, but it would be proper to call Chaco a city, in Paul Wheatley's (1971) sense of a ceremonial city or center (further developed by Meyer 1991 and Smith and Reynolds 1987; see also Rapoport 1993). I use, without overmuch embarrassment, the term "ceremonial city" or simply "city," *sensu* Wheatley, for Chaco, Paquime, and Aztec.

There are remarkable differences in our knowledge of each of these three sites. A century of sustained research gives us a huge set of data from Chaco (reviewed by Lister and Lister 1981). Paquime is known almost exclusively from a single research program, that of Charles Di Peso, who excavated about one-third of the site in the 1960s (Di Peso 1974). Paquime (also known as Casas Grandes) is less well researched than Chaco. Chaco Canyon has seen five large-scale research programs over the last hundred years; Paquime has had only one, in the late 1960s (Di Peso 1974). Survey is adding to our knowledge of its region (Whalen and Minnis 1996b), but Paquime proper belongs to Di Peso.

At Aztec, we have barely scratched the surface. Earl Morris excavated one of half a dozen Great Houses and the National Park Service excavated one of at least three tri-walled structures (Lister and Lister 1987). The total Aztec sample is much smaller than Di Peso's from Paquime. Ongoing Chaco work continually reevaluates earlier research; Di Peso's (1974) report stands as a monument to detailed publication; but Aztec was dug early and never fully reported. In short, we know much less about Aztec than we do about either Chaco or Paquime.

During the 11th and early 12th centuries, Chaco Canyon was a ceremonial city with a highly developed tradition of monumental building (chap. 2). Huge sandstone masonry buildings defined a central precinct of several square kilometers. Chaco was the center of a 40,000 km² regional network of "Great Houses" which incorporated most of the southern Colorado Plateau (chap. 3; Crown and Judge 1991; Doyel and Lekson 1992; Lekson et al. 1988; Vivian 1990.) Planning was rigid, formal, and geometric: Precise symmetries, solar and cardinal orientations, and dramatic use of natural features all operated on scales incorporating the individual building, settlement, landscape, and region.

From about 1250 to perhaps 1500, Paquime was the premier city of the Southwest, with a five-story, poured-adobe, Pueblo-style core of homes, workshops, and warehouses (figs. 3.1, 3.2). The central building was surrounded by a remarkable mix of Mesoamerican and Southwestern public and ceremonial monuments: ballcourts, great kivas (Unit 11, Room 38, see fig. 3.3; Lekson in press e), platforms, effigy mounds. Paquime's planning and formality surpasses Chaco's.

Like Chaco, Paquime was the largest site of its time and place. Its local region extended over much of the northern Chihuahuan desert, in the state of Chihuahua and southern New Mexico (among others, Di Peso, Rinaldo, and Fenner 1974a:1–7; Minnis 1989; Whalen and Minnis 1996b), but its influences

Figure 3.1. Paquime (courtesy of Adriel Heisey). A few of the largest northern Rio Grande sites may compare with Paquime in architectural mass, but no Southwestern site rivals the southern city's social and material complexity. There was nothing like Paquime—outside its immediate dependencies—in the 14th and 15th century Southwest; it stood alone.

were felt throughout the southern Southwest and along the Rio Grande (Schaafsma 1979). We are only beginning to understand the larger social and political implications of Paquime, but it is evident that Paquime was hugely important both for its time and for subsequent Pueblo history.

Between the end of construction at Chaco (ca. 1125) and the beginnings of Paquime (ca. 1250) an intermediate center rose at Aztec Ruins (fig. 3.4). We are only beginning to understand Aztec. It has usually been considered a late, secondary Chacoan center—perhaps a colony of refugees leaving a failing Chaco. It was much more. The sandstone masonry West Ruin at Aztec, excavated by Earl Morris in the 1910s (Morris 1919, 1921, 1924a, 1924b, 1928), is only one of perhaps six Great Houses in the complex. The equally large East Ruin remains largely unexcavated (Richert 1964) and, incredibly, the other great houses remained, until lately, largely unknown. The work of Peter McKenna and John Stein (Stein and McKenna 1988; McKenna and Toll 1992; and ongoing research

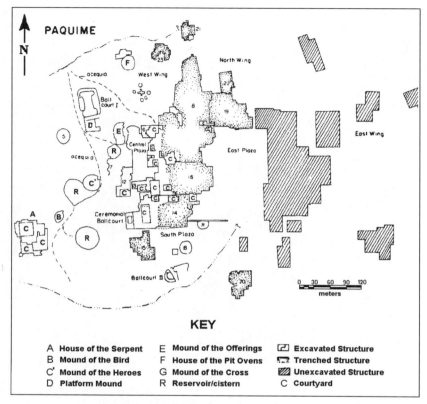

KEY

A House of the Serpent	E Mound of the Offerings	☑ Excavated Structure
B Mound of the Bird	F House of the Pit Ovens	⬜ Trenched Structure
C' Mound of the Heroes	G Mound of the Cross	▨ Unexcavated Structure
D Platform Mound	R Reservoir/cistern	C Courtyard

Figure 3.2. Paquime (reproduced from David Wilcox, "Changing Contexts of Pueblo Adaptations, A.D. 1250–1600," courtesy of University of Arizona Press). This map, compiled by David Wilcox from Di Peso's reports, shows the unexcavated east wing—often omitted from second-generation Paquime maps. Di Peso's keeness for decorative graphics made his published maps difficult to use—or even, in some cases, to understand. A number of post-Di Peso compilations exist; Wilcox's is the most complete. Note the possible separation of "Great House"-sized units, conjoined to form a very Pueblo-like city.

by Thomas Windes) has revealed an urban complex comparable to the earlier city at Chaco.

Chaco-scale construction began at Aztec just as large-scale building ceased in Chaco. The Aztec city encompassed huge Great Houses, landscape symmetries manifest in tri-wall structures and Great Kivas, and a remarkable array of roads, mounds and berms (Stein and McKenna 1988). There had been no earlier settlements of any size at Aztec; it rose *de novo* (McKenna 1998). More than 275 new tree-ring dates demonstrate that construction in Chacoan

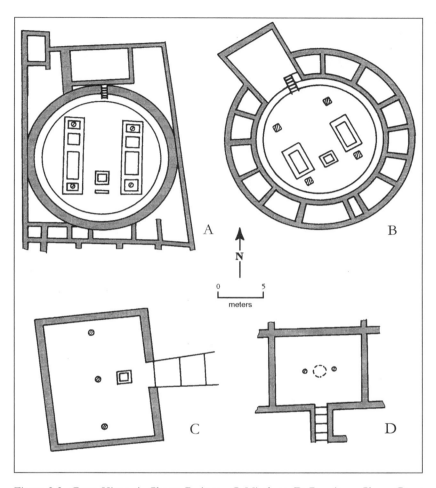

Figure 3.3. Great Kivas: A, Chaco; B, Aztec; C, Mimbres; D, Paquime. Chaco Great Kivas were generally subterranean and freestanding. Aztec Great Kivas were often incorporated or even surrounded by building. Some Aztec-era Great Kivas were rectangular; for example, Fire Temple and Long House at Mesa Verde. Mimbres Great Kivas were rectangular, and may have been replaced by rectangular enclosed plazas toward the end of the Mimbres phase. The single candidate Great Kiva at Paquime (Unit 11, Room 38) is rectangular, incorporated into the House of the Serpent.

styles and scales began about 1110 and continued until about 1275 (McKenna 1998; McKenna and Toll 1992). Contrary to earlier interpretations of discontinuity at Aztec, with "Chacoan abandonment" and "Mesa Verde replacement" (Morris 1919; Lekson and Cameron 1995), it seems clear that the Aztec complex had a continuous architectural history over one and a half centuries.

Figure 3.4. Aztec. The excavated building at Aztec Ruins (called West Ruin) was only one of a half-dozen very large Great Houses in the Aztec area. Three of these—East, West, and North ruins—form the core of the Aztec complex. Note the Hubbard Tri-wall, lower right.

Aztec was intermediate between Chaco and Paquime, and there was an intermediate between Chaco and Aztec: Salmon Ruins (fig. 3.5). Built about 1090–1095, Salmon Ruins was the original terminus of the Great North Road (discussed below) and perhaps the first site selected for the New Chaco (also discussed below). But Salmon Ruins never developed into a ceremonial city; that role shifted almost immediately to Aztec. We will return to Salmon later in this and other chapters.

Size and Scale

Chaco and Paquime seem, on first blush, so unalike. Chaco was built of sandstone, Paquime was built of adobe; Chaco pottery was black-on-white, Paquime pottery was polychrome; Chaco had kivas, Paquime had ballcourts. Substantial differences, but inconsequential for my argument. I'll deal with stone and adobe, black-on-white and polychrome, kivas, and ballcourts in due time; let us get past those bright, shiny, superficial differences and plunge into deeper, murkier similarities.

Figure 3.5. Salmon Ruins (courtesy National Park Service, Neg. # 18005). Comparable in size, plan, and labor investment to Pueblo Bonito and Chetro Ketl, buildings such as Salmon and—later—Aztec, continued Chaco-scale construction in the Totah district, around Farmington: the New Chaco.

Chaco and Paquime were both big, by far the largest sites of their times, and probably larger than any other puebloan sites up to protohistoric times. Consider scale and population. The central precinct at Chaco (fig. 2.15) encompassed over 6 km^2, including open space (Lekson 1986a). Di Peso estimated the area of urban Paquime at about 0.35 km^2 (Di Peso 1974:370). For comparison, Taos pueblo today encloses about 0.04 km^2, and Sapawe, perhaps the largest of the protohistoric Rio Grande pueblos, covers about 0.12 km^2 (cf. plans of other pueblos, ancient and modern, in Morgan 1994).

The total roofed space for the eight major structures in "downtown" Chaco (not including scores of known smaller buildings) is about 67,500 m^2 (Powers, Gillespie, and Lekson 1983: table 41); the total for Paquime, including both central and peripheral ("ranch" style) architecture, is 33,500 m^2 (Di Peso, Rinaldo, and Fenner 1974a: fig. 127–4).[3] Thus "downtown" Chaco included about twice the roofed area as Paquime; indeed, Chetro Ketl (the largest Chacoan building) alone was comparable to the main Paquime pueblo structure (23,395 m^2 and 25,943 m^2, respectively).

Chaco was larger than Paquime, but architectural and residential density was much higher at Paquime. Population estimates for all of Chaco Canyon range as high as 5,600 (Hayes 1981:50), but the central Chaco area (the central 6 km^2) contained no more than 2,500 to 3,000 people (Lekson 1986a, 1988c), and more conservative (or would that be radical?) estimates place the core population at less than 1,000 (Windes 1984, 1987a). Di Peso estimated population at Paquime of about 3,000 (Di Peso, Rinaldo, and Fenner 1974a: fig. 127–4) and, in my opinion, his estimate was low by perhaps one-third to one-half (that is, the population of Paquime may have approached 5,000; Lekson 1989c). Pick the estimates that please you, but my estimates—made long before I thought Chaco and Paquime might be related—have Chaco at about one-half the population of Paquime.

Aztec is less well known, but we can safely say this: It was no small potatoes. It was nearly off the spud scale. Aztec's core area (fig. 3.6), with buildings dispersed over a Chaco-style landscape, covered about 0.75 km^2, with a combined Great House roofed area about one-third larger than Paquime's (Stein and McKenna 1988). The newly revealed scale of Aztec is as remarkable as its new dating. Surveys of the area immediately around the West Ruin-East Ruin complex reveal a staggering concentration of monumental Great Houses, Great Kivas, roads, and smaller presumably domestic structures (Stein and McKenna 1988). The Aztec complex was clearly close, in scale, to the Bonito-Chetro Ketl-Alto core of "downtown" Chaco. Other Great Houses in the Aztec area may extend both the size of Aztec to rival that of the whole ten-mile length of Chaco Canyon (McKenna and Toll 1992).

If architectural volumes of all the buildings at Chaco were compressed into a cube of rooms, that cube would enclose about twice as much volume as Paquime. We know less about Aztec, but I estimate that its total volume falls about midway between Chaco and Paquime. Thus, the total volume of the three centers decreases, sequentially: Chaco was largest, Aztec about three-quarters the size of Chaco, and Paquime about two-thirds the size of Aztec. The total ground area covered by each center decreases much more dramatically: As noted above, downtown Chaco covered over 15 times more area than Paquime. Again, Aztec falls between somewhere between: half the size of Chaco, eight times the size of Paquime. The density of architecture, in effect, increases: The ratio of roofed space to ground area at Chaco increased by a factor of four at Aztec; Aztec's ratio increased almost five times at Paquime. To summarize: From Chaco to Aztec to Paquime, total roofed area decreased by a factor of three-quarters and then two-thirds, total city area decreased to one-half and then one-eighth, and architectural density increased by a factor of four and then five.

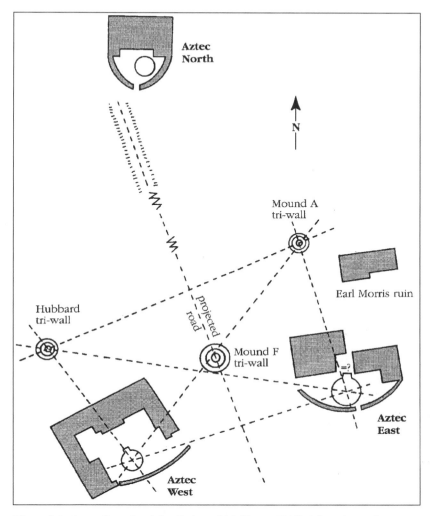

Figure 3.6. Aztec Complex (after Stein and McKenna 1988). There is much more to Aztec than meets the eye. A visitor to Aztec Ruins National Monument sees Earl Morris's house (now the visitors' center), the West Ruin (excavated by Morris) and the Hubbard Tri-wall (now backfilled). That is just the beginning—figuratively and literally. This composite map suggests some of Aztec's size and complexity. The National Monument, established early in 1923, included only the West Ruin—probably the first major construction at Aztec. The East Ruin (built after the West Ruin) was added to the monument five years later, and three more tracts were annexed by 1948; negotiations to acquire Aztec North are ongoing. Big sites are not uncommon in the northern San Juan, but none rival Aztec; it is surprising that Morris made so little of Aztec's extraordinary size. Morris's tenure at Aztec was reportedly frustrating and disappointing; perhaps those difficulties led to an ambivalence about the site.

Form

The difference between the areas of Chaco (6 km²) and Paquime (0.35 km²) reflects larger historical trends in Puebloan building. Each exemplifies the architectural "rules" of its time. Pueblo villages of the Chacoan era (11th century) were dispersed clusters of single or extended family units, with central public or community-identifying facilities (Great Houses and Great Kivas) (Lekson 1991). The spatially extensive composition of Chaco Canyon paralleled, on monumentally larger scales, that of several hundreds of other contemporary, smaller Pueblo communities in the region.

So, too, Paquime paralleled contemporary 14th-century Pueblo town-planning (fig. 3.2). As mapped by Di Peso, Paquime was a massive, terraced, U-shaped pueblo-style building surrounding a central plaza (Di Peso's "east plaza," Di Peso, Rinaldo, and Fenner 1974a: fig. 125–4; see also Lekson in press e). The view from the central plaza would have been much like Taos Pueblo today: terraced adobe roomblocks surrounding a large, well-defined plaza. Like Taos, ceremonial architecture and mounds are located around the outside of the building.

This comparison does not imply a direct historic linkage between Paquime and Taos, but corrects widespread misconceptions about Paquime's form. Di Peso excavated the ritual and ceremonial precincts outside the pueblo itself and only nibbled at the edges of the massed adobe roomblocks, all but ignoring the real central plaza of the site. His presentations (and later versions) of the site's layout are severely biased by this excavation strategy (e.g., Di Peso, Rinaldo, and Fenner 1974a: fig. 124–4, comparing "domestic and public/ceremonial settlement patterns" at Pueblo Bonito, Paquime, and Tula). Paquime was a profoundly Puebloan site—with a great many Mesoamerican appurtenances. Contemporary Mesoamerican and north Mexican architecture did not include anything like Paquime's pueblo-style form, but there's no denying the ballcourts, colonnades, and other non-Southwestern features (Lekson 1983b).

While Chaco itself was spatially extensive, its major buildings (such as Pueblo Bonito and Chetro Ketl) originated the massed, terraced form later so characteristic of Pueblo towns; the big Chaco buildings were the icons of the Pueblo style (Lekson 1990a; Fowler and Stein 1992). But Chaco buildings were not residential "Pueblos": Up to 80 percent of the roofed space of buildings like Pueblo Bonito and Pueblo Alto lacked any evidence of domestic functions. They may have been warehouses, palaces, monuments, or something else altogether, but the lack of living features indicates that they were not, in any useful sense, pueblos. It was only after Chaco, in the 12th and 13th centuries, that Plateau towns assumed the apartment-like form that we today call "Pueblo": tightly aggregated massing, terraced around a central enclosed plaza (Adler 1996; Morgan 1994). That happened first, of course, in Mimbres in the 11th century (chap. 2), and Mimbres, as we shall see, is implicated in Paquime's beginnings.

It was this Pueblo form, in a highly dramatic expression, that we see at 14th-century Paquime. Paquime was the ultimate 14th–15th-century pueblo: densely massed, terraced around a central plaza, and very big. Other pueblos of its time, and later, mirrored its form (again, see Morgan 1994). Should we expect Chaco and Paquime to look alike? No, if we take into account the century (or two) that separates them.

Aztec hints at intermediate forms, spanning that century. The Aztec Ruins complex is Chacoan in its use of space (fig. 3.6): Great Houses, Great Kivas, tri-walled structures, and an array of roads and earthen architecture spread over a large area. The West Ruin would be comfortable in Chaco, but the later East Ruin seems to "deconstruct" the old Great House model, emphasizing the plaza over the roomblocks (Stein and McKenna 1988). The massed 14th-century Pueblo form is not yet evident, but neither was Aztec a rote repetition of Chacoan canons. And people demonstrably *lived in* Aztec (Morris 1919; Lekson and Cameron 1995); its rooms are filled with trash, burials, mealing bins, and firepits.

The forms of Chaco and Paquime reflected general rules of Pueblo town-planning for their respective eras—although "reflect" is perhaps too passive a term. Chaco and Paquime look very different, but they differ in the same ways other Pueblo settlements *of their times* differ. A Chaco-era community of scattered units does not look like a Paquime-era pueblo with roomblocks massed around a central plaza. They express two different stages in the evolution of Pueblo building. Aztec may provide transitional forms: separate Chaco-style buildings (Great Houses) but more closely packed into an urban core intermediate between the spacious array of Chaco and the high density of later Pueblo town-planning.

All three cities were clearly planned, with complex internal geometries and formal canons of design (Di Peso 1974: 370ff.; Fowler and Stein 1992; Fritz 1978; McKenna and Toll 1992; Sofaer 1997; Stein and Lekson 1992). (Selected aspects of city planning will be discussed further, below.) Chaco used a great deal of space; there was distance between the Great Houses of Downtown Chaco. At Aztec, Great Houses and tri-walls were much more densely packed in the core of the ceremonial city; built and unbuilt spaces are more nearly equal in area. Paquime reached very high densities of construction, with open space limited (and delimited) by a central plaza and a narrow outer zone of ballcourts and "pyramids." I likened Paquime to Taos, as comparable compact puebloan forms, but Di Peso et al. (1974; see also Wilcox in press b) saw Paquime as an assembly of contiguous "houses," separated by small interior plazas, alleyways, or unfenestrated walls. It is tempting to see Paquime as multiple Great Houses ordered into a single, contiguous city plan—the formal "culmination" of decreasing spacing and increasing density from Chaco to Aztec to Paquime. While Paquime was profoundly Puebloan (Lekson in press e), it was also highly unusual—in this and many other ways. Like Chaco and Aztec, Paquime's form was simultaneously unique and iconic in its time and place.

Cardinal Knowledge

Cardinality and, particularly, meridian alignment were rare in Southwestern architecture (Morgan 1994) and in prehistoric North America generally (see, for example, Aveni 1977; but see also Ashmore 1991). The scarcity of cardinal construction may reflect the unimportance of the meridian for agricultural calendrics. North is a useless direction; it doesn't help you plant. Indeed, for many years it was assumed by white scholars that the cardinal orientations so evident in Pueblo ritual and world view were borrowed from Spanish and American maps and compasses. Thus the appearance of meridian alignments is noteworthy. Two of the most conspicuous and most important Pueblo places that address the meridian were Chaco and Paquime.

The cardinality of Chaco Canyon and its architectural organization around a meridian were noted two decades ago by John Fritz (1978). The exact north-south siting of Pueblo Alto and Tsin Kletsin—both conspicuous mesa-top buildings (fig. 3.7)—is a matter of public record, so familiar that it evokes little comment in the vast Chacoan literature.[4] Variously esoteric equinoctial, lunar, and other astronomical alignments have been argued for Chaco (e.g., Sofaer and Sinclair 1987; Sofaer 1997); they meet with some resistance and varying objections (e.g., Zeilik 1987). But the cardinal orientation of major walls at Pueblo Bonito, the meridian geometry of the central Chaco core, and meridian alignment of the North Road are beyond contest and cavil. The meridian was the major defining axis of Chaco.

At Paquime, the cardinals and particularly the meridian were also conspicuously important. The Mound of the Cross (fig. 3.8) was a cardinal monument (Di Peso, Rinaldo, and Fenner 1974a:287–288). Di Peso suggested that the Mound of the Cross "served as a cardinal direction datum for the builders who aligned the city in terms of its orientation" (Di Peso 1974:409). The meridian is manifest in the symmetry of the pueblo around the central plaza (Di Peso's "East Plaza"). Major plaza-defining walls were north-south (fig. 3.2). Room walls at Paquime vary from the cardinals to minor degrees, but the basic cardinality of the pueblo's underlying grid is evident and obvious (see plans in Di Peso 1974 and Di Peso, Rinaldo, and Fenner 1974a, b). The place

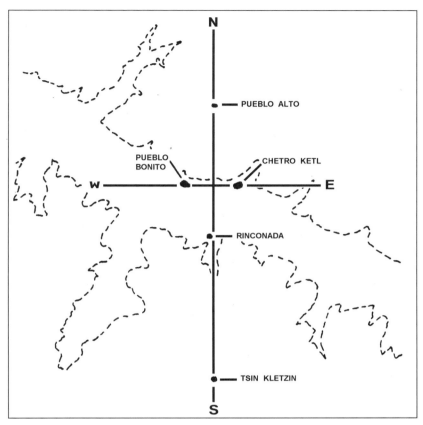

Figure 3.7. John Fritz's Chaco (reproduced from John Fritz, "Paleopsychology Today," 1978; courtesy of Academic Press). Fritz's minimalist diagram defined a north-south meridian, marked by Pueblo Alto and Tsin Kletsin, as the principal axis of Chaco Canyon. At the time, in the late 1970s, archaeologists evinced interest, but no great enthusiasm. Fritz later expanded his ideas (1987). Other important aspects of Chacoan planning have been defined by Anna Sofaer (1997) and the Solstice Project. Ongoing work by John Stein and his colleagues (Fowler and Stein 1992; Stein and Lekson 1992; Stein, Suiter, and Ford 1997) reveal a simple but highly ramified geometry of the ceremonial city.

looks like it was designed on an Etch-a-Sketch, turning one dial at a time (fig. 3.9). Di Peso was so impressed by Paquime's cardinality that he used a stylized version of the Mound of the Cross as his symbol for the city in maps and charts.

The importance of the north-south axis was more strongly reflected at Paquime than at any individual buildings at Chaco Canyon; the meridian at Paquime works on the same scale as the north-south axis of downtown Chaco. Chaco grew around its meridian axis, while Paquime incorporated

Figure 3.8. Mound of the Cross (courtesy of Adriel Heisey). A monument to the meridian? Charles Di Peso thought so. Di Peso's archaeological reports were famous for their pictorial embellishments. Throughout his long and productive career, he asked draftsmen and artists to populate his monographs with dogs, kids, turkeys, family squabbles, and other incidents of ancient life. Di Peso had a passion for graphics. He was so struck with Paquime's cardinality that, throughout the Casas Grandes report, he used a stylized representation of the Mound of the Cross as the primary symbol for Paquime.

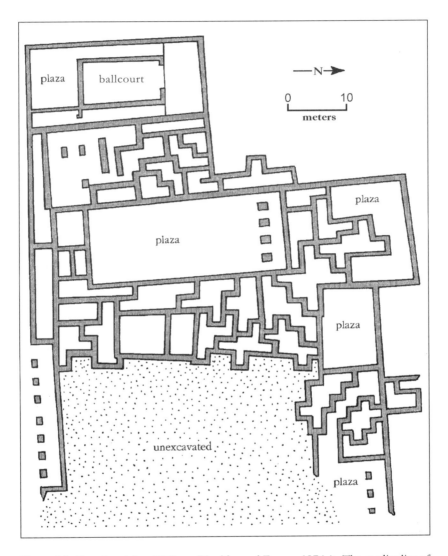

Figure 3.9. Paquime (after Di Peso, Rinaldo, and Fenner 1974c). The cardinality of Paquime is evident in the grid patterns of its east-west north-south walls. This section of the House of the Pillars is representative. Multiple right-angled corners produced extraordinary cruciform and butterfly-shaped rooms. Those corners also helped, structurally, in the successful construction of four-storied building with poured adobe—not a material-of-choice for that purpose. "Folding," with many corners and alcoves, corrugated the walls, and made them much stronger.

the meridian as an axis of its grid plan. Historically, grid-plan cities are *new* cities, cities built to a simple, measured masterplan. Not all new cities are rectangular grids, but it is rather difficult to evolve a grid organically.

Chaco and Paquime employed the meridian as the major axis of planning; Aztec did not. Aztec was planned around a central axis (fig. 3.6), much like Chaco's meridian; but Aztec's axis orientation was to the southeast (an azimuth of about 160°), manifest as a road running northwest from the Aztec complex toward Mesa Verde (Stein and McKenna 1988, McKenna and Toll 1992). The major sandstone buildings (East and West ruins) face toward the reverse of this angle (that is, south-southeast). The third major great house (North Ruin—built of massive puddled adobe), sits on the bluffs above East and West ruins. It faces conspicuously to the south, but not precisely (Richard Friedman, personal communication 1996). And, to anticipate discussions in chapter 4, Aztec's very location was predicated on cardinal knowledge, due north of Chaco. The *place* of Aztec was meridian.

Why north? North was not an everyday direction; that is, north was not important to daily, seasonal, or annual life. The time-scales of calendar, economic year, and ritual cycles were measured by the movements of the sun, along the eastern and western horizons. Sun, moon, and stars were constantly but erratically wandering; those celestial orbs were anything but fixed.

North, however, was a fixed point—though at 1100, a void (Polaris was off the mark)—around which all the heavens revolved. Indeed, North was the *only* fixed direction. The sun, moon, planets and stars peregrinated in dizzying loops and cycles; even the equinox was a relative measure. Before maps, before globes, before geography, north was the only direction that did *not* change.

So why north? Because it was the only obvious, immutable, real direction. Pueblo people call north "the heart of the sky."[5] South, at Chaco's latitudes, was invisible, below the horizon; no celestial feature marked south. South could only be the linear projection of north, a complement to the sky's heart. North was esoteric—it played no practical calendrical role—but it was not arcane. Everyone knew north—everyone could see the stars revolve around the Heart of the Sky. When charged with meaning, north was especially potent because it was manifest and knowable: You could see it, even if you could not understand it.

Fabrications

City planning and construction details at Chaco, Aztec, and Paquime will be compared and contrasted at some length in following sections. Why not, in our first reactions, be superficial, skin-deep? Judge these books by their covers: Chaco and Aztec are postcard paragons of Anasazi sandstone masonry, while

Paquime used massive adobe to monumental effect (fig. 3.10). Historically, Southwesternists set great store on wall type and style. Surely, the dichotomy of sandstone and adobe is fatal to my argument? Perhaps not; Aztec provides an intermediate condition, both stone and mud, for those who might be comforted by smooth transitions and synoptic series.

Chaco was built of sandstone masonry; Paquime's walls were poured or puddled adobe. Most major construction at Aztec—East and West Ruins—is of Chaco-style sandstone masonry. The third largest Great House at Aztec, the North Ruin, was constructed of massive puddled or poured adobe (McKenna and Toll 1992). North Ruin was a very large building: 100 plus groundfloor rooms, in a typical Great House D configuration—a footprint comparable to Wijiji at Chaco Canyon. Its adobe mound covers an area about 60 x 45 m and stands 3 m tall. North Ruin remains undated; it is tempting to think of it as late, a transition from Chaco's stone to Paquime's mud.

In fact, similar massive adobe walls occurred at a Great House nearer Chaco: Bis sa'ani, a few kilometers northeast of the canyon. Bis sa'ani was a small Great House, well dated to 1130–1140—just after construction ended in downtown Chaco. It was built principally of massive poured adobe walls, with Chaco-style sandstone masonry used for some exterior walls (Breternitz, Doyel, and Marshall 1982). Thus, massive poured or puddled adobe wall techniques, much like those of Paquime, were used at Bis sa'anni by the early 12th century.

There are, of course, local histories of adobe technology in the northern Southwest (Cameron 1998), and post-Mimbres horizons used coursed adobe. The point is this: Massive adobe walls were used in very late construction near Chaco; it was a major element at the North Ruin at Aztec; and massive adobe was the principal technique at Paquime. For those who recoil from immoderate change, here perhaps, is continuity.[6]

God Dwells in the Details

Chaco, Aztec, and Paquime shared remarkable parallels of detail: distinctive architectural elements found uniquely and conspicuously at Chaco and Paquime, and—to a lesser degree—Aztec. Most of these parallels were originally noted by Charles Di Peso (Di Peso, Rinaldo, and Fenner 1974a:208–211). My self-appointed job at the Chaco Project was to refute Di Peso's claims; and I did (Lekson 1983b). I argued that most of Di Peso's parallels could be dismissed, defused, or otherwise explained away; but a pesky residuum of unusual features, apparently unique to Paquime and Chaco, defied easy rejection. In fairness to myself, I noted those residual features (and one more of my own; Lekson 1983b:189). But, having disposed of almost all of Di Peso's parallels, I thought my job was done, and I simply ignored the remainders. They returned to haunt my rest.

3.10a.

3.10b

3.10c

Figure 3.10. Walls: a, Chaco; b, Aztec; c, Paquime. Chaco used an excellent local sandstone to create its impressively patterned masonry. Aztec did the best it could with inferior sandstones. Paquime's valley offered only river cobbles and basalts (at some distance); they chose adobe. The silly-looking fellow is me.

Specifically, those details include: colonnades, room-wide platforms, stone disk post foundations, platform mounds, and tri-walls. I found the first three disturbing in 1984; now I find them compelling. I reserve mounds and tri-walls for separate treatment, below; they too are remarkable, but less specific to Chaco, Aztec, and Paquime. (T-shaped doors, another Di Peso detail, are ubiquitous; they are discussed in appendix A.)

It is useful to think of colonnades, room-wide platforms, and disks as very different manifestations of architectural symbolism: public, private, and hidden. Colonnades are quite public; they appear on exterior walls and face large open, public spaces (plazas, courtyards, etc.). Room-wide platforms were installed within rooms; they would have been effectively private, affecting only those who had access to those rooms. Stone disk foundations were invisible, hidden after construction. Only those involved in planning and construction would know stone disks were in place.

Colonnades (fig. 3.11) have been long been identified as Mesoamerican forms, unique within the Southwest to two sites: Chaco and Paquime (Di Peso, Rinaldo, and Fenner 1974a:211, 264–266; Ferdon 1955:4–5; Lekson 1983b:185–186). At both Chaco and Paquime, colonnades are plaza-facing (i.e., exterior), ground-level features. At Chaco, a remarkable thirteen-pillar colonnade occurs at Chetro Ketl and a more problematic example has been identified at Bc 51; at Paquime, there are seven colonnades with from two to seven pillars. In the Chaco colonnades, the pillars are rectangular stone masonry and rise from a low base wall; most Paquime colonnades had rectangular cast adobe pillars, but one was a portal-like construction of wooden posts, and all were full height (i.e., they rest on the floor level). The Mexican provenance of colonnades has been treated elsewhere (Ferdon 1955; Di Peso, Rinaldo, and Fenner 1974a). To my knowledge, the Chaco and Paquime colonnades are unique in the greater Southwest. We know of no colonnades at Aztec, but only one major building has been excavated at that huge complex.

Room-wide platforms (fig. 3.12) are ubiquitous at Chaco, Paquime, and Aztec (Di Peso, Rinaldo, and Fenner 1974a: 238–246: Lekson 1983b:189, 1986a:38; Morris 1928). To my knowledge, they are found nowhere else in the Southwest. Room-wide platforms (Di Peso's "bed platforms") were very deep shelves, built with primary and secondary beams much like roofs, midway between floor and ceiling in both ends of rectangular rooms or in room-sized alcoves. They were a conspicuous element in original room design, and they would have altered completely the uses to which a room could be put. Their purpose is obscure; Di Peso thought they were for sleeping while I thought that they were storage facilities, doubling the floor area available for nonstackable goods. In any event, they are distinctive private architectural elements, known only to those who actually used them, and they are found only at Chaco, Paquime, and Aztec.

3.11a

3.11b

Figure 3.11. Colonnades: a, Chaco; b, Paquime. There is one colonnade at Chaco, at Chetro Ketl (and another candidate, which I find unconvincing, at Bc 51). Had Chetro Ketl not been excavated, we would not know its colonnade. Only one Great House has been investigated at Aztec. The absence of colonnades at Aztec may be a simple sampling problem: to find rare features, dig more sites. There are seven colonnades at Paquime. The next nearest colonnades to the south are in Zacatecas, at La Quemada and Alta Vista, which predate Chaco and Paquime. Colonnades are not conspicuous at West Mexican sites, but we know very little of their architecture.

Massive stone disks (fig. 3.13), 0.6 to 1.2 m in diameter and about 10 cm thick were placed under major roof-support posts in Chacoan Great Kivas, the Aztec Great Kiva, and a number of unusual rooms at Paquime (Di Peso 1974:214; Di Peso, Rinaldo, and Fenner 1974b:230–234; Lekson 1983b:189; Vivian and Reiter 1960:91). At Chaco and Aztec, these disks

3.12a

Figure 3.12. Room-wide platforms: a, Chaco; b, Aztec; c, Paquime. An inele-gant term for an important feature. Di Peso called them "bed platforms," but at Chaco they appear to be storage features. In ruins, they might appear to be a collapsed roof or second story; recognition of room-wide platforms may require preservation of walls to at least half their original height. Their current distribution is limited to Chaco, Aztec, and Paquime, but there are suspicious beam-socket-sized holes in the uppermost story of Casa Grande (near Phoenix)—currently interpreted as astronomical apparatus.

3.12b.

3.12c.

Figure 3.13. Sandstone disks: a, Chaco; b, Aztec; c, Paquime. Colonnades are rare and might be missed in limited excavations; room-wide platforms could disappear, if a ruin was reduced to low wall stubs. But no archaeologist should miss 600 kg or 1200 pound stone disks. At Chaco and Aztec, they appear beneath Great Kiva columns; at Paquime, the support piers or columns were in several apparently important rooms.

were "stacked" up to four deep; at Paquime, they were usually single, but in one case, two disks were "stacked" together. Turquoise and shell offerings were frequently placed on or below the disks at all three sites. Stone disks served as structural foundations, but the "stacking" of disks and the presence of offerings suggests that architectural symbolism may have been as much a concern as structural stability. Disks, in any event, were hidden; after installation, they were far beneath the floor level and could not be seen.[7]

So, there are three architectural features unique to Chaco, Aztec, and Paquime: very public colonnades, private interior room-wide platforms, and the hidden sandstone disks beneath major roof support posts. There are two other architectural features of particular interest, but these are perhaps less distinctively associated with these three sites: platform mounds and multiwalled structures.

Platform mounds (fig. 3.14) are a Southwestern structural type with a complicated provenance (most notably, a polemical and as-yet-unresolved history of platform mounds in the Hohokam region, e.g., Elson 1998). At Puebloan sites they are limited to Pueblo Bonito at Chaco Canyon and Paquime (Lekson 1986a:74, 143–144; Di Peso, Rinaldo, and Fenner 1974a:209, 270). The two

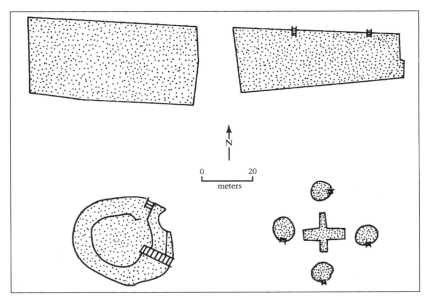

Figure 3.14. Mounds: upper, Pueblo Bonito; and lower, Paquime. Many native communities in eastern North American and most of Middle America piled up dirt. In the Southwest, the Hohokam are famous for their platform mounds. It would be remarkable if ancestral Pueblo peoples did *not* use earth for architecture; and, in fact, they did. Chaco era earthen architecture was multifaceted and widespread (see fig. 2.7); Aztec almost certainly continued this tradition (three large mounds in front of the Aztec Great Houses are now gone, but berms and mounds dot the terraces behind Aztec). Moundbuilding at Paquime reached complexities unmatched in the Southwest, not so much in size as in diversity. Effigy mounds were unique to the southern city: a bird mound may reflect the center's aviary interests, and a remarkable linear plumed-serpent effigy stretched almost 250 m long. The plumed serpent was at the extreme west margin of the city; it was oriented very nearly north-south, with the head just west of north and the tail to the south.

rectangular, masonry-walled, adobe-surfaced mounds at Pueblo Bonito probably date to 1075–1105 (Lekson 1986a:144). Masonry-walled mounds at Paquime date to the Paquime phase, 1250–1450 (although Di Peso assigns one mound to the earlier, but now-problematic Buena Fe phase; Di Peso, Rinaldo, and Fenner 1974a:270). Paquime mounds take a variety of shapes: rectangular, round, cross-shaped, and zoomorphic. There are no precise matches between the simple, rectangular Chacoan form and the wide variety of forms at Paquime. Neither Chaco or Paquime mounds appear to derive from Hohokam Classic Period (ca. 1300–1500) platform mounds, which supported (residential?) structures—although my mind remains open on this question. Aztec clearly employed earthen architecture and masonry-walled terracing (Morris 1928), but the true form of the now-vanished Aztec "mounds" remains a mystery.[8]

Tri-walled and multiwalled structures (fig. 3.15) may be the architectural signature of the Aztec region, comparable to Chaco's Great Houses and Paquime's ballcourts (an idea pursued below). Tri-walled structures, certainly, were prominent and important at Aztec Ruins (fig. 3.6).[9] There was a single tri-wall at Pueblo del Arroyo, one of the last structures built (and then razed) at Chaco Canyon—a "transitional" link between late Chaco and early Aztec.

Was there anything similar at Paquime? The remarkable structure atop Cerro de Moctezuma (Di Peso, Rinaldo, and Fenner 1974b:866–867), some 7 km southwest of Paquime comes to mind. Those who have visited Paquime will know how Cerro de Moctezuma visually dominates the Casas Grandes valley and Paquime itself, and how it looks north unobstructed to the Mimbres Mountains. The structure at its peak is one of a class of sites that Di Peso called *atalayas*, fire communication stations that spanned a vast area (and another candidate marker for Paquime's region, as discussed below). Cerro de Moctezuma was by far the largest and most elaborate of the known *atalayas* (Swanson 1997); it consists of a massive round tower rising from the center of a series of irregularly circular terraces. Di Peso mapped these terraces as a spiral, but recent remapping reveals that these terraces were in fact concentric (John Roney, personal communication 1996; Swanson 1997).[10] Was Cerro de Moctzuma a tri-wall?

Minor Artifacts and Major Dudes

But what about pottery? Isn't pottery the critical criterion in Southwestern archaeology? Gallup Black-on-white (the signature type of Chaco) doesn't look like Ramos Polychrome (the type fossil of Paquime)—see figure 2.4. Nor does Lino Black-on-gray look like Mesa Verde Black-on-white, or Mesa Verde Black-on-white look like Cieneguilla Glaze-on-yellow—but most of us believe they were made by ascending and descending generations of the same people.

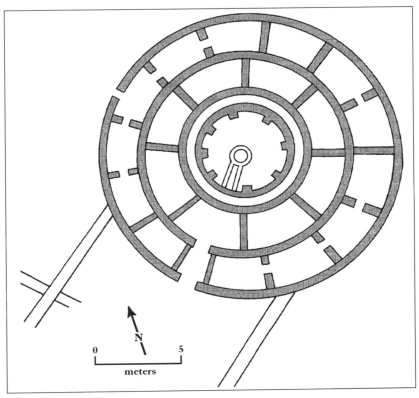

Figure 3.15. Hubbard Tri-wall at Aztec (After Vivian 1959). Perhaps the last major public structure built at Chaco was the tri-wall behind Pueblo del Arroyo, the only example of this building type at Chaco. That structure was apparently razed shortly after its construction, about the time building began at Aztec. Building and unbuilding meant more than construction or destruction; it seems likely that functions of the Pueblo del Arroyo tri-wall were transferred north along with its form (but not its fabric!), and the older, replaced building was decommissioned. Bi- and tri-walled circular structures are central nodes of the Aztec city plan (fig. 3.6); others are known at secondary centers in northern San Juan, more will almost certainly appear in future attempts to define the Aztec region. No such features are known from the Mimbres or Casas Grandes areas, but the remarkable Cerro de Moctezuma—Paquime's mountaintop observatory—had two low concentric ring walls around its massive round tower. The parallel is intriguing. North approximate.

The Chaco-Aztec-Paquime progression spans five centuries. That's a long time, and through those many years, material culture changed broadly across the greater Southwest. Gradual changes were, cumulatively, marked and dramatic: layering the 15th-century Southwest directly over the 10th-century Southwest, and we might think replacement, not continuity. (The striking differences between historic pueblos and ancient ruins led early explorers and settlers to suggest that Mesa Verde and Chaco were, in fact, the Aztec homeland; Lister and Lister 1987). Aztec was not Aztlan, but things *did* change. Architectural languages evolved, ceramics changed, more powerful bows were introduced, and corn hybridized. The material landscape of Chaco-Aztec-Paquime power altered and evolved in response to forces and circumstances beyond the control (or even beyond the ken) of elites or commoners at those centers. A lot can happen in five centuries.

We expect to see material continuities when a group moves from place A to place B. Pots, to a great degree, still equal people. Since midcentury, we've tried to anticipate and tabulate indicators of post-migration culture (Haury 1958). But Chaco-Aztec-Paquime was not a migration, nor a folk movement; it was an elaborately staged shift in a ceremonial city, directed by elites who show themselves, archaeologically, in different ways than nonelites. For example, Chaco elites did not make their own pottery. We know this from Chaco, where Great House assemblages were *at least* 50 percent (and probably more) imported pottery. People conspicuously consumed pots at Pueblo Alto, but they probably didn't make many pots there. Elites manifested themselves in architecture and exotica, not serving dishes.

The movement, up and down the meridian, *was not* a migration; it was a political maneuver, by a small but powerful elite. When the capital shifted first to Aztec and then to Paquime, the elite moved—perhaps 1,000, less than a multitude, but more than enough to reproduce, both biologically and socially. Should we expect major transformation—sea-changes—in local pottery, metates, axes, and arrowheads when a group of parasitic non-producers arrive? Maybe not.

Elites co-opt local popular symbolism and overlay new configurations of exotica and monumental building. We need not exhaustively explore the minor artifacts of Chaco, Aztec, and Paquime, but a brief example from Chaco and Paquime might suggest how such a survey should be framed—not with tempers, motor habits, and motifs, but in dramatic contextual parallels. This is the parable of the odd pots and the Major Dudes.

At Pueblo Bonito at Chaco Canyon, a cache of 192 (of 210 known) "cylinder jars" (fig. 3.16) were located in a complex of rooms which also housed the highly unusual wooden crypt of the two most elaborate burials in the canyon. Cylinder jars have a literature all their own (summarized in Toll 1990) with Mesoamerican implication and refutations. They are (approximately) cylindrical in form, averaging 24 cm tall and 11 cm in opening diameter (Toll 1990:273). With a few red-slipped exceptions, all are white-slipped. Most are Gallup or Chaco Black-on-white, but painted deco-

3.16a

3.16b

Figure 3.16. A, Chaco cylinder jars; b, Paquime hand drums. The functions of ceramic cylinder jars and hand drums are uncertain, but contextual evidence, presented in Chapter 3, suggests parallels. Both are of about the same size, approximately 20–30 cm tall. Cylinder jars have opposed lugs with small openings, suited to a thong—lashing for a skin drum head? But the bottoms of cylinder jars are closed, an acoustic contradiction. Paquime hand drums are open on both ends; about one-third had perforations (not lugs) for thong or twine.

ration includes a range of styles (including Puerco and McElmo); many are unpainted. No one is quite sure what cylinder jars were. They might be standard measures, but their volumes are too variable. They have four or more lugs or small handles that could have secured skins for use as drums, but their bases are closed, not open as they presumably would be for drums.

The cylinder jars came from the central warren of tiny, old rooms which also contained a remarkable inventory of wooden "canes" or "wands," turquoise jewelry, arrows, and other items. In the floor of the room adjacent to the cylinder jars, there was a unique wooden plank crypt containing the extended burials of two middle-aged men—Major Dudes—with fabulous quantities of turquoise jewelry. Scattered above the crypt were the disarticulated remains of 12 individuals—perhaps retainers. (Akins 1986; Akins and Schelberg 1984; Frisbie 1978).

Hand drums (fig. 3.16) were a ceramic form unique in the Greater Southwest to Paquime (Di Peso, Rinaldo, and Fenner 1974c:356–365). Similar in size to cylinder jars (average height 17.6 cm, average opening diameter 11.7 cm), hand drums were shaped like bottomless wine glasses. Presumably, skins were stretched over the larger end. They were decorated in a variety of styles (Babicora, Ramos) but most were plain or textured. Over 80 percent of the 109 known hand drums were found in a single cache on the floor of an old room which, with an adjacent room, "contained two elaborate subfloor tombs with which a large number of ceramic hand drums were associated. These two subfloor tombs . . . were covered with board planking . . . Both of these graves contained a large quantity and diversity of artifact accompaniments compared with burials from other architectural units" (Ravesloot 1988:32). The crypt burial contained a dozen other individuals, five of whom were disarticulated above the principal internment: a middle-aged man, matched by another middle-aged man in the crypt next door (Di Peso, Rinaldo, and Fenner 1974e 387–396; Ravesloot 1988:34). Ravesloot (1988:70) and Di Peso (1974:419) suggested that the highest status burials at Paquime were three secondary burials in a chamber of the Mound of the Offerings. After that group, the crypt burials in Unit 13 were judged the next-highest-status (Ravesloot 1988:69). I'm not sure we know who the secondary burials in the big Ramos pots were, but the two middle-aged men in the wooden crypts were Major Dudes.

The striking similarities of unique vessel caches with equally unique crypt burials at both Pueblo Bonito and Paquime tell us more, I think, than the comparatively minor differences between black-on-white cylinders and polychrome hand-drums. (We have no comparable Major-Dude-with-unique-pots from Aztec but, again, we have excavated much less of Aztec than Chaco and Paquime.) To follow elites, we must look away from bulk artifacts and common crafts and seek instead uncommon contexts and *rarae aves.*

Hecho en Mexico

Both Chaco and Paquime have been strongly implicated in Mesoamerican "connections." In ancient times and modern archaeology, they are magnets for Mexico. Aztec, despite its pioneer-days naming, has largely escaped extra-territorial allegations.

More than any other Pueblo sites, Chaco and Paquime have been explained by, or related to, or denied any Mexican associations (see, among others, reviews by Di Peso, Rinaldo, and Fenner 1974a:208–211; Judge 1991:29–30; Lekson 1983b; Mathien 1986; McGuire 1980, 1989, 1993a). Why? Because Chaco and Paquime appear so unusual or anomalous in Pueblo prehistory, they invite *deus ex machina* Mexican explanations.

There is, of course, lots of corroborative evidence. Both Chaco and Paquime traded heavily with societies to the south; macaws, parrots, copper bells, shell, and other artifacts originating far to the south were found in relative abundance at both. Architectural forms, such as colonnades (Chaco, Paquime) and I-shaped ballcourts (Paquime), and possibly platform mounds (Chaco, Paquime) refer to Mesoamerican or, more likely, West Mexican models.

Prevailing consensus denies a significant Mesoamerican presence or causal role at Chaco (e.g., Vivian 1990:416–417). Paquime, with its many Mexican details, is more frequently and less contentiously linked to the south, but even at Paquime current thinking runs against direct intervention (e.g., McGuire 1993a:38; Minnis 1989). Of course, Paquime is actually *in* Mexico, which helps Mesoamerican arguments; but, before 1848, so was Chaco.

Birds, bells, and shells most clearly show Chaco and Paquime's southern connections; but, as discussed above, Mexican exotica are often dismissed as low-volume trinkets, vastly outweighed by tons of honest Southwestern sherds. I argued in chapter 2 that macaws and their ilk are far more important to political-prestige economies than mountains of local pottage.

Copper bells and other copper artifacts, particularly abundant at Paquime (Di Peso, Rinaldo, and Fenner 1974b:507–510), probably came from West Mexico (Vargas 1995; but see Hosler 1994:221 for a contrasting view). Scarlet macaws also originated in west Mexico—their natural range is at least 1,000 kms south of the Southwest (Hargrave 1970). The idea of backpacking big, angry thick-billed parrots or macaws over long distances makes one pity the porter—what a nasty job. Live birds were carried north to Mimbres and on to Chaco. It is not impossible that attempts were made to breed birds in the Mimbres area—shell has been found—but probably without any great success.[11] Macaws were definitely bred, on commercial scales, at Paquime, where more than 500 were found (Di Peso, Rinaldo, and Fenner 1974e:272). Elaborate breeding pen complexes (fig. 3.17) attest to the importance of macaw production at Paquime (Di Peso 1974:598–601; Minnis 1988; Whalen and Minnis 1996c). Thus, Chaco was a conspicuous 11th-century consumer of macaws; Paquime was a 14th-century producer.

Aztec Ruins and its region have not produced many foreign curios. Very few copper bells have been found in the northern San Juan: one from Aztec (Morris 1919:100); one bell from Goodman Point near Cortez, Colorado (a large site with a Chaco era component; Vargas 1995: Table 5.1); two bells from the Shield Site (Hayes and Chappell 1962; Mark Varien, personal communication 1996), a Chaco-era ruin very near Goodman Point; and a reported bell from Edge-of-the-Cedars near Blanding, Utah (Vargas 1995:75), another large site with a Chaco-era Great House component (Hurst 1998). Compared with the numbers of bells from Chaco Canyon (about 25), the Mimbres region (about 25), or the Hohokam region (about 150), the Northern San Juan is cupricly challenged: very few bells from this most intensively investigated area.

There were more birds than bells. Excavations at Salmon Ruins produced macaws in a wide range of contexts (Philip Shelley, personal communication, 1996), and (as noted below) a few from Aztec. Macaws or parrots are frequently depicted on Mesa Verde Black-on-white pottery (Crown 1994:149) and Mesa Verde rock art. No birds have been recovered from the scores of Aztec-era sites excavated in the Northern San Juan; Aztec and Salmon had the birds.

The Northern San Juan has been extensively excavated, but we know less about Aztec itself than we might like. Morris found only one copper bell at Aztec West, two macaws (Lori Pendelton, personal communication 1997) and one macaw feather (Morris 1919:64). But, of course, Aztec West is only one of the half-a-dozen large buildings at Aztec. What a different picture we would have of Chaco, had only Chetro Ketl and not Pueblo Bonito been excavated! With the current data, however, it appears that long-range exchange (so spectacularly evident at Chaco in the 12th century and at Paquime in the 14th century) was greatly reduced at Aztec during the 13th century (Lekson and Cameron 1995).

Marine shell represents another class of exotic material. Most shell came from coastal Mexico and the Sea of Cortez; much less came from the California Pacific coast. I rely here on Rona Bradley's (1993, 1996) excellent summaries. Based largely on species assemblages, she concluded that there were two major shell production and distribution systems in the Greater Southwest: a Hohokam system and a Paquime system. These two systems were largely sequential, with the Hohokam system dominating prior to about 1275, and Paquime replacing the Hohokam system thereafter. Hohokam shell reached Chaco in impressive quantities. Aztec and Wupatki—both post-1125, pre-1275 centers—were also in this network, but they produced far less shell than Chaco. Paquime's shell products supplied Pueblo villages far to the north and northwest.

Mimbres, an area that shared bells and macaws with Chaco, occupies an interesting position in Bradley's (1996) analysis: Pre-Mimbres sites shared species with Hohokam shell assemblages, but later Mimbres phase shell

Figure 3.17. Macaw pens at Paquime. Macaws were bred at Paquime, in startling quantities. Macaws eat fruit when they are at home, but fruits are not abundant in the Chihuahuan desert. Whatever the Paquime macaws ate, they lived long enough to hatch eggs; but they were probably not happy birds. The stone rings and heavy stone plugs seem excessive, but a crabby macaw is an unpleasant beast: sharp beaks, long talons, and an evil disposition.

more closely resemble Paquime patterns. Mimbres (1000–1150) is, of course, substantially earlier than Paquime (1250–1500). Thus, Mimbres area shell appears to originate with Hohokam suppliers but later developed an independent acquisition network, mirrored by the depictions of Sea of Cortez fish on Mimbres pots—Mimbres artists went to the beach (Jett and Moyle 1986). Species similarity suggests that those Mimbres networks were continued (on greatly expanded levels) in the subsequent era of Paquime. Shell links Mimbres and Paquime across the dark age of post-Mimbres reorganization. Like macaws, the quantity of shell at Paquime eclipses that at Chaco and Aztec. Di Peso found one-and-a-half *tons* of shell at Paquime.

Regional Integration

Chaco, Aztec, and Paquime shared remarkable architectural features. The regional contexts of each were also strikingly parallel: Chaco, Aztec, and Paquime was each, in its time and place, the largest, most important, central settlement within its region.

I noted above that we know most about Chaco, much about Paquime, and surprisingly little about Aztec. There is a remarkably symmetrical imbalance, among the three areas, between the intensity of archaeological research and the definition of regional systems. Chaco has been well researched (Vivian 1990), and the Chacoan region is reasonably well defined (Lekson 1991). Aztec's region—if Aztec had a region—is among the most intensely researched archaeological districts on earth: the Mesa Verde district (e.g., Varien et al. 1996). Despite an unmatched history of excavation and survey, Aztec regional hegemony within the Mesa Verde district is currently no more than a suggestion. (And a very unwelcome suggestion, to many Northern San Juan archaeologists.) Chihuahua remains practically unknown, compared with Chaco or the northern San Juan (Fish and Fish 1994; Phillips 1989), yet we have confident (and contradictory) maps of the Paquime polity (discussed below). Recent projects (e.g., Whalen and Minnis 1996a, 1996b; Kelley and Villapando 1996) have begun to develop reliable geographic knowledge of Paquime's region; it is fair to say that the archaeology of northwestern Chihuahua is today where Mesa Verde was five decades ago.

The Chacoan region is delimited by the distribution of Great Houses, Great Kivas, and roads (e.g., Lekson 1991; Wilcox 1996a). We may have a dozen different readings of what that region means, but the reality of Great Houses and their regional distribution are not in serious question, at least in my book. This is *my* book: If you have read chapter 2, then we may take "as read" the Chacoan Regional System.

This new understanding of Aztec as a ceremonial city naturally raises the question of a comparable, Chaco-scale region. We are only *beginning* to understand Aztec. Its architectural canons continued those of Chaco, so it is possible that many "Chaco outliers" in the northern San Juan region may someday be recast as "Aztec outliers." Almost every excavated Chacoan Great House in the northern San Juan—like the Bluff Great House—continued to be occupied through Aztec times. From surface data alone, it would be extremely difficult to differentiate Aztec-era from Chaco-era Great Houses.

Given its size and scale, it seems almost certain that the 13th century in the northern San Juan was the era of Aztec. Aztec was enormous. No other northern San Juan site came close in size and formality. Even the very largest towns of the Montezuma Valley pale by comparison. The core of Aztec was four times larger (in numbers of rooms) than Yellow Jacket, the very largest Montezuma Valley village. Indeed, the Montezuma Valley may well have been to Aztec what the Chuska Valley was to Chaco: The densest populations were not clustered around either Chaco or Aztec, but 60 to 100 km to the west.

A hypothetical Aztec "region" (see fig. 4.4) could encompass the northern San Juan, an area normally termed the Mesa Verde Region (e.g., Varien et al. 1996). That name says it all: For over a century, our understanding of the 13th century in the northern San Juan has been dominated by Mesa Verde—a lovely park, but a bit of a backwater. We must filter out the tremendous visual impact of cliff dwellings. History and hype gave us "Mesa Verde" where other geographic tags might better serve. Huge masses of "Mesa Verde" pottery (fig. 2.4) have been excavated from the La Plata district, from Salmon Ruins, and from Aztec Ruins (and points south, Roney 1995). If Aztec had been excavated before Wetherill stumbled onto Cliff Palace, that same pottery might well be called Aztec Black-on-white.

Mesa Verde Black-on-white may provide a gross ceramic index of the Aztec region—not the elites, but the base population. Mesa Verde Black-on-white is found in the Northern San Juan in a region of about 50,000– 60,000 km². If that distribution is extended south of the Colorado-New Mexico line (a boundary some Mesa Verde archaeologists decline to cross: e.g., Varian et al. 1996: fig. 7.1), that area would double (Roney 1995: fig. 3). Indeed, if New Mexico "Mesa Verde" is included, Aztec is not offset to the east of its putative region, but geographically central.

Architecture provides safer signs than pottery; buildings cost a lot more to make and they don't move around. Architecture—Great Houses, Great Kivas, roads—was the principal criterion defining the Chacoan region. Ball-courts (discussed below) provide a comparable index for Paquime. What might be the architectural signature of Aztec? As noted above, Great Houses and Great Kivas were parts of both Chacoan and Aztec built environments. We need a form specific to Aztec's time and place. Tri-wall structures are spectacularly prominent at Aztec (fig. 3.15), and perhaps they could be used to define its region. Circular bi- and tri-wall structures are found through much, but not all, of the Northern San Juan "Mesa Verde" region (Churchill et al. 1998; Germick 1985; Lekson 1983a; Vivian 1959). Bi- and tri-walls are limited to a zone between Aztec and Escalante in southwest Colorado—an area of perhaps 10,000 km². Recall the tri-wall at Pueblo del Arroyo, in Chaco Canyon; two other extreme southern tri-walls at Tohatchi Flats and Kin Li Chee (Lekson 1983a) would triple the region, and approach the outermost limits of Mesa Verde Black-on-white pottery (Roney 1995). Tri-wall research has yet to be mounted that would rival the sustained outlier hunts of the 1970s and 80s.[12] I found the Kin Li Chee tri-wall quite by accident, looking for a place to take a picture of a Navajo corn field; the Tohatchi Flats bi-wall turned up in a highway right-of-way.

Paquime, most archaeologists agree, was the primate center of a large region (Di Peso 1974; Di Peso, Rinaldo, and Fenner 1974a:208; LeBlanc 1986b:116, 1989:192, 202; Minnis 1989; Wilcox 1996a, b). But we disagree on just how large that region was (table 1). Di Peso (1974:328) suggested an area of 85,000 km², based on primarily on the distribution of Paquime ceramics (see also Wilcox 1996a); Schaafsma (1979) expanded that area to about 200,000 km² by including the El Paso phase; Minnis (1984, 1989) countered with a much more modest 55,000 km². Subsequent work by Whalen and Minnis (1996a, b) seems bent on downsizing. Their most recent work concludes that "the area of a day's walk around Paquime thus seems to represent the apogee of several of the system's activities" (Whalen and Minnis 1996a:744); following Wilcox's dictum of 35 km (22 miles) per day, that gives us a central Paquime region of under 4,000 km². Whalen and Minnis are shrinking Paquime from within; others, like John Douglas (1992, 1995) are snipping away its dependencies from without.

Table 1. Regional estimates, in square kilometers.

	Chaco	Paquime
Conservative	30,000 *Vivian 1990: fig. 8.2*	55,000 *Minnis 1989: 305*
Median	75,000 *Wilcox 1990: fig. 2*	85,000 *Di Peso 1974:328*
Expansionist	150,000+ *Lekson 1991: fig 3.10*	200,000 *Schaafsma 1979: map 1*

A day's walk seems a bit too small—more like a 1970s catchment area than the hinterland of a great Southwestern city, a site with more exotic materials than all the other excavated sites in the Pueblo Southwest combined. Architectural evidence favors Minnis's original 55,000 km² estimate over his more recent mini-Paquime. What Paquime architectural signatures fill the role of Chacoan Great House or Aztec tri-walls? The obvious candidate is the I-shaped ballcourt (fig. 3.18). These spectacular public structures are some of the most impressive features at Paquime and, despite thin survey coverage, we know that similar I-shaped ballcourts occur over a fairly large area—about 55,000 km² (Naylor 1995; Whalen and Minnis 1996a). Whalen and Minnis (1996a) note that ballcourts of the interior zone—the Paquime core—were larger, fancier, and more numerous than ballcourts beyond the day's radius. Given the very pioneering state of survey in Chihuahua and Sonora, I question their conclusion "that the number of courts is low" (Whalen and Minnis 1996a:742)—this seems hasty, given that only 300 km² have been systematically surveyed within the 55,000 km² enclosing the few documented ballcourts (see also Naylor 1995).

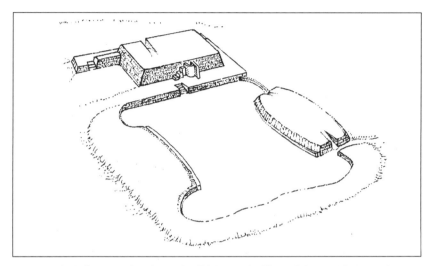

Figure 3.18. Ballcourt at Paquime (after Di Peso, Rinaldo, and Fenner 1974a). Whatever the oval Hohokam "ballcourts" were (or were not), there is no doubt that Paquime played in the big leagues. Paquime had the most and the largest I-shaped courts, but at least one is known from extreme southwestern New Mexico. In ruin, I-shaped courts can appear as short, parallel earthen berms. It would be worth revisiting some of the enigmatic Chacoan road segments that cluster around outliers; from the surface, they look not unlike provincial Paquime ballcourts.

Perhaps the most telling examples are ballcourts in southwestern New Mexico, most notably at the Joyce Well site (Whalen and Minnis 1996a: fig.4). The boot-heel of New Mexico was a distant province of Paquime (see figs. 2.17 and 4.3), but it has seen more archaeological activity than any other part of the Paquime region (reviewed in Lekson 1992b). Despite a series of surveys and excavations, the Joyce Well ballcourt remains all but unpublished, word-of-mouth data, confirmed principally by personal visits. How many more ballcourts are lurking in the unstudied or understudied valleys and bolsons of northwestern Chihuahua? We can, I think, assume the answer will be: more than a few.

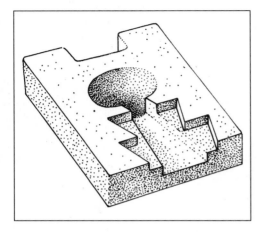

Figure 3.19.
Paquime hearth (after Di Peso, Rinaldo, and Fenner 1974a). The very distinctive raised-platform hearth is unique to Paquime and its dependencies. I am not aware of any comparable features at Chaco, Aztec, Mimbres or El Paso sites. Examples are known, however, from Paquime-related sites in southwestern New Mexico. (McCluney 1968, n.d.).

Joyce Well is 140 km from Paquime—four day's journey, at regulation rates. We do not know the extent of Paquime's region, but southwestern New Mexico ballcourts and fire-hearths (fig. 3.19) suggest that Minnis's original 55,000 km² scale is far more likely than a day's walk. A day's walk, 55,000 km²—*autant d'hommes, autant d'avis.* The range of sizes for the Paquime region tells us as much about contemporary practices and personalities of archaeology as it does about prehistoric conditions.

THEIR CHEQUERED CAREERS

Chaco and Paquime have long been linked in archaeological argument. Aztec has not, until now, played much of a role. This section follows the parries and ripostes of archaeological thinking on Chaco, Paquime, and—lurking in the wings—Aztec.

Current views of Chaco are generally projections of or reactions to the results of the last major research, the National Park Service's Chaco Project, from 1971 to 1986. The Chaco Project party line, in the early 1970s, explained Chaco as a Mesoamerican creation (Hayes 1981; Lister 1978). Changes in leadership brought changes in direction and the new mid-70s group did not ratify their predecessors' free-trade agreement. What was this all this loose talk about Mesoamerica? Where was it coming from? The obvious candidate for a Mesoamerican (or at least cadastrally Mexican) source was Paquime, which burst upon the archaeological scene in a magnificent 1974 eight-volume report. Paquime was a real contender.

Di Peso originally dated Paquime to 1060–1340 (Di Peso 1974; Di Peso, Rinaldo, and Fenner 1974a:8–35); Chaco in the '70s was dated to 900–1125 (fig. 3.20). Di Peso knew Chaco's dates, and he stretched Paquime's chronology to its elastic limits, to argue contemporaneity with Chaco (Di Peso 1974:653). Detailed Paquime-Chaco comparisons (Di Peso, Rinaldo, and Fenner 1974a:208–211) made it clear that Di Peso had Chaco squarely in Paquime's sights. The "Chaco Alamo" (J. Charles Kelley's exasperated tag) reacted predictably: "Where is the archaeological evidence to establish connecting links between Chaco and . . . Casas Grandes [Paquime]?" asked Bob Lister, the Chaco Project's first director, who was in fact a strong advocate of "Mesoamerican influence" at Chaco (Lister 1978:240).

Di Peso did more than hint at Paquime-Chaco connections, but he hedged his bets by also asking if Chaco and Paquime could have been the products of the same Mesoamerican *pochteca* explorer-merchants, or—presaging my arguments in this book—whether "remnants of the Late Bonitian peoples, after abandoning Chaco, could have gone to Casas Grandes [Paquime] about the time that the Paquimians began their urban renewal project ca. A.D. 1205" (Di Peso, in Di Peso, Rinaldo, and Fenner 1974a:211). Di Peso covered Chaco to win, place, or show in the chronological race. The research of the Chaco Project through the later 1970s and early 1980s was at least in part an evaluation of Mesoamerican influences including, particularly, Paquime. "Influences" and "events" did not sit well with New Archaeology. The Chaco Project could account for the evolution and operation of Chaco within local ecological scales, so no Mexicans need apply (Judge 1989:233–249; Lekson 1983b; Mathien 1983, 1986). A war raged hot and cold between the defenders of the "Chaco Alamo" and *pochteca* promoters. And in the end, Chaco's victory over Mexican expansionists came not from Chaco data, but from the internal collapse of the overstrained Paquime chronology. Di Peso's early dating of Paquime (1060–1340) had been attacked by a wide range of authors (including some otherwise friendly to Mesoamerica in the Southwest), culminating in Dean and Ravesloot's dendrochronological re-study (1993:96–98). Dean and Ravesloot demonstrated that Di Peso's Paquime chronology was simply wrong. They conclusively redated Paquime from no earlier than 1250 to no later than 1500. The redating was a statistical extrapolation, and the actual dates are probably closer to 1300–1450. The chronology of interaction had been turned on its head: Paquime could never have caused or even affected Chaco, because Paquime was at least 100 years later than Chaco (fig. 3.20). While specters of Mesoamerica still flutter around the dark corners of the Chacoan world, the main contender—Paquime—was knocked from the ring. The result has been a draconian devaluation of Di Peso.

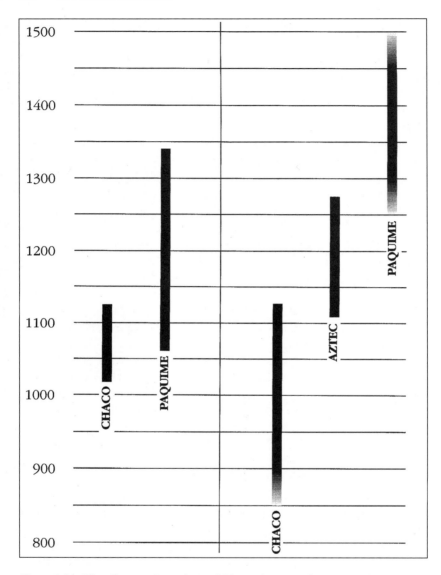

Figure 3.20. The slippery chronology of Chaco, Aztec, and Paquime. Dates on the left indicate Charles Di Peso's dating of Paquime and the Bonito Phase at Chaco (Di Peso, Rinaldo, and Fenner 1974a: fig. 136–4). Dates on the right represent the chronology as it is currently understood, from the work of Dean and Ravesloot (1993), McKenna (1998), and Windes and Ford (1996).

Two recent multiauthor publications that address Chaco and Paquime demonstrate the sweeping rout of Paquime-Chaco connections, real or imaginary: *Chaco and Hohokam* (Crown and Judge 1991) and *Culture and Contact: Charles C. Di Peso's Gran Chichimeca* (Woosley and Ravesloot 1993). Chaco authors in the Chaco-Hohokam volume do not even mention Paquime (the single reference coming obliquely, in a Hohokam chapter). The "Gran Chichimeca" volume makes several references to Chaco, but beyond historical summaries of Di Peso's discredited arguments, Chaco and Paquime are linked precisely twice: first, to deny their contemporaneity ("it is no longer necessary to stretch the archaeological record to identify dubious parallels between Paquime and Chacoan sites," Dean and Ravesloot 1993:102); and second, in a valiant effort by J. Charles Kelley to sustain the connection in light of the new chronology ("Mesoamerican merchants . . . sparked the initial organization of Chaco. . . . When locally deteriorating ecological conditions forced abandonment of the [Chaco] area ca. A.D. 1170, they retreated to a previously established minor base in northwestern Chihuahua [Paquime]" Kelley 1993:249). Kelley, true to his vision, stood alone among the dozen authors of these two volumes, historically linking Chaco and Paquime.

And so it stands today. No one thinks of Chaco and Paquime together, except as anecdotal fodder for history of the field. But Di Peso's throw-away speculation on Chaco-to-Paquime migrations rises from the ashes of his old dead chronology. Maybe those remnants of late Chaco peoples really did walk a long nonwinding road, the old straight track to Paquime.

And where was Aztec in all this brouhaha? Nowhere. Aztec never entered into Chaco-Paquime discussions. "Aztec" appears repeatedly in the several indexes of Di Peso's report, but almost exclusively in reference to the empire of Tenochtitlan. Only once does "Aztec" refer to the National Monument in New Mexico. "Aztec" doesn't even make the cut in Stephen Plog's (1997) new Southwestern textbook, *Ancient Peoples of the American Southwest*, and only once in Linda Cordell's (1977) *Archaeology of the Southwest*, as a historical footnote to the development of dendrochronology.

Over the years, Aztec Ruins was first seen as a refugee colony of fleeing Chacoans, then as an Chacoan agricultural outpost (Lister and Lister 1987:86), or a Mesa Verde site with a small barrio of Chacoans (Ferguson and Rohn 1987:155). In the mid-1980s, Jim Judge hinted that Aztec may have been more: "I submit that there was a shift in the administrative and ritual locus from Chaco to the San Juan area, perhaps to either Aztec or Salmon" (Judge 1989:247). It was Aztec: Aztec became a major player in Southwestern geopolitics.[13]

New dates, new maps, and new understandings have completely changed our view of Aztec. It was not the last twitch of a dying Chaco, but a shift of political power to a new capital. There is nothing like Aztec in the northern San Juan (i.e., Mesa Verde) region: Its monumental construction is unmatched by any of the scores of large Mesa Verde sites I know through visits or descriptions or both. Aztec did not compete with Chaco; Aztec replaced Chaco and, in its turn, was replaced by Paquime.

NOTES

1. For example, the Blue Mesa site just south of Durango, Colorado (see fig. 4.3). Blue Mesa appears to be the very largest Pueblo I (A.D. 700–900) site in the northern Southwest (Fuller 1988; Wilshusen 1991), four or five times larger than any other site of that period. About 250 households lived there—for about one generation (Wilshusen 1991). The pattern for earlier large sites was short-term occupation and mobility. Despite its brief occupance, it is worth noting that Blue Mesa's great size and location are somewhat unusual—and only 10 km off the later Chaco meridian. And, of course, the largest *excavated*Basketmaker site, Shabik'eshchee, is at Chaco Canyon. Make of that what you will.

2. "Uniquity" is a real word; you'll find it in *really*big dictionaries.

3. Di Peso made a 13.1% adjustment for walls in his calculation; a similar adjustment brings the Chaco total down to about 58,600 m².

4. Cordell (1984:273) gives it a sentence, and about the same in the 1997 edition; Vivian 1990 doesn't even mention it; Plog (1997:108) limits it to a couple of paragraphs. The north-south alignment of Alto and Tsin Kletsin is simply a curiosity.

5. Zenith and nadir were consistent, but not visibly fixed. The Chacoan world spanned sufficient latitude to make one person's zenith another person's declination. "Up" and "down," while important on the building scale, was (literally) surficial on the regional scale. "Up" and "down" must differ from place to place, whether your earth is flat or round. But celestial north remains constant.

6. Sandstone seems to have been the stone of choice, but Great Houses were built out of whatever was handy: river cobbles, adobe, sandstone, petrified wood. Great House architects went to great lengths to achieve particular forms, but they did not always go to great lengths to acquire materials.

7. A sandstone disk, much like these, was observed next to a Great Kiva by Adolph Bandelier at Las Ventanas (Bandelier 1892:321); and one can still be seen near a pot hole at that site. Others, presumably from Las Ventanas, are rumored to exist edging gardens in the nearby town of Grants. Las Ventanas is a medium-sized outlier, about 7 km east of the meridian; it is the southernmost "complete consensus" outlier, about 130 km south of Chaco (Marshall, Stein, Loose, and Novotny 1979:187).

8.   Earthen architecture was far more common at Anasazi sites than we previously thought (Stein and Lekson 1992). Berms, trash mounds, terraces, building platforms, and other earthen structures are typical at Chaco and extra-Chaco Great Houses. They pushed a lot of dirt around and stacked it up in piles. The Bonito and Paquime mounds, in contrast, were masonry-walled and surfaced, with thick mud or adobe-plastered capping floors (at Pueblo Bonito). The Pueblo Bonito and Paquime mounds were walled, surfaced platforms. (I discount claims made for a pyramid at Pottery Mound; Hibben 1966.)

The Bonito and Paquime platform mounds may not have been unique in the Pueblo Southwest. My particular epiphany came in the Tonto Basin, observing the excavation of Salado platform mounds. Salado (or Classic Period Hohokam) platform mounds were built with internal divisions, compartments or cells, which look rather like rooms. (Indeed, it was difficult for a Plateau archaeologist to observe Tonto Basin platform mounds and not think: pueblos.) Tonto Basin archaeologists would agree that some of the cells *were* rooms. If platform mounds were composed of rooms or room-like spaces, what are we to make of the doorless, featureless rooms/cells in the Pueblo Bonito trash mounds or in the tri-walls (see note 9, below)?

9.   Another form of tri-walled platform requires brief comment: Shortly after we had dismissed Di Peso's architectural claims, Jonathan Reyman (1985) served up the startling idea that tri-wall structures were West Mexican platform mounds. According to Reyman, the concentric rings were infilled and terraced up a third story platform/tower, perhaps with an inset kiva. At the time, I hooted with the rest: Tri-walls were, well, tri-walls. We didn't know *what* they were but, certainly, they weren't Mexican wedding-cake platform mounds!

The uneasy revelation of empty-cell platform architecture in Salado and Bonito mounds paralleled developments in our understanding of Chacoan architecture. It now seems possible that "rooms" at Great Houses, like Pueblo Bonito, were as much massing as containers. That is, first story rooms at Great Houses may simply elevate the second story. Our view of Chacoan building has changed, and Reyman's premise, today, no longer seems such a stretch. Perhaps tri-walls *were* wedding-cake platform mounds. Stranger things have happened to Anasazi architecture. With the passing of time and the erosion of youthful surety, I feel we may have done Reyman a disservice in this (and other things).

10. The *atalaya* of Cerro de Moctezuma resembled Reyman's reconstruction of the Hubbard Tri-wall at Aztec Ruins (see note 9 above). It *stuck up.* Compare Di Peso, Rinaldo, and Fenner 1974b: fig.239–5 and Reyman 1985: fig. 31. Note, however, that Di Peso got it wrong: The Cerro de Moctezuma tower is not a spiral, but concentrically walled (Swanson 1997). The Cerro de Moctezuma *atalaya* sits on the north-facing crest of the mountain at longitude 107° 59' 48"; Aztec Ruins (measured at the central tri-wall) sits at 107° 59' 50" while the adobe North Ruin, on the bluffs above Aztec, faces south on longitude 108°. As discussed in chapter 4, naked-eye surveying precludes this kind of accuracy, except by chance.

11. The "buttresses" along the south wall of Kin Kletso and the west wall of Kin
     Bineola resemble, vaguely, the breeding pens of Paquime. Neither are structurally
     convincing as "buttresses." The Kin Kletso example was excavated in 1934
     with, unfortunately, no surviving notes about its contents (Vivian and Mathews
     1964:44); I think that canyon lore would tell us, however, if the Kin Kletso
     "buttresses" were found full of macaw bones.

12. Many more tri-walled and bi-walled structures will probably appear, much as
     Great Houses multiplied in the 1980s (e.g., Churchill, Kuckelman, and Varien
     1998). Where are the tri-walls in the New Mexican "Mesa Verde" region? The
     earliest dated tri-wall was built, at Chaco Canyon, about 1105, (Lekson 1983a);
     tri-walls served as principal elements of Aztec planning troughout the history
     of that city, ending about 1275. Other multiple-walled structures—D-shaped
     buildings with double exterior walls—appear rather late in the Four Corners
     and may well represent a continuation of the Chacoan form (Bradley 1996).

     The single, very conspicuous tri-wall structure at Chaco, behind Pueblo del
     Arroyo, was one of the last major construction events in the canyon, and it was
     razed after completion (Judd 1959: 108–119). The Pueblo del Arroyo tri-wall
     might be seen as a "bridging" form, like the North Ruin at Aztec "bridges" the
     architectural transition from Chacoan sandstone to Paquime adobe. I don't
     require seamless transitions, but continuities comfort my colleagues—a subject
     to which we will return in chapter 5.

13. I rejected Judge's arguments for a northward slide at the time (Lekson 1984a:
     267–269)—a strange reaction from someone (myself) who worked at Salmon
     Ruins before coming to Chaco. (I was misled by the carbon-painted pottery at
     Chaco, a deadend beyond the scope of this footnote and book.) Judge's sug-
     gestion of a Chaco-to-San-Juan shift were further developed by Lynne Sebastian
     (1992: 135–136). David Wilcox took things even farther, suggesting that the
     Aztec complex developed as a competing military center, a peer polity chal-
     lenging Chaco's supremacy (Wilcox 1993, 1996a). Wilcox's argument requires
     Chaco to live well beyond its last tree-ring dates, an interpretation I once favored
     (Lekson and Cameron 1995) but which I now recognize as a losing rear-guard
     defense of Chaco against Judge's northern San Juan hypothesis. The dendro-
     chronological facts say otherwise.

     Chaco continued to be remembered and certain buildings (Great Kivas, in
     particular) were maintained; but after about 1125, large-scale building ceased.
     Whatever Chaco had been, it was something else—something *less*—after 1125.
     Aztec, from 1100 to 1275, was huge. Chaco and Aztec were sequential, not
     contemporary.

4

"A Beautiful Fact Killed by an Ugly Theory"

> The geography may be a little difficult to arrange.
>
> Rick Blaine, *Casablanca*

Chaco, Aztec, and Paquime are north-south of each other, on approximately longitude 107° 57' 25"—the "centerline" of Chaco Canyon, defined by the conspicuous alignment of Pueblo Alto and Tsin Kletsin (fig. 3.7; Fritz 1978). I will call that line the Chaco Meridian.

I say these three sites are on the Chaco Meridian, but they are not precisely on the same longitude. Charles Di Peso reported Paquime's location as 107° 58' (Di Peso 1974:24) but that was an error: Recent GPS determinations place Paquime's plaza datum at 107° 56' 49". The difference between the Chaco Meridian and Paquime (measured to the site's principal datum) is thus about 36", or an east displacement of about 1 km. The central tri-walled structure at Aztec is located at 107° 59' 50"—about 4 km west of Fritz's Chaco centerline. The three sites are therefore not really on the same longitude, precisely, but the Chaco Meridian was a constructed feature, not a geodetic line. The errors are about what we would expect, given terrain and technology, and are described below. (And good enough for government work: The east boundary of New Mexico, a line of longitude comparable in length to the Chaco Meridian, has a 3.7 km jog.)

Error is relative: These errors are relative to the Chaco Meridian. Which longitude, exactly, was Chaco's? I use Fritz's longitude because it was demonstrably significant at Chaco (fig. 3.7), but the canyon spans about 5 minutes of longitude from Una Vida to Penasco Blanco. Aztec really is due north of Penasco Blanco; Paquime really is due south of the highest point on the south-facing cliffs of Chaco's South Mesa.

Picking points is an inherent difficulty in this line of work. I am a constant critic of archaeoastronomers at Pueblo Bonito, a semicircular building with radial walls and windows that, in plan, closely resembles a plastic school protractor; look out Bonito's windows and you can span the entire northern sky, look in and you pick up the southern half. There are lots of radial lines at Bonito, and there are lots of celestial bodies out there to align them with. Is it any surprise that Bonito's windows sometimes frame one star or another? With enough points, something will invariably line up with something else. To avoid arbitrary selection, I begin with the Chaco Meridian: We will go with 107° 57' 25".[1]

The fact that Chaco, Aztec, and Paquime shared a meridian, with allowable errors, should not be at issue: It's on the map. But was that alignment intentional? I argue in this chapter that it was. Chapter 3 reviewed some remarkable architectural parallels between and among these three ancient cities. Those shared features and details, found at these three and nowhere else, suggest that *something* was going on. But 720 kilometers—from Aztec to Paquime—is a mighty long way: Why do it? Here, I move beyond material similarities to questions of technical plausibility and cultural meaning, questions of how and why. In this juristic age—the last few years have seen at least five "trials of the century"—I present my case as means, motive, and opportunity. Could they do it, technically? Would they do it, ideologically? Did they have the time to do it, chronologically? Courtroom cliches, perhaps, but my goal is to demonstrate, beyond reasonable doubt and by a preponderance of the evidence, that the Chaco meridian structured the political history of the Pueblo Southwest.

MEANS: "THEY DO THINGS DIFFERENTLY THERE"

Did Chaco, Aztec, and Paquime possess the knowledge and technical ability to create a 720 km long alignment on a meridian? Yes: That technology was demonstrated in the early 12th century, when they built the Great North Road linking Chaco and Aztec.

One of the most remarkable features of the Chacoan region was its network of roads (Stein 1989, Lekson et al. 1988). Chacoan roads, where we can see them, were wide (ca. 9 m), very straight, and carefully engineered with cut-and-fill and elaborate ramps and stairways at slope breaks (Kincaid 1983: chaps. 6, 9). At least two (and perhaps three) roads, with all those formal characteristics, fan out from Chaco Canyon. The South Road runs south-southwest to Hosta

Butte. The West Road (if it is real) runs west-northwest toward a peak in the Chuksa Mountains. The North Road runs due north from Pueblo Alto to Aztec Ruins—to a city, not a mountain.

In the 1980s, we thought that roads radiated out in all directions from Chaco, linking the center to its outliers. We could see roads fanning out from Pueblo Alto (Windes 1987a), but outside the canyon, only a few roads were ever fully studied—it is expensive to research a 60 km long site that, more often than not, is invisible on the ground. The North Road and the South Road, at least, were real (Kincaid 1983; Nials, Stein, and Roney 1987). At most outliers, we could see short road segments pointing back to Chaco or to the next outlier and, given the reality of the North and South roads, we assumed that it was safe to "connect the dots" between those segments. John Stein and I prepared a map for *Scientific American* (fig. 2.8), showing known and projected roads like spokes of a gigantic wheel (Lekson et al. 1988).

Happily, that map clearly differentiated "known" and "projected" roads, because roads don't work that way. Most of the roads radiating out from Pueblo Alto end after only a few kilometers. John Roney revisited roads projected between prominent outliers and found nothing (Roney 1992). Apparently, it was sufficient to build a short segment pointing in the proper direction; that symbolic alignment did whatever roads were supposed to do. Roads routinely connect nearby sites, but over longer hauls, start points and end points were enough.

So most roads run only a few kilometers, at most; only two or three roads were actually built over long distances. The most impressive of those few was the Great North Road (Kincaid 1983; Sofaer, Marshall, and Sinclair 1989). It was a product of later Chacoan times; based on dating of associated structures and ceramic scatters along its route, the North Road was built no earlier than the 1080s and more likely the early 1100s (Stein and McKenna 1988:57). The North Road (fig. 4.1) begins at Pueblo Alto in Chaco Canyon and runs at about 15° east of north 3 km to Escavada Wash. At the Escavada, the road corrects its course and runs north (within an approximately 1.0 km wide corridor) for 56 km from Pueblo Alto to Twin Angels Pueblo. For short lengths along this route, the route is represented by double or even quadruple parallel roadways. The road recombines into a single roadway and then reaches an elaborate stairway and descends into rugged Kutz Canyon and then, presumably, on to Twin Angels Pueblo, almost exactly north of the road's point-of-beginning at Chaco Canyon. Twin Angels Pueblo is an odd outlier (Carlson 1966); most outliers were central to communities of small unit pueblos (Lekson 1991), but Twin Angels sits in splendid isolation. There is no associated community, no reason for Twin Angels except its positions along the North Road.

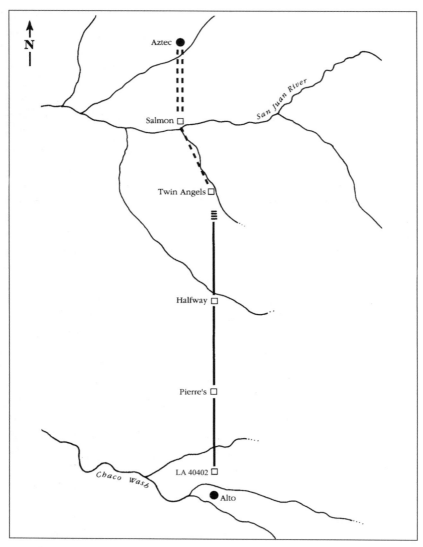

Figure 4.1. The Great North Road. The North Road was named "great" for the famous Roman road running north through England; Randall Morrison probably first proposed the name. This map combines elements from the Bureau of Land Management surveys (Nials, Stein, and Roney 1987) and the Solstice Project (Sofaer, Marshall, and Sinclair 1989), along with my own projections. We have not found the segment linking Salmon and Aztec, but I'm betting some small part of my reputation that it's there. The North Road was not perfectly straight—it careened, ever so slightly, within a 1 km wide corridor, and "dog-legged" a few kilometers at Kutz Canyon. But its northern orientation is nevertheless remarkable.

At Twin Angels Pueblo, the road turns briefly away from north. To that point, the North Road traversed mostly level lands, with only low ridges and a few small valleys breaking the line-of-sight. The terrain beyond Kutz Canyon is very different: authentic badlands, a moonscape of deep clay canyons and precipitous cliffs. I will argue below that landscape, by and large, was no obstacle to Chacoan engineering; but these people were not idiots. At Twin Angels, the Road almost certainly angled about 30° west of north and continued 15 km down the level bottom of Kutz Canyon to Salmon Ruins. Twin Angels and Salmon Ruins mark its route; the bottom of Kutz Canyon has, of course, been heavily eroded over the last eight centuries. The Kutz Canyon offset puts the road a few kilometers west of its initial longitude at Chaco Canyon. From Salmon, the North Road almost certainly ran precisely north, again, 16 km to Aztec Ruins (Stein and McKenna 1988:57) although this segment has not yet been located on the ground. Aztec Ruins, 85 km north of Pueblo Alto at Chaco Canyon, is less than 4 km west of the Chaco Meridian—an angle error of only 2.5° (Sofaer 1997: table 3).

Our best evidence for Chacoan surveying is the North Road. The road is not an assertion or an inference, it actually exists on the ground. We can see it and study it. The North Road shows us, concretely, Chacoans could survey a long meridian line over broken terrain.[2] We know they did it, and we can speculate on how. Only two specific techniques were necessary to survey the North Road: determining north and prolonging a line.

Determining north was easy—but not by reference to the pole star Polaris, which was well off celestial north in the 11th–13th centuries. A range of simple techniques are known for fixing the parallel (i.e., east-west) from a solar passage or the rotation of stars from horizon to horizon.[3] North was then fixed by the perpendicular of the east-west parallel (Kim Malville, personal communication 1995). This process required no complex equipment. "For sighting and meridian determination, the [ancient] Egyptians used a plumb bob, which was observed through a slit cut in the end of a palm leaf" (Multhauf 1985:57) and we can assume that Anasazi technology was at least that complex. Experiments at Chaco with string or poles determined north with accuracies of about 40' for a single sighting, and less than 20' for repeated, visually "averaged" measurements (Rolf Sinclair and Anna Sofaer, personal communication 1988).

Accuracy came from repeated measurements. The periodicity of the measurement is thus of some importance. Unlike the annual cycles of solstices and 18+ year lunar standstills, north can be measured daily. Repeated observations of north were easy, and considerable accuracy could be achieved. Significantly, building orientations at Chaco Canyon were very precise for the meridian (less than one degree off at Pueblo Bonito, Hungo Pavi, and Tsin

Kletzin) but far less accurate for proposed solstitial and lunar alignments, with their much longer observational cycles (Sofaer 1997).

The North Road (and the Chaco Meridian) would have been surveyed by physically prolonging a line by visual alignment of targets. It would not be possible for Chacoans to go to Aztec or Paquime and determine longitude from the stars or other landmarks. Independent determination of longitude was far beyond the technical capabilities of the New World (and Old, until relatively recently; Howse 1980; Sobel 1995). It was simply impossible to locate Aztec or Paquime on the Chaco Meridian without actually staking out a north-south line, beginning at Chaco. That line could be surveyed, on the ground, by backsighting and foresighting on range poles or plumb lines. Experiments in naked-eye surveying at Chaco demonstrate that lines could be prolonged over broken terrain with remarkable accuracy, for example about 1 m of error over 2 km (Rolf Sinclair and Anna Sofaer, personal communication 1988). Surveying from backsight to foresight was simple and straightforward, until terrain blocked the backsight. Every ridge or valley would break the line-of-sight. Then it would be necessary to reestablish north, and begin the process again—a problem which actually increased accuracy (as described below).[4]

We can see the results of Chacoan surveying in the North Road. The road, in some segments, runs very close to the true meridian (Kincaid 1983), but not along its entire length. From ridge to ridge, it careens ever so slightly, back and forth within a corridor of about 1 km width. There appear to have been very slight changes of direction at each ridge line, each break in the line-of-sight, each place where it would have been necessary to reestablish north. Each time north was reestablished, error was introduced. As we shall see, that error was "self-correcting.[5]

There was nothing complicated about laying out the North Road. A panel of astronomers and archaeologists concluded that only "simple technology—probably not a corps of engineers—was required to perform such tasks as aligning the roads" (Young 1987:231). A troop of Boy (or Girl) Scouts could lay out the North Road with three poles, a spool of rope, and a box of truck flares. Surveying the North Road might have required time and patience—the Scouts might have passed from Cub to Eagle by the time they reached Aztec—but no technical equipment or esoteric knowledge.[6]

Whatever the methods used, Twin Angels Pueblo is less than 1' off the longitude of the North Road where it begins its meridian route, at Escavada Wash—an error of less than 500 m over a length of more than 55 km. The key to this accuracy may be the breaks in the line-of-sight and the need to repeatedly reestablish north and the line's direction. At least three and perhaps four ridge lines break the line-of-sight. A meridian line prolonged by segments, with independent measurements establishing and reestablishing north at each new segment, can actually be more accurate than a single line of equal length projected from a single, initial measurement. This is because random errors of measurement, introduced each time north is reestablished, cancel each other out. We can actually see that in the route of the North Road.[7]

How might that work over the longer span from Chaco to Paquime? Chaco and Paquime are 630 km apart—thirteen times the distance of the North Road from Alto to Twin Angels Pueblo (fig. 4.2). The error observed on Chaco walls aligned on celestial phenomenon—including solstices and lunar cycle—is typically no more than 2° (Rolf Sinclair, personal communication 1996). A initial 2° error would create an error of over 22 km if continued, unabated, over 630 km. But, in fact, the Chaco-Paquime error was only 1 km. This accuracy was achieved because the Chaco-Paquime line (like the North Road) must have been prolonged in short segments. There are about a dozen major breaks in the line-of-sight between Chaco and Paquime.

The Chaco-Paquime meridian spans five major plains of 50–60 km width (fig. 4.2). From north to south, these are: the southern San Juan Basin, the North Plains, the Plains of St. Augustine, the Deming Plain, and Llano de Carretas. At its southern end, the Rio Mimbres and Rio Paquime valleys, which align roughly along this meridian, create a combined 250 km length of relatively flat terrain (incorporating the Deming Plain and the Llano de Carretas).

Between these long plain segments, a series of ridges, hills, and mountains interrupt visibility along the meridian line. From north to south, these are (with their approximate latitudes): the Dutton Plateau (Borrego Pass, 35° 30'), the east foothills of the Zuni Mountains (Gallo Peak, 35°), the Sawtooth Mountains (34° 15'), Crosby Mountains (Sugarloaf Peak, 34° 8'), Indian Peaks (33° 30'), west slopes of the Black Range (from Alexander Peak 33° 30' to Mimbres Peak 32° 45'), Carrizalillo Hills (31° 45'), and the southeast foothills of the Sierra Alta (Cerro Grande 31° 8') (fig 4.2).

Most or all of these features would be useful for very long back- and fore-sights (theoretically, up to 160 km). That is, these high points could have been beneficial in running the meridian line over intervening plains. Only the Black Range, with about 80 km of uninterrupted mountain ridges, poses a major terrain challenge. But the Black Range probably requires no different techniques, merely more time and labor. And field checks indicate that the Black Range could have been spanned in only one or two jumps, by "wiggling in" (see note 4).

So ridge lines divide the Chaco-Paquime line-of-sight at approximately 50–60 km intervals; at each ridge, a new sighting measurement would have been necessary. Thus, the Chaco-Paquime line required at least 11 to 13 separate measurements for 11 to 13 segments of relatively equal length.

Figure 4.2. The Chaco Meridian. A, North half; b, south half.

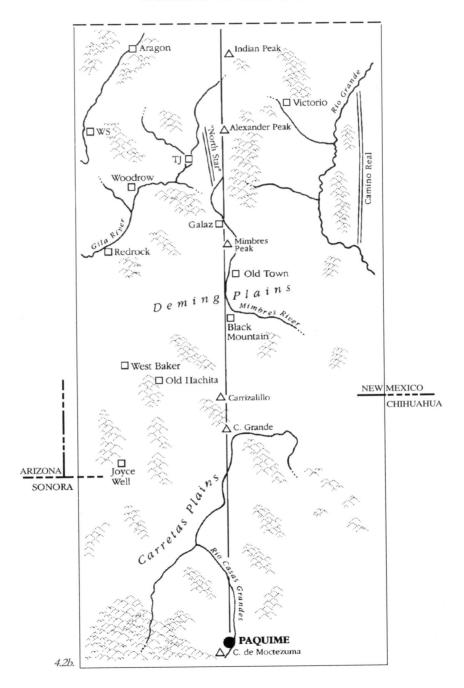

4.2b.

Recall that Chaco and Paquime are only about 1 km apart in their meridians; that is, the east-west displacement or error is only 1 km over 630 km distance. That's good shooting; but is it unreasonably good? Given the necessity for reestablishing north at least a dozen times, a 1 km error is not astonishing. In fact, it is predictable.

Formulas have been developed for calculating theoretical errors inherent in repeated measurements, such as segmented meridians. A formula for multiple "independent uncertainties" comes from John R. Taylor's *Introduction to Error Analysis* (Taylor 1982:52–59)—as explained to your mathematically challenged author by Professor Taylor himself, who must be held blameless for any subsequent misuse. All that is needed are the average angle error, the total length, and the number of segments. Chaco and Paquime were 630 km apart. The likely error for naked-eye sighting at Chaco has been estimated to be no greater than 2° (Rolf Sinclair, personal communication, 1996). The number of ranges between 11 and 13 segments of approximately equal length. (For those following Taylor's text, I assume that the segments were of exactly equal length, without doing great injustice to topographic reality.)

Error for multiple segment, "independent uncertainties" is a quadratic sum, rather than a simple sum; that is, the errors accrue as the square root of their summed squares, rather than directly. The theoretical error for a multiple segment model (based on formulas in Taylor 1982) for 13 measurements would be about 6 km and, for 11 measurements, about 6.6 km—a considerable reduction from the simple compounded 2° error of 22 km! And, of course, my estimate of the number of segments is minimal; the alignment may have incorporated many more segments, many more measurements and, thus, an even smaller theoretical error.

A theoretical error of about 6 km is not incommensurate with the actual error of 1 km. (The theoretical error similarly computed for the North Road to Twin Angels Pueblo is 775 m, not far off the observed error of 500 m.) One kilometer, still, is more accurate than 6 km. Should this concern us? I think not: They got lucky. The theoretical error is, in fact, a statistical bell curve: a 6 km span about a mean, with the chances of 1 km error much higher than an error of 3 km. It is not remarkable that an error of 1 km was achieved on the first (and presumably only) attempt to trace this line on the ground. Had the error been 22 km, for example, we would have to consider nonrandom sources for error. A displacement of 1 km was fortunate, but not fabulous.

Complementing the results obtained from Taylor's formula, Joey Donahue of Los Alamos National Laboratory simulated an alignment of 200 miles (320 km) with twenty segments of 10 miles (16 km). At each segment, an independent random error with a standard deviation of 2° was introduced. The model was run 10,000 times, and produced a mean predictably very close to zero and, more important, a standard error of only 0.35 miles, or about 0.56 km (Joey Donahue, personal communication 1996). While the distance in Donahue's simulation is about half that of the actual Chaco-Paquime alignment, it is evident that considerable precision was possible over longer, segmented distances.

Keith Kintigh of Arizona State University developed a similar program to simulate the alignment process. I quote from his letter, reporting the results (Keith Kintigh, personal communication 1998):

> If one assumes a 630 km meridian divided into thirteen equal segments (of 48.5 km) and an angular error uniformly distributed between −2° and +2°, simulating the survey 100,000 times provides a mean error near 0, as it should because the error is random, not biased to the east or west (the mean is actually 13 m and the standard deviation is 3.5 km). The more important result is that a survey will produce a displacement less than or equal to the observed 1 km displacement about 22 percent of the time. Thus, we would expect them to do as well or better than they actually did better than one out of five times. The average displacement (ignoring direction) is about 2.8 km. . . . Errors of more than 10 km are quite unlikely. Similar results are obtained if the angular error is normally distributed with a standard deviation of 1°. A survey would result in a displacement of 1 km or less about one out of four times (26%) and the average displacement is 2.4 km.

Greater accuracy, reducing the 2° and even the 1° error, could have been achieved by repeated determinations of north at each segment and "averaging" the results; recall that experiments at Chaco obtained north with accuracies of less than a degree by simply repeating measurements. Accuracy could have been improved by running the entire 630 km Chaco-Paquime meridian many times and "averaging" the location of the final station at Casas Grandes. But we should not demand this Teutonic precision of the ancient Pueblo peoples. Why would they hammer themselves for accuracy? Indeed, how could they even know they were in error? Longitude was a mystery: They had no way of knowing that there was any error to correct. Standing at Aztec or Paquime, there was no way to judge how close or how far they were from the Chaco Meridian. They could only know that a line had been run, a deed had been done. One line was probably fine—and, thanks to "independent uncertainties," they (almost) nailed it with one try.

MEANS (CONTINUED): "CAN'T GET THERE FROM HERE"

Did the meridian route from Chaco to Paquime cross unknown lands? We know that they knew the Chaco-Aztec segment; they built a road on it. But from Chaco south to Paquime is rather new territory, for archaeology if not for ancient Pueblo people.

The meridian route from Chaco to Aztec spanned 630 km of mountain ranges, hills, plains, and valleys (fig. 4.2). What knowledge of this long span would Chaco, or Aztec have? Recall that the meridian could only be surveyed *from* Chaco *to* Paquime; no other sequence of alignment was technically possible. Thus, it would be convenient for my argument if Chaco (and, thus, Aztec) knew something about the sunny South before they got there.

Looking south from Chaco, the first 200 km lies firmly within the Chacoan region (fig. 4.3); whatever the Chacoan Regional System was or was not, we can be reasonably certain that the first 200 km was anything but terra incognita to Chaco or Aztec. So the first third of the meridian was well known. Only 100 km separates the southern edge of the Chaco region, as conventionally drawn, from the northern borders of Mimbres (fig. 4.3). Skipping, for now, that 100 km gap, let us revisit Mimbres (chap. 2, fig. 2.7).

The 11th-century Mimbres region (fig. 4.3) encompasses the final, southernmost 330 km of the Chaco-Paquime meridian, including the site of yet-to-be-built 14th-century Paquime (cf fig. 4.5). Chaco and Mimbres were exactly contemporary and notably north-and-south. The Chaco meridian crosses the Mimbres River near the modern town of Mimbres, where the river leaves its narrow mountain valley; it passes within 4 km of Old Town, perhaps the largest Mimbres Valley village (fig. 2.17, 2.18, 4.3).

In chapter 2, I suggested that Chaco and Mimbres knew each other and that Mimbres was actually incorporated to some degree into the Chacoan world. Chaco and Mimbres were conspicuous consumers of Mesoamerican trade items, specifically macaws, shell, and copper bells. In the 11th- and early 12th-century Pueblo world, these items were notably concentrated at Chaco Canyon and the Mimbres valley. Chaco and Mimbres were, at the very least, on the same trade circuit and, I think, allied (and aligned) within the larger world order. The routes between Chaco and the Mimbres valley must have been well-known (and probably well-beaten) in the 11th century.

It's tough country, between the southernmost edges of the Chaco region and Mimbres area (fig. 4.2b, 4.3). The Mogollon Uplands includes one of the very earliest declared "wilderness areas." It is easy to see why. Eighty kilometers of mountains separate the Plains of St. Augustine from the Mimbres Valley. Likely routes, for us, would not follow the Chaco Meridian across the west flanks of the rugged Black Range (fig. 4.2). Instead, projected "trade routes" follow river valleys: far to the west, up the Gila River, over a low divide to the San Francisco River valley, and then upstream to the Plains of St. Augustine; or far to the east along the Rio Grande (Kelley 1986; Riley 1976, 1995:Map 10;). Both routes were later marked (even entrenched) by Spanish, Mexican, and Territorial roads. They seem reasonable—that's how *we* would do it.

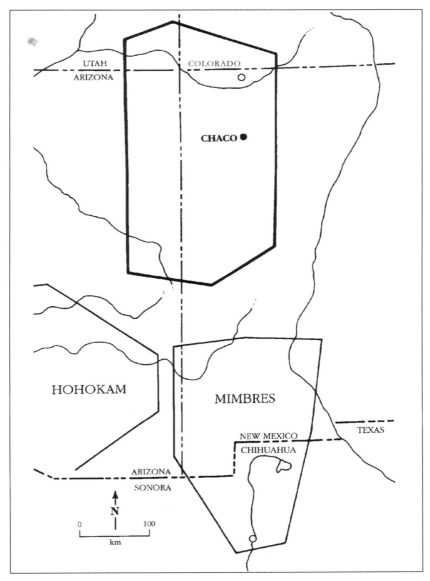

Figure 4.3. Chaco, Mimbres, Hohokam. The three major regional entities in the 11th- and early 12th-century Southwest were Sedentary Period Hohokam, Mimbres, and Chaco. Hohokam and Chaco, separated by the Mogollon Rim and the uplands, ignored each other. Only at either end of the Rim—at Flagstaff and near the Rio Grande—could north and south meet, with very interesting results. Mimbres—on the east end—was a fantastic moire of Chaco and Hohokam. On the west, Wupatki-era Sinagua was a phenomenal fusion of Southwestern monumental traditions: ballcourts, Great Houses, and Great Kivas.

Carl Sauer, in his seminal study of *The Road to Cibola*, used European logistics to reconstruct native routes: "Men on horses had the same need of saving distance, of finding easy passes and stream crossings, and of food and drink, that directed the Indian's travel afoot. Footpaths and pack-trails rarely differ." (Sauer 1932:1). But anyone who has tried Jackson Staircase at Chaco Canyon knows that the only way a horse goes up or down that incline is in pieces. Pueblo trails and Chaco roads were not equine-friendly. Navajo people built wagon roads over most of the Chaco region, and they don't retrace the Chaco routes.

Sauer, and all who followed him, assume that colonial roads define the principal precolonial trade routes, and many may. But foot traffic really can move differently than horses, remudas, and wagons. The mechanics are simply not the same; a porter has radically different requirements for "food and drink" than a horse. Indian trails could go straight over mountains and molehills, and many did. Certainly, Chacoan roads favored straightness over ease.

When we look at the modern map, there is, in fact, a road through the Mogollon uplands, closely parallel to the Chaco Meridian (fig. 4.2b). It is today called the North Star Road, and it (reportedly) began as a 19th-century military road. It was a wagon road, and winds tortuously over the ridges and through the valleys of the west flanks of the Black Range. The history of the North Star Road remains to be written, but it is not too far-fetched to suggest it traced a far older route, deviating to accommodate new transportation technologies.

The 100 km "gap" between Chaco and Mimbres was almost certainly not a gap in knowledge during the 11th century. But at 1275, when Aztec ends, archaeological maps for the Mimbres area are blank. As discussed in chapter 2, the standard version has the Mimbres Valley more or less abandoned at about 1125 (LeBlanc 1983). Erasing Mimbres opens the Chaco-Paquime gap to dangerous lengths (fig. 4.3). But, as noted in chapter 2, Mimbres had not vanished. It just changed clothes.

The lower Mimbres Valley and the desert beyond was occupied by post-Mimbres populations that continued the Mimbres line, if not the Mimbres fashion (fig. 4.4). The iconography and ideology changed, but memories—good or bad—of both Mimbres and Chaco would almost certainly remain. The spatial gap between Chaco and Paquime's site was only slightly greater than the earlier gap between Chaco and Mimbres. Of knowledge there was probably no gap at all: Mimbres knew Chaco, Chaco knew Mimbres, and post-Mimbres peoples would have remembered it all.

When the post-Mimbres people shifted their center-of-gravity to the south, the northern frontier of the former Mimbres region was effectively depopulated (LeBlanc 1989). Into that brief breach charged populations with Tularosa Black-

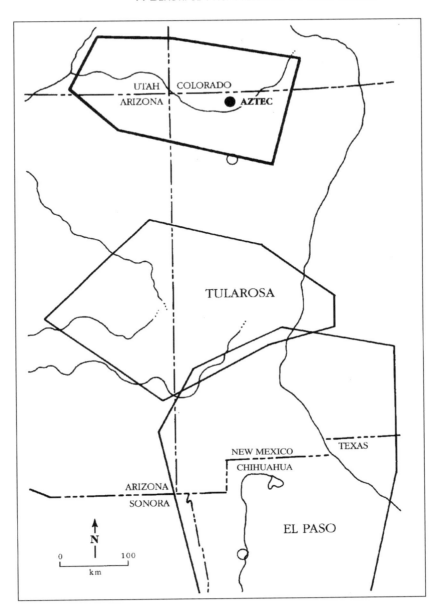

Figure 4.4. Aztec, Tularosa, El Paso. The broad east-west band of Tularosa Black-on-white and allied types mirrors the northern band of Mesa Verde Black-on-white. The Tularosa horizon prefigures the Pinedale style, a key element in the emergence of post-Chaco ideological developments (Crown 1994).

on-white pottery, part of a much larger post-Chaco Tularosa Horizon (fig. 4.4) that centered on the Zuni and Acoma districts (Lekson 1996b). The Tularosa Horizon continued the Great House community pattern in the old Chacoan region (Fowler and Stein 1992; Kintigh, Howell, and Duff 1996). The southernmost Tularosa post-Chaco Great Houses (of which I am aware) are the Victorio site on Alamosa Creek (Laumbach 1992; Laumbach and Wakeman in press) and, I think, the WS Ranch site on the Rio San Francisco, about 300 km south of Chaco. (The excavator of WS Ranch, James Neeley, would probably *not* agree.) Sites of the Tularosa Horizon enjoyed stronger southern links than the remote, northern Aztec domain. For example, the Tularosa phase pueblo at Turkey Creek produced 12 macaws (Hargrave 1970:44) and 8 copper bells (Vargas 1995: table 4.2)—more than Aztec.

Along the line of the Chaco Meridian only 80 km separated a small Tularosa community near the old Mimbres TJ Ruin from the huge, post-Mimbres Black Mountain site (fig. 4.2). In less mountainous districts, Tularosa and post-Mimbres archaeologies are virtually in contact: Post-Mimbres villages were only a few km downstream from both Victorio and WS Ranch (a large early El Paso phase site at the mouth of Alamosa Creek and an early Salado site just below WS Ranch). If anything, the 100 km "gap" of Chaco and Mimbres times was diminished by 1275—the end of Aztec and the beginning of Paquime.

During the Aztec polity's last decades, the southern half of the old Chaco world was booming. The Tularosa Horizon was huge: Enormous pueblos were built, left, and replaced in an unbroken historical chain that leads ultimately to the modern Pueblos of Zuni and Acoma. The Chaco Meridian runs right down the traditional "boundary" between Zuni and Acoma territories—archaeological and modern (Ferguson and Hart 1985; Ruppe 1953). Zuni and Acoma are the modern Pueblos closest to the Chaco Meridian—an interesting fact, considering their traditional histories (discussed later in this chapter).

To summarize the preceding two sections, Chacoan techniques demonstrably could survey accurate meridians over long distances and broken terrain. We can see and measure their results in cardinal alignments of Chaco buildings and the Great North Road. Surveying the meridian from Chaco to Aztec or Chaco to Paquime would not require complex technical achievements. Moreover, they were almost certainly familiar with the route. The flow of exotic goods demonstrates distinct material connections between north and south in the 11th and early 12th centuries; the distributions of Mimbres and Chaco, and post-Mimbres and Tularosa sites nearly overlap. The Chaco Meridian traversed well-known country. It did not boldly go where no man, woman, itinerant merchant, or priestly delegation had gone before. They knew the route. They could do the job. All they needed was a reason.

Motive: "Roads Through Time"

Chacoan roads are enigmatic: no wheeled vehicles, no horses or mules, no bulk transport other than porters. There was no obvious practical reason to construct a 9 m wide freeway where a foot path would suffice. Following straight lines, Chacoan roads climbed steep slopes when easier, porter-friendly alternate routes were close to hand. What are we to make of this? We can probably conclude that Chacoan roads served purposes beyond (but including) pedestrian travel.

The North Road, like other Chacoan roads, was originally interpreted as a transportation corridor, analogous to modern roads (Ebert and Hitchcock 1980). This was not a foolish projection of present into past: Bulk goods (construction timbers, pottery, and probably corn) were indeed transported into Chaco Canyon from distant sources. We don't know if those goods followed roads or if they moved along trails—easier to walk but harder to find archaeologically.

The bulkiest bulk material was construction timber. A great many beams were brought into Chaco, and perhaps the width of the road reflects the length of the timber (Snygg and Windes 1998). Or, perhaps, it was not goods, but people. There are situations in which people move in groups; suggestions range from pilgrim processions going into Chaco (Judge 1989; Malville and Judge 1993; Malville and Malville 1995) to troops marching out (David Wilcox, quoted in Roberts 1996:98). Either or both are possible.

But roads had symbolic value, perhaps more important than any pedestrian use (e.g., Roney 1992). The North Road, in particular, has been interpreted as nonfunctional: a "cosmographic expression" of spiritual or mythical values (Marshall 1997; Sofaer, Marshall, and Sinclair 1989). This interpretation proceeds from the premise that the North Road had "no clear practical destination" (Sofaer, Marshall, and Sinclair 1989:374)—a road to nowhere, ending at Kutz Canyon (fig. 4.1).

In the teeth of Southwestern archaeology's relentless functionalism, this was a bold stroke. Ritual roads (e.g., Gabriel 1991) are a radical departure from corn-beans-and-squash prehistories that we routinely offer the public, and I admire Sofaer, Marshall, and Sinclair's vision. But, alas, I cannot write off the North Road as a road to nowhere. The route of the road is described in some detail above—to recap, the road reaches Kutz Canyon and descends into it via an elaborate wooden stairway. The physical evidence of a road will be absent in the eroded bottom of Kutz Canyon, but Twin Angels Pueblo demonstrates that the road continued at least that far beyond the stairway along the bottom of the canyon (fig. 4.1). Salmon continues the line, and Aztec (due north of Salmon) ends it. As noted, we lack a road between Salmon and Aztec, but we have not committed comparable resources to this segment that the San Juan

Valley Archaeological Project, the National Park Service, the Bureau of Land Management, and the Solstice Project (among others) expended on the North Road from Chaco to Kutz Canyon.

The North Road was not a road to nowhere; it was a road from Chaco to Aztec (via Salmon), and it ran due north. But there's something odd about the chronology of its termeni (fig. 3.20). Large-scale construction at Chaco Canyon ended about 1125. Salmon Ruin rose about 1088 and building began at Aztec about 1110. The North Road—more difficult to date than buildings—appears to have been constructed between the late 1080s and the early 1100s (Kincaid 1983, Sofaer, Marshall, and Sinclair 1989)—during the initial planning and construction at Salmon and Aztec. The road did not connect existing places; it connected an old place with a new place, an *emerging* place.

At several well-studied locations, Chacoan road segments connect non-contemporary, sequentially-built Great Houses and pueblos (Fowler and Stein 1992). In Manuelito Canyon near Gallup, New Mexico, a road links a Chacoan Great House (ca. 1050–1150) to a post-Chaco Great House (ca. 1150–1250) about 3.75 km away; a second linkage, spanning the 3 km distance between the post-Chaco Great House and a larger, later pueblo ruin known only as "Big House" (ca. 1250–1325), may also exist. The pattern of roads connecting sequential, noncontemporary Great Houses and pueblos is known from a number of widely separated districts, from Mesa Verde to east central Arizona (Fowler and Stein 1992:116–118).

John Stein and Andrew Fowler call these "roads through time." Chacoan "roads" can be seen as "time bridges, symbolic umbilicals that linked one age to another" (Fowler and Stein 1992:117). Roads through time monumented and commemorated the historical linkage between Chaco Great Houses and post-Chaco formations. They legitimized the ritual and social roles of post-Chaco Great Houses and pueblos by a material, landscape reference back to a locus of mythic or historic power. At the local scale, those linkages spanned distances of 2 to 6 km; but roads through time could cross longer spans. One of the longest roads, the North Road, linked Chaco and Aztec, built in different eras. The North Road was not a transportation corridor for beams, troops, or pilgrims—although these may have moved along the road. It was a monument— an interpretation first offered by Fowler and Stein (1992:119).

Why north? I don't know; but we do know that north was important in Chacoan cosmology, as that cosmology was expressed in the layout of the ceremonial city and its monumental Great Houses. As noted above, Chaco itself was planned around a meridian axis (fig. 3.7). Pueblo Alto and Tsin Kletsin were themselves cardinal in orientation and together their alignment defined Fritz's Chaco Meridian. Alto was early, built in 1020s over an even earlier Great House structure (Windes 1987a, 1987b). Tsin Kletsin was constructed much later, in the early 1100s, we don't know if it covers an earlier shrine or monument (Lekson 1986a).

Pueblo Bonito could not be shifted from its original solar or lunar orientations (Sofaer 1997), but the cardinals found expression in the latest construction at that most important building. Late, prominent, cardinal walls enclosed and divided the great plaza at Pueblo Bonito (Frontispiece). The dividing wall, perhaps the last major architectural statement at Bonito, runs just a fraction off true north. It was oriented with care and difficulty; its line crossed a large subterranean kiva. The wall spanned that chamber's wide roof (itself near the maximum limits for Chacoan building) on paired wooden beams. That structural solution was both awkward and dangerous, but it was evidently more important to align the wall with north than to shift a few degrees east and miss the kiva. We don't know what north meant, but we do know that it was very important.

To summarize: A formal Chacoan regional geometry was expressed by alignments, physically monumented by short "road" segments and, rarely, by major continuous roads.[8] Roads commemorated linkages between places within the larger region: between contemporary settlements, between "outliers" and Chaco, or—most significantly for this chapter—between sequentially constructed Great Houses and pueblos. The North Road served this last purpose, linking Chaco to Aztec. The North Road projected the Chaco Meridian; the Chaco-Paquime alignment prolonged that same meridian.

OPPORTUNITY: "HOW CAN YOU BE IN TWO PLACES AT ONCE . . . ?"

"How can you be in two places at once, when you're not anywhere at all?" That '60s acid-vaudeville tag not only dates your author, it describes the chronological conundrum of archaeologists trying to make sense of Chaco and Paquime. Initially, Charles Di Peso stretched the Paquime tree-ring dates to make the two contemporary—contemporaneity made sense, given the remarkable parallels between those two major centers. The redating of Paquime by Dean and Ravesloot (1993) revealed that Chaco (900–1125) was more than a century older than Paquime (1250–1450). The dates had changed, but the parallels remained, suggesting connections across that century gap (fig. 3.20). As Di Peso insisted, Chaco had *something* to do with Paquime, or vice versa. Despite their differing ages, Chaco and Paquime remain an item.

How to cross that missing century? That was the problem when I began to rethink Chaco and Paquime, several years ago. A series of new dates from

Aztec and a new realization of Aztec's scale and importance—primarily the work of John Stein, Peter McKenna, and Tom Windes—filled the gap (McKenna and Toll 1992; McKenna 1998; Stein and Mckenna 1992). Aztec, once dismissed as a "secondary Chacoan center" was in fact the New Chaco—and the chronological, political, and geographic transition from Chaco to Paquime.

Construction at Aztec began—in a previously unimportant valley—just as major construction ended at Chaco. From 1110 through about 1275, Aztec was the premier site in the northern San Juan. Construction ended at the Aztec complex about 1275. Several other very interesting things coincide, approximately, with that date: the beginnings of the "Great Drought"; the depopulation of the Four Corners; and the initial construction of Paquime, sometime after 1250 and before 1300.

Paquime rose in a previously unimportant valley, almost 700 km south of Aztec. Times changed, but one idea remained, proclaiming political continuity: meridian alignment.

CLOSING ARGUMENTS: "HIGH CRIMES AND MISDEMEANORS"

Chaco-Aztec-Paquime planners had means (engineering and terrain knowledge), motive (roads-through-time, positional legitimation) and opportunity (sequential chronology) to design and produce the Chaco-Paquime alignment. It could still be a coincidence; it could *always* be a coincidence. In these final arguments I address issues of coincidence, and then offer suggestions—history, ecology, process—about the alignment's meaning.

Coincidence

The alignment of Chaco, Aztec, and Paquime could be pure chance. Circumstantial evidence, alone, cannot leap that hurdle: We will always arrive back at the beginning of the Mobius strip. Surely, dots on a map are *testable*. What are the statistical probabilities that the alignment of Chaco, Aztec, and Paquime was simple coincidence? Testing for simple coincidence raises complex questions.

There are statistics for testing linearities, lines of sites. Ley lines—the peculiarly British obsession with site alignments—have been subjected to statistical analysis.[9] Alfred Watkins, the first and most appealing of the "ley hunters," recognized the need for statistical tests in his 1920s publications: "what really matters . . . is whether it is a humanly designed fact, an accidental coincidence, or a mare's nest that mounds, moats, beacons, and mark stones fall into straight lines" (quoted in Broadbent 1980:111). Somewhere about mid-century, ley lines took a sharp turn from Watkins's "Old Straight Track" to New Age earth-energy mysteries. I have reviewed, but not exhausted this literature—indeed, the reverse: The literature exhausted me. It has a prurient, Roswellian, X-File interest, but let me state plainly: I am not personally interested in earth-energies, UFOs, or *feng shui*, despite the fact that I now live in Boulder, Colorado, and (in a previous life) resided in Santa Fe, New Mexico.

Pro and con partisans attempted to statistically test ley alignments (e.g., Pennick and Devereux 1989:232–236). The statistical questions asked of ley lines were two: first, how to discover ley lines and, second, how to evaluate proposed ley lines. In both instances, the crux of the problem was the development of statistical distributions of "colinearities" within a spatial field of uniform, independent, random points—a hypothetical array of candidate sites for alignment.

It will come as no surprise that discovery statistics were developed by ley line hunters, while evaluation statistics were developed by skeptical statisticians. The latter are of far more interest for the Chaco-Aztec-Paquime alignment than the former. A celebrated example concerns fifty-two megaliths scattered over Cornwall—the "Old Stones of Land's End" (e.g., Broadbent 1980; Kendall and Kendall 1980; Michell 1974, 1977). Various ley lines had been proposed for these monuments, and several statisticians evaluated methods for testing their validity. The logic of their tests rested on the numbers of three-point alignments, within fifty-two random points, which might be expected through chance alone. Statistical distributions of those potential random alignments were calculated, and the number of alignments actually observed in the Old Stones of Land's End compared with that distribution—with mixed results. There were more alignments observed than predicted by pure chance. A sizable portion of the alignments could be dismissed as chance occurrences, but which (if any) were "real" ley lines and which were random alignments?

There is a difference in the Chaco-Aztec-Paquime problem, and it is enormously important: The points on the Chaco Meridian alignment were not elements of a larger uniform set of points, but were themselves unique. Chaco, Aztec, and Paquime are not just any sites. There was only one Chaco, one Aztec, and one Paquime during each of their respective epochs. And the alignment itself is not an independent line within the 360° of possible alignments. The alignment is precisely north-south, along the meridian, a direction of demonstrable cultural importance at Chaco and Paquime. Thus the question does not involve *any* three points along *any* line, in an open field of random independent points: The three points are unique, and the line unique as well. Indeed, the statistical situation should be restated as a four-point problem: Chaco, Aztec, Paquime, and North. Thus, the question is not—as for ley lines—"what is the statistical probability that X proportion of a field of N points align?," but rather, "what is the chance that three unique, precisely sequential points align, along a fourth geodesically unique direction, the meridian?" It's not a chip-shot statistical issue.

Let us sneak up on the same problem from another angle. If we begin with all known sites in the Southwest, we will certainly find many sets of three (and more) that line up. If we restrict our field to sites over 100 rooms with over a century of occupation, that number drops, and with it the probability of chance alignments. If we further restrict the set to Pueblo primate regional centers, rich with exotic artifacts and monumental architecture, the number falls to exactly three: Chaco, Aztec, and Paquime. When the sample equals the population, all statistical bets are off.

I put this problem, casually, to several statisticians (who will remain anonymous, here; no need to drag them through this muck). They found the ley-line machinations engrossing, questioning small points of logic but generally approving the British approach. But as various criteria and arguments reduced the set of potential points to smaller and smaller numbers, they became less and less interested. When I made the case that Chaco, Aztec, and Paquime were each unique in their own times and places, and that they were precisely sequential, and that North was culturally charged, they dismissed the case as nonstatistical.[10]

The question is not: What chance that Chicago shares a meridian with Tuscaloosa? (which, by chance, it does) but, rather, what are the odds that the capital of United States is due north of Teotihuacan or El Mirador? If Washington *had* been built due north of Teotihuacan (near Aberdeen, South Dakota?), we would question coincidence, and search Pierre L'Enfant's papers for a Mexican travel diary. (Accidents *will* happen: Washington and Cahokia share a degree of latitude.)

Statistical probabilities, in this case, are obviated by intention, for there was overriding historical direction in the Chaco Meridian. Our evaluation of Chaco, Aztec, and Paquime cannot be purely statistical. "Chance only matters when it can be shown not to be chance. If it does, but cannot be, it does not" (Hawthorn 1991:9).

Coincidence, Again

Moving away from statistical evaluations, we can look at the places involved, the local ecologies and histories. Why were they *there?* Were there particular point-specific reasons—beyond, before, or besides the meridian—for the locations of Chaco, Aztec, and Paquime?

Chaco's location has always been troublesome (fig. 4.2). Despite the efforts of Vivian (1990) and Sebastian (1992) to create a kinder, gentler Chaco, the canyon remains one of the least inviting settings in northwestern New Mexico. No rain, short growing season, long nasty winter, no wood, no water—there's nothing to recommend Chaco but sandstone. Chaco was not "there" because of any overwhelming *local* advantages of its canyon; small populations lived there for centuries before Pueblo Bonito, but there were no physiographic quirks that presaged the Chaco phenomenon. As discussed above, I favor out-of-favor explanations that link Chaco's rise to its remarkably strategic position, central to the far richer margins of the Chaco Basin—location! location! location! So, it's there because it's there because it's there: Chaco was literally a central place. Its fate and fortune were fixed by its position.

Aztec was a much nicer place, alongside the Animas River. Aztec had water and trees. But there are lots of comparably nice places in Aztec's neighborhood, a point well attested by the masses of archaeology that litter the margins of the Animas, La Plata, and San Juan rivers. There was no particular reason to build Aztec on the Animas instead of the La Plata or the San Juan, and no particular reason for its precise location on the Animas—no springs, no odd rock formations, no point specific resource (indeed, the sandstone used for Aztec's construction was brought from quarries several kilometers away). In fact, there was no deep history at the site of Aztec itself; the surrounding area was essentially unoccupied before that great center was built (McKenna 1998). Aztec was built on new ground. Aztec was there because it was north of Chaco, at the end of the Great North Road.

Paquime was located at a *really* nice spot: just below the narrows where the Rio Casas Grandes enters its most productive valley. (Similar settings were favored by the earlier Mimbres towns to the north; Lekson 1992b). There were other streams that flow from the Sierra Madre out into the northern Chihuahuan desert—Santa Barbara, Conchos, San Pedro, Santa Clara, Santa Maria, Carretas, and others—over about three degrees of longitude. Those river valleys are full of archaeology (Di Peso, Rinaldo, and Fenner 1974b: fig. 284–5; Whalen and Minnis 1996b). Paquime could have been built along any of half a dozen these rich riverine oases, which lie well outside the meridian. The Rio Casas Grandes is the largest of the rivers flowing northeast out of the Sierra Madre, but any of the major streams probably *could have* supported Paquime. Sapawe—one of the very largest northern Rio Grande sites, comparable in size (and age) to Paquime—sits beside a much smaller creek than the Rio Casas Grandes. Paquime was built on the biggest river, but it did not have to be.

Paquime, like Aztec, appears to have sprung fully formed from the gravel terraces of the Rio Casas Grandes. Low numbers of people lived along the river, at small hamlets like the Convento Site (Di Peso, Rinaldo, and Fenner 1974a). At Paquime itself, there are a few pithouses and miscellaneous features that predate the city, but Di Peso's Buena Fe Phase—pre-Paquime—has been exploded (Dean and Ravesloot 1993). In my opinion, there is no visible architecture at Paquime that can be securely dated before 1250, or even 1300. The principal question of Casas Grandes archaeology, in my opinion, is the nature of the area's population between the end of the Mimbres phase (about 1130) and the beginnings of Paquime (between 1250 and 1300). Whalen and Minnis (1996b) have been looking for post-Mimbres, pre-Paquime sites for a decade, without a great deal of luck (Paul Minnis, personal communication 1998). Ben Nelson and Roger Anyon (1996) introduced the idea of "fallow valleys" in the Mimbres region, of which the Rio Casas Grandes valley was a part. Mimbres valleys were heavily occupied and then abandoned for several generations, allowing their depleted resources to recover, before they were reoccupied. It appears that this is the case for the Rio Casas Grandes valley: Despite our quests for local continuity and archaeological sequence, there is thin evidence for significant populations immediately prior to Paquime. (That's why Di Peso called in the Mexicans.) They might be buried beneath the later big sites—but not, apparently, at Paquime itself.

Paquime was essentially *de novo*. Di Peso found a few earlier pit-structures below the great city, and I interpret these thin remains as *much* earlier than Paquime. His report makes it clear that no sizable community, producing significant architectural ruins, preceded Paquime (Di Peso, Rinaldo, and Fenner 1974a, 1974b). Paquime's people probably came from elsewhere, perhaps from the post-Mimbres villages of the El Paso region (Lekson 1992b). Its rulers—I think—came from farther north.

Chaco was there for a reason—centrality within the Chaco Basin. Aztec and Paquime were located along attractive rivers, but their rivers were differentiated from other nearby equally attractive rivers only or principally by their intersection with Chaco's meridian.

Agriculturally, the progress from Chaco to Aztec to Paquime was indeed progressive. Let us descend from the airy realms of prestige economies and meridian alignments, and regain the terra firma of subsistence, to corn-beans-and-squash archaeology. The sequence from Chaco to Aztec to Paquime tracks increasing control of agricultural productivity.

Chaco was the center of a rainfall adaptation: Chaco-era populations had long traditions of mobility, repositioning themselves to adapt to shifting rainfall. For the Chaco-era subsistence economy, space was more important than place—except for the heavily subsidized center. At Chaco itself, rainfall was gathered and tweaked to a degree unknown elsewhere in its world (Vivian 1990, 1991); but there was little or no stream diversion because, at Chaco, there was little or no stream to divert.

Chaco crashed, and Aztec rose on the Animas (after a possible false start, at Salmon on the huge unruly San Juan River). The Rio Animas was a fine small stream for simple, pre-pump diversion irrigation and, of all the Northern San Juan sites, Aztec appears most likely to have had real stream diversion canals (Greiser and Moore 1995; Howe 1947). Aztec irrigated, but its regional population continued to rely on rainfall (Van West 1996). Aztec failed when rains failed, over its larger region, in the Great Drought. Aztec itself had considerable control over its local subsistence base. The regional population was still dry-farming and still vulnerable. The Great Drought never dried up Aztec's canals but no one else had canals.

Paquime was at the best location of these three for *really* serious canal irrigation. No one ever dry-farmed the Chihuahuan desert; canals were not optional, they were necessary. The long growing season of the Chihuahuan desert and the moderate flow of the Rio Casas Grandes provided an ideal setting for Hohokam-scale irrigation in Mimbres times and after. It was the best spot due south of Chaco: The Meridian also crossed the Rio Mimbres, where canals had fueled the Mimbres achievement a century earlier. But that nest was fouled (Minnis 1985)—salinated, deforested, dotted with ill-omened ruins of a repudiated society. (Recall the remarkable eclipse of Mimbres iconography and architecture, chap. 2.) The Paquime polity rejected the rainfall water-control subsistence of the Plateau (Schmidt and Gerald 1988 contra Di Peso 1974). Paquime's was a canal economy (Doolittle 1993) and so was its hinterland's.

The sequence, then, from Chaco to Aztec to Paquime was an adaptive transition from Chaco dry farming, to ditches at Aztec, to full regional commitment to canal irrigation at Paquime—progressively greater and greater control over the means and modes of agricultural production. For those of us who still harbor ecological, evolutionary aspirations for the Greater Southwest, the sequential locations of Chaco, Aztec, and Paquime make a degree of sense.[11]

Pueblo prehistory shows, in general, a trend from dry-farming to small-scale water control to canal irrigation. Is there reason to think that the Chaco-Aztec-Paquime sequence was in any way different or independent of larger trends? Much of what we see archaeologically at these three sites reflects background patterns of pottery design, weapon technology, food processing methods, and so forth that developed or evolved unrelated to whatever political shenanigans may or may not have engaged the residents of the big centers. In this case, however, the cities *may* have led the way: Water control at Chaco was in advance (chronologically and technically) of other Pueblo districts; canal irrigation at Aztec was all but unique on the Plateau; and the scale of Paquime's putative canal systems was both larger and earlier than Rio Grande systems. These are points for research—I am by no means certain that these assertions are entirely accurate—but the need for local surpluses at these ceremonial cities might well have driven innovation in subsistence economies. From Chaco to Aztec to Paquime, the cities increased their control of production.

Positional Legitimation

A shift from water control at Chaco, to small canals at Aztec, to big canals with a long growing season at Paquime might make sense; but the Meridian doesn't. At least, not in any practical, corn-beans-and-squash sort of way. Meridian alignment, I argue, represents the attempt by Aztec's and Paquime's planners to link their new cities symbolically to the first center at Chaco. Meridian alignment with Chaco legitimized Aztec and Paquime by reference to an immediate historical and (later) mythical past, using Chaco's own remarkable spatial language. "The belief that superior magical or mythical power or sanctioning can be derived from lands and peoples outside the home society can also be used to legitimize the origins of ruling houses" (Helms 1992:161). They situated Chaco within its regional system to monument social and political relationships by *alignment* with roads, or road segments; as they did later at Aztec and Paquime.

Legitimation by reference to a real or mythic past is a common strategy in emerging political formations. "New developments are more secure when they are invested with the authority of the past" (Bradley 1993:116). Just as the Aztecs appropriated mythic/historic Tula and the ruins of even earlier Teotihuacan, peoples all over the world have claimed association with larger-than-life, never-to-be-equalled pasts. Ben Nelson, in a conference paper (Nelson 1996) suggested a process of "simultaneous disintegration and expansion" on the Post-Classic Mesoamerican northern frontier. As frontier centers waned, their leaders moved north and northwest to new areas. They established power through symbols and ceremonies, and claims of ancestry from those failed, near-mythical earlier centers. Paquime, Nelson suggests, was the northernmost of those cities. I like this model; it's the same case I'm making, but I'm making it from north to south. Paquime may have been such a remarkable place—the most astonishing achievement of the Pueblo past—because it was the place where Mesoamerica and Pueblo political power finally, physically met.

Mary Helms—whose insights into the power of distance were an inspiration (Helms 1988)—explored the relationship of kingly towns or cities to two kinds of "outside centers," creative centers that exist mythically, on a cosmic vertical axis mundi or, more tangibly, on a horizontal axis mundi, "out there" at some distance from the kingly center (Helms 1993:173–175). Chaco must have been both, first to Aztec and later to Paquime. "Spatially/temporally outside centers are regarded as foci of initial cultural origins and creation, and thus places of cosmological power" (Helms 1993:173). The center of "here and now" appeals to the "center-out-there" through ritual, highly crafted objects, recognizable material styles; and "pilgrimages to the sacred distant place over the horizon" (Helms 1993:175). The Chaco Meridian was a monument, marking a political tactic manifest in (but not unique to) the ancient Southwest: positional legitimation.

In noncartographic societies, place and landscape have an immediacy and importance they sometimes lose when they are literally reduced to two dimensions. Landscape features, celestial phenomena, and the very directions themselves have a potential for meaning we can probably never recapture. I suggest that Chaco, Aztec, and Paquime used directional symbolism for major social and political ends. Other societies do this. Cuzco's *ceques* radiated out to Inca dependencies and borders; a strong case has been made for one *ceque* running about 300 km from Cuzco to Tiahuanaco, a form of positional legitimation not unlike Chaco, Aztec, and Paquime (Zuidema 1982:439). On an even larger scale, Islam's 900 million adherents—from Java to the horn of Africa—oriented themselves, their places of worship, and their worlds to the Black Rock of the Qabah in Mecca. They did this in medieval times, too, without complex surveying technologies, but with remarkable accuracy.[12]

Chaco, at some point, became the stuff of myth and history. It could not easily be forgotten—Chaco transformed the ancient Southwest and set trajectories that carried Pueblo peoples through the 13th, 14th, and 15th centuries. Chaco Canyon—as a place—must have retained enormous ideological and political importance. Any new political formation on Chaco's scale would have to address the historical fact of Chaco, and either appropriate or reject that first center's memory. "Images of the past commonly legitimate a present social order. It is an implicit rule that participants in any social order must presuppose a shared memory" (Connerton 1989:3). Chaco was just about everywhere, and everywhere people must have remembered Chaco—it was a shared memory, like a great comet or a volcanic eruption. Paquime appealed to Chaco's memory for validation, through repetition (or appropriation) of Chacoan architectural symbols (colonnades, mounds, massing, cardinality, roads, etc.) but even more through the physical alignment through prolongation of the Chacoan regional geometry. The North Road, a road-through-time that continued the old axis mundi of Chaco, was projected south beyond the Colorado Plateau into the Chihuahuan desert. The Chaco Meridian was the mechanism and manifestation of positional legitimation.

Alignment between the new (Aztec, Paquime) and the old (Chaco) demonstrated these connections both actively and passively: by the act of alignment, and by monuments such as the North Road and the Mound of the Cross.

The act itself was probably as important as the monument. The procedure of alignment, while technically simple, must have been a major, memorable event. It required coordination of labor over large areas and considerable time—perhaps decades. Recall my aging Boy Scouts: The Chaco-Paquime alignment would have taken a considerable length of time and, with attendant pomp and ceremony, it would have been a remarkable performance for all Southwestern peoples to see. Chaco was nothing if not show, there was little that was modest or subtle about Chacoan architecture (Great Houses, for example, were typically sited to visually dominate the land around them). Imagine the effect of a procession marching 630 km south from the ancient city of Chaco, cutting trees for lines-of-sight, lighting flares and bonfires for backsights, performing ceremonies and rituals.

Everybody in the Southwest knew about Chaco in its heyday, if only by rumor; and everybody would have known about the monumental operations of meridian alignment. There were sound political reasons for public display during the process: The point of positional legitimation is not simply to comfort the rulers, but to convince and persuade the ruled.

The Chaco Meridian, as positional legitimation, is remarkable only for its scale. So too are the huge Hohokam canals of the Phoenix Basin, unmatched in ancient Mexico (Doolittle 1990). Sometimes things happened in the Southwest that exceed our expectations, our frames-of-reference, our conventional archaeological vision of the Southwestern past.

Historical Connections

What was it, exactly, that was moving north and south along the Chaco meridian? Not hordes of people: While Chaco, Aztec, and Paquime played out this grand geographic game, the other 99 percent of Pueblo peoples were just trying to make a living. The population bases of the Chaco, Aztec, and Paquime regions were profoundly local. Chaco, Aztec, and Paquime were centers of political prestige economies. The effects of their political tumults and turmoils on larger, regional populations might have been profound and disturbing, but affairs of state need not affect the countryside's larders.

Why did Chaco "end"? I think its demise was political (but take your pick: Judge 1989, Sebastian 1992, Tainter 1988, Vivian 1990). The lack of effect on the larger region argues against drought, famine, war, pestilence, or death. Whatever the "cause," monumental building ceases about 1125. When Chaco shifted to Aztec, hardly anyone else on the Colorado Plateau budged. But when Aztec fell, the entire Four Corners was abandoned—an unnecessarily complete depopulation (Van West 1994) and an indication of centralized, political decision-making. Paquime's rise was accompanied by an explosion of Pueblo peoples over the Mogollon Rim and out into the low deserts—the business we used to call "Salado" (Lekson 1992d, in press c).

The shifting center was *not* necessarily a harbinger of larger migrations. In the first instance—Chaco to Aztec—there was little concomitant disruption of larger populations; in the second—from Aztec to Paquime—much of the Pueblo Southwest was up and moving. The meridian machinations reflected smaller, more singular groups. The elite of Chaco numbered in the several hundreds— perhaps a thousand—the residents of its major Great Houses. With its supporting population, the whole of Chaco Canyon never numbered much above 2,500–3,000. Aztec was perhaps smaller; Paquime slightly larger. The key sector was that small elite, decision-makers who perpetuated their power through architectural and landscape symbolism, a few hundred elites and their retainers. Whether that elite moved south from the northern San Juan, or another newly emerging elite looked north from the old Mimbres region to the mythical center at Chaco, I do not know; but their decisions reflected a vision of power that transcended local regions and local economies.

When, about 1275, tens of thousands of people left the Four Corners, most stopped at the arc of pueblos that stretched from Hopi to the Rio Grande (fig. 4.5). The forces behind that movement were powerful: Some Four Corners people exploded far beyond the present Pueblos, moving south off the Plateau entirely to found Kayenta villages near Tucson (Woodson 1995) and Mesa Verde towns near Truth-or-Consequences (Lekson 1996b:172). The southward sagging of the Tularosa Horizon (fig. 4.4) and the phenomenal migrations of some Four Corners peoples brought the post-Chaco world into the post-Mimbres region.

Paquime itself, even further south, rose in a sparsely populated valley. Paquime was Chacoan in its scale and labor; who built it? Who was the base population on which Paquime was founded? The 13th- and 14th-century populations of southern New Mexico and northwest Chihuahua were probably historical descendants of the Mimbres (Creel 1997; Lekson 1992b and in press c; Turner 1993). Some portion of that population relocated to the Rio Casas Grandes, and accepted Paquime's legitimacy. If, as I argue, Paquime's rulers based that legitimacy on an appeal to Chaco, the local population had to recognize the symbols and understand the architectural language and positional legitimization that linked the new city to the older northern center. That is, those post-Mimbres populations had to remember Chaco; otherwise, the architectural details, the symbolism, and the meridian alignment itself would carry no meaning, and might only distance and alienate, rather than legitimize, Paquime's brave new world. Paquime's base population had to know the rules so Paquime's elite could play the game.

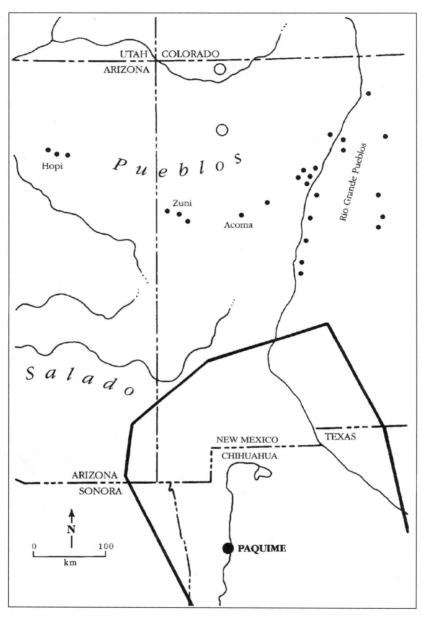

Figure 4.5. Paquime, Salado, Pueblos. The "Pueblos" are schematic representations of proto-historic and historic locations. "Salado"—once the conquering tribes of the north—is now an extremely diffuse distribution of Gila Polychrome, but it retains its magic appeal. Salado may be down, but it's not out.

Mimbres, I think, provides the bridge. Mimbres knew Chaco (chap. 2), and post-Mimbres peoples presumably remembered Chaco during the fragmented Aztec era. Those memories provided the historical context—the stage setting—for Paquime.

Historical Connections, Continued

These events—if they happened—were momentous, dramatic, climactic. Chaco, Aztec, and Paquime should be remembered in Pueblo histories, and I think that they are. They may be central to key passages in the origin histories of several Pueblos. Those histories offer a different perspective on historical connections between Chaco, Aztec, and Paquime.

Oral history is tricky. Professor Henry Jones, Jr., perhaps the most influential archaeologist of our time, warned us: "We cannot afford to take mythology at face value," but we should not dismiss Pueblo origin stories as mere myth. Early anthropologists, like Robert Lowie, did; they summarily dismissed Pueblo and Navajo traditions as sources for history. Elsie Clews Parsons parodied origin stories in her classic *Pueblo Indian Religion*:

> Pueblo history and geography are a series of archaeological or topo-graphical legends, almost as naive and fanciful about near events as about remote or cosmic ones. The general outline is simple: "We came up, we moved southward (or eastward) and built houses, something happened, a quarrel or choosing a fateful egg or being stung by mosquitos, we moved again, we kept on seeking the middle place until we found it here, where we are to live forever." (Parsons 1996:215)

Parsons's offensive, dismissive view ignores threads of history amid the rich tapestry of cosmology, eschatology, moralizing, and pure poetry that shapes traditional histories. Origin stories serve many purposes, and chronicle is only one among many duties that shape their rhetoric and content.

Joe Sando, a Pueblo historian, champions the accuracy of oral traditions, maintaining that traditional history "was not tilted to adorn the reputation of one or another. . . . Nor was it changed or distorted to supply credibility to the demands of a powerful political structure" (Sando 1992:21). But history may be layered within larger narrative themes. Writers Tessie Naranjo and Leslie Marmon Silko honor the metaphorical nature of traditional stories (Naranjo 1995; Silko 1995). "All stories are considered valid. There is never one version of any story" (Naranjo 1995:248). Meaning transcends historical detail.

Oral traditions—like all good history—are perhaps best understood as *both* historical and metaphorical, varying in degree. Peter Nabokov, in an insightful essay on Native American views of history, concludes:

> The spectrum of American Indian narratives, behaviors, and symbols which carry any information faintly deemed 'historical' actually falls on any number of different points between the idealized poles of chronology (history) and cosmology (mythology). (Nabokov 1996:9)

I am convinced that Pueblo and Navajo traditions carry rich lodes of history. Analyses of specific Pueblo oral traditions of intertribal clashes (Nabokov 1996:14–15), volcanic eruptions (Malotki and Lomatuway'ma 1987), and the Pueblo Revolt Wiget (1982) concluded that those accounts were accurate in both chronology and detail, embedded in expositions of cultural rules and world-views.

> When such information as encoded in these narratives enters the public life of the community, articulated as a statement of shared values, represented by shared symbols, then such material has a high degree of durability and, when properly decoded, a high degree of reliability. (Wiget 1982:197)

Native American advocates urge archaeology and history to accept tribal oral histories (DeLoria 1995; Dongoske et al. 1997; Echo-Hawk 1993, 1997; Nabokov 1996; Wilson 1997). And, indeed, oral traditions have equal status with archaeology and academic history as evidence in laws such as NAGPRA. Tribal scholars and anthropologists who work closely with tribes declare that "real history is embedded in Native American oral traditions" (Anyon et al. 1997:83), and Indian scholars suggest that traditional history may extend back into the Pleistocene (Echo-Hawk 1993, 1997:91). How are archaeologists to use traditional history? The challenges are daunting, but the possibilities are important and consequential. New archaeological approaches encourage historicity; new social attitudes encourage it; and new laws demand it. Lynn Teague has pioneered the integration of traditional history and archaeology in the Southwest, with her analysis of late Hohokam prehistory and O'Odham and Hopi traditions (Teague 1993). Her innovative approaches have yet to reach the Plateau.

There are protocols for the critical study and use of oral histories (e.g., Vansina 1985), but those techniques may not be suitable or appropriate to Pueblo oral traditions. For many reasons, those traditions—still vital—are not accessible for systematic study. More and more Pueblos are adopting policies prohibiting discussions of history with outsiders. Limited to published accounts or "unofficial" versions, we must take what we can get, opportunistically, weaving site locations, sherd-counts, and tree-ring dates with traditional sequences, descriptions, and narrative details. If we use published information with both ingenuity and respect, we might even show how more open exchanges could lead to even greater insights.

"Scientific methodology may not be appropriate for the research of oral traditions, where more humanistic, holistic, and qualitative approaches are sometimes warranted" (Anyon et al. 1997:83). Most of us are not trained in those methods (I am not), and mainstream archaeology does not welcome them. There is a narrow penumbra, outside the light of tribal trust but not quite in the utter darkness of old-style ahistorical New Archaeology, in which useful things can, perhaps, be done. Gliding through that thin air, you appear from above as an Icarus and from below as a UFO—either way, most interesting when you crash. Non-Indian scholars must tease out places and events, at considerable risk of error and unintended offense. Felipe Fernandez-Armesto (1987:154) rightly warns us against "the aetiological enthusiasm of some historians . . . to detect real places and events in the undergrowth of any myth or legend." It's so easy to be wrong—but why stop now?

White House, a place prominent in Pueblo origin stories, is a case in point. White House was a seminal center, common to several Pueblos histories, where things happened that shaped subsequent Pueblo life. At White House, the kachinas lived with, fought with, and then left the people—after teaching them the dances and ceremonies that would continue the vital converse between spirit world and this world. White House was a wonder, but the events that transpired there were not ultimately happy or even correct (Lekson and Cameron 1995).

Florence Hawley, then in the employ of the Wetherill Mesa Project at Mesa Verde, determined that Mesa Verde was White House (Ellis 1967). I have suggested that White House was Chaco (Lekson and Cameron 1995). Pueblo colleagues have told me that White House, today, refers more to the Four Corners region rather than any one site. A particular problem of White House is its common legacy: Too many tribes claim White House in their heritage for it to be any one place, like Mesa Verde—there's not enough room for all those people. The same objection might be made for Chaco but, as the primate center of the Pueblo world, Chaco was the one place that could be shared among many different Pueblos' and clans' histories. Chaco transformed the Pueblo world; people remember things like that. And Chaco, in decline, played a role in the rise of kachina ceremony: Chacoan ideology failed and left a void that needed filling.

Kachina images appear first on Mimbres pottery, and post-Mimbres rock art, from about 1050 to perhaps 1200 (Schaafsma 1994). Kachina ceremonialism could have come only very late (if at all) to Chaco. Based on the absence of images on pottery or rock art, it did not travel to Aztec. Aztec perpetuated Chaco's old time religion; whatever that might have been, it wasn't the kachina ceremonialism that appears so clearly on the Upper Little Colorado, at about the time that Aztec ends (Adams 1991).

Chaco may well have been White House. I suspect that White House also refers to Aztec or, most likely, to Chaco *and* Aztec, where important political and ceremonial decisions were played out, spectacularly and (in the end) unsuccessfully. Chaco and Aztec were very definite places. White House was both a place and a metaphor for events—some of bad memory—that shaped later Pueblo life.

Paquime appears, I believe, as a very specific place—if unlocated—in the traditional stories of Acoma and, perhaps, Zuni. Evidence comes from key passages in the origin stories of these Pueblos, before the peoples reached their middle places and became Acoma and Zuni. The narratives were first recorded by Ruth Bunzel (1932), Mathew Stirling (1942), Leslie White (1932), and Frank Hamilton Cushing (1896); my understanding of those texts has benefited from conversations with Petuuche Gilbert at Acoma and Ed Ladd from Zuni.

Acoma accounts (recorded by White and Stirling) are most fully developed. In these stories, the people left White House. "They decided to go to the south, where lay a place called Ako. They wished to go there and raise parrots [macaws]" (White 1932:145). They travelled due south, following directions given to them by deities, crossing four mountain ranges and four intervening valleys or plains.

The people carried two bird's eggs, one a macaw and the other a crow, given to them by a deity or semidivine heros; they were to choose and open one egg when they reached their destination. One egg was a beautiful blue and the other was dun-colored and plain; no one knew which egg was the macaw egg and which was the crow egg. When they reached Acoma (Ako), they divided into two groups by choosing eggs. The people who chose the blue egg, which they assumed was the macaw's, knew that they would stay at Acoma. But when the blue egg was broken, out flew crows. The people who had chosen the other egg continued far to the south. "The rest must journey on to Kuyapukauwak and take the other egg with them. . . . This was a very sad time for both groups. The parrot group left toward the south and it is not known how far they went" (Stirling 1942: 83). (Parsons 1996:223 adds, in a dismissive footnote, a statement from an unnamed informant: "No one knows where they are now, perhaps in Central America!")

The Zuni story is very similar (Cushing 1896:386–387; Dutton 1963:112 n. 404; Tedlock 1972:264–266). The people choose between two eggs, and a sizable group follow the parrot or macaw from the plain egg, far south to the Land of Everlasting Sunshine (Ferguson and Hart 1985:22). However, this event is said to have taken place west of Zuni, presumably in the valley of the upper Little Colorado (Ferguson and Hart 1985:21). Ed Ladd (personal communication 1996) adds some important points to the published

Zuni accounts. The division of the people occasioned by the choice of eggs happened before either Zuni and Acoma were established. Thus, the people who went south were not Zuni or Acoma and, through time, developed their own language; but they looked very much like Zuni people. After the southern people had established their homes in "the land of eternal summer," a few returned as traders, bringing macaw feathers, live macaws and parrots, and sea shells.

Macaws, at every contemporary Pueblo, symbolize the direction south (Dozier 1970:Table 8). They are today associated with the sun (Tyler 1991:13), and macaws and their feathers are specifically and especially associated with modern kachina *sacra* (Parsons 1996:398). Indeed, macaws, their feathers, and their images were key icons in the early development of kachina ceremonialism. Macaws and parrots appear frequently in 11th-century Mimbres art, alongside the earliest kachina-like images (Dutton 1963: 166–167 n. 501), and, later, with readily identifiable kachinas on 15th-century kiva murals (e.g., Hibben 1975; Smith 1952). Trade in macaws was interrupted by the Spanish conquest (Tyler 1991:22–23) and has never quite recovered, but the association of macaws and kachinas is still strong. Macaws were apparently integral to the early development of kachina ceremonialism and to other "cults" of the post-Chaco world (e.g., the "Southwestern cult" of Crown 1994:149,167). (Hamilton Tyler states that crows and ravens were more directly associated with kachinas than were macaws; what interesting implications for the Acoma story!; Tyler 1991:173ff.)

Macaws were important to Chaco, before kachinas; recall the macaw feather sash found in Utah, at the far edge of the Chaco world (chap. 2). Numbers of macaws increase dramatically *after* Chaco, and I think this is directly related to their association with rapidly spreading kachina ceremonialism—demonstrated in kiva murals from Hopi (Smith 1952); and the Rio Grande (Hibben 1975). Recall that 17 macaws were found at Mimbres sites and 34 at Chaco. Only a few were found at the Aztec complex—the New Chaco—and other 12th- and 13th-century sites in the northern San Juan, like Salmon Ruins. Chronologically, the next macaw "hot spot" was Wupatki (1135–1195), which may well have played a critical role in the crystallization of kachina ceremonialism (Christian Downum personal communication 1997). After Wupatki, the number of macaws explodes, for example, in the late 13th- and 14th-century pueblos of the uppermost Little Colorado (Hargrave 1970). Paquime bred the birds and was probably the principal source for a hugely expanded market.

We do not know the nature of Chacoan ceremonial, but it must have been directed, controlled, institutional. Priests, not shamans, built those grim formal buildings. The investment of labor to assure permanence suggests a formality and repetition of performance transcending individual practitioners: Those settings were designed for the long haul. We may assume that—at least by the second generation—Chacoan builders knew that their handiwork would outlast their own lives. Whatever Chaco was, it was not a democracy, and its ceremony might not have been socially encompassing. Kachina ceremonialism, in contrast, is inclusive: Theoretically, everyone can be associated with one society or another. Everyone, potentially, can get into the act. At Chaco, feathers were a controlled substance; at Pueblos with developed kachina societies, feathers were a public necessity.

Kachina ceremonialism becomes dramatically evident at exactly the same time Aztec ends and Paquime began (Adams 1991), and macaws were ubiquitous in its artistic expressions. Paquime, and a handful of its surrounding settlements (Whalen and Minnis 1996c) were the only Southwestern Pueblos to commercially produce macaws—thousands of macaws. Paquime was the major and probably the sole source for parrots and macaws for 14th- and 15th-century kachina ceremonialism. "The people wished to go south, and raise parrots," according to the Acoma and Zuni stories; and that's exactly what they did.

There is a specificity to these accounts that belies the generalities of White House. Acoma origin stories even name the southern place: Kuyapukauwak (Stirling 1942:83). This, despite the fact that the people who went south were forever separated from those who stayed behind. The Zuni parrot group— "those who were to go in coral's direction" (Tedlock 1972:265) passed from the scene and almost from memory, returning only as traders carrying macaws and shells. White House was Pueblo history, and thereby subject to metaphorical displacement; Kuyapukauwak was someone else's history and perhaps less useful for Pueblo moralizing. The history of the parrot-raisers, leaving Acoma and heading south into memory, was freed from the narrative duties of White House, which was the world before, and Acoma itself, which is the world today. White House and Acoma itself are matters for metaphor, Kuyapukauwak was a *place,* incidental and therefore real.

It is geographically telling that Zuni and Acoma (and Zia and, perhaps, Laguna) recount this story; it is, evidently, not part of the common heritage of Hopi or of the other Pueblos along the Rio Grande (Parsons 1996:223). Acoma and Zuni lie just east and west of the Chaco meridian, about 120 km south of Chaco. The meridian line itself coincides closely with the boundary separating Acoma's and Zuni's territories, both modern and ancient (fig. 4.2). The meridian passage occurred during a time of remarkable population growth and cultural formation at both the Zuni and Acoma (Kintigh 1985, 1996; Roney 1996)—a pivotal period for these two closely related, yet linguistically distinct cultural traditions.

The origin histories of Acoma and Zuni were tied to the Chaco Meridian or, at least, to the events it represented and the places it linked. It is not "legend, naive and fanciful" that Acoma and Zuni origin stories recall macaw eggs and "parrot peoples" journeying far to the south—not myth, but history: momentous events, accurately remembered and poetically told. Pueblo peoples' memories transcend the time scales of modern archaeology.

Navajo (Dine) peoples have stores of knowledge about Chaco and its region. The Navajo probably entered the northern Southwest several centuries after Chaco and Aztec; yet there is a specificity about Navajo traditional histories of Chaco that demands our attention (e.g., Kelley and Francis 1994; McPherson 1992). Navajo people adopted much from the Pueblos: weaving, corn, sheep and—presumably—a great deal of the knowledge and traditions specific to the country. They were more than neighbors: Economic mutualism, intermarriage, co-residence, ritual exchange, warfare and raiding, and even alliance linked Navajo clans and particular pueblos at various times. Navajo clans living in and around Chaco could well carry stories of its ancient times—Pueblo history of these Navajo places. And, of course, there remains the possibility that the Navajo were in the area before their consensus archaeological appearance.

One important cycle of stories tells of Noqoilpi, the Great Gambler, a ruler who lived at Chaco Canyon. There are many variants of the Gambler story (e.g., Judd 1954:351–354; McPherson 1992:87–93 and citations therein). Many versions have details that correspond almost exactly to the archaeological reconstruction presented here (for example, in some accounts, the Gambler was shot *due south* from Pueblo Alto into Mexico; John Stein, personal communication 1998). Other versions name places and describe events inconsistent with my hypothesis (e.g., in one story, the Gambler was exiled to Tiz-na-zinde, about 18 miles west of Pueblo Alto; Judd 1954:354).

Rather than picking and choosing details and variants that best fit the Chaco-Aztec-Paquime sequence, it is more useful to present elements common to most of the Noqoilpi stories. The Gambler cycle tells the rise and fall of the Chaco Anasazi. Noqoilpi reduced surrounding peoples (perhaps all the different tribes) to vassalage or slavery, by unfailingly winning gambling contests, and then "demanded that they build the huge pueblo for his house" (McPherson 1992:87)—Pueblo Alto, the "Chief's House." After a despotic career, the Gambler was overthrown by the gods (either directly through a cessation of rainfall or by their agents) and ejected—in many versions, shot into the sky like an arrow. "The underlying theme is that they had an extensive knowledge that led to a haughty uncontrolled pride and eventual destruction" (McPherson 1992:91). The Gambler might be a

Pueblo person, but he is usually identified as a foreigner: Spanish or Mexican (which may mean a Mexican Indian; David Brugge personal communication 1998), or even an Anglo—someone of different origins and status.

The Gambler story describes emergent hierarchy at Chaco. It is specific to that place. Although the rise-and-fall plot is common to many (all?) mythologies, commonalities of the Gambler stories and Pueblo accounts of White House are telling: personal aggrandizement, institutionalized political power, and forced departure. These things did not happen elsewhere or anywhere in the Southwest. They happened at White House: at Chaco Canyon and Aztec.

Historical Connections, Concluded

The fundamental question facing the Chaco Meridian is: coincidence or intention? Intentional alignment has major implications for Southwestern prehistory and a cascade of archaeological ramifications. If the alignment was indeed coincidental, then that vista of historical possibilities hits what 18th-century British landscape architects called a "ha-ha": a boundary offering enticing views but blocking passage into that new country. "Ha-ha" indeed: The joke's on me and on the long-suffering reader, whose patience probably reached its limits some pages past.

Statistical approaches to unique phenomena are futile: The Chaco-Aztec-Paquime alignment was unique. We cannot hope for statistical decision, but we can mimic statistical logic. Begin with a null hypothesis: The alignment was random. What set of conditions would refute the null? Independent sets of data cumulatively decrease the probability of chance alignment: internal details unique to these sites, the primate role of each site, the cardinal direction of their alignment, their near-precise sequence, and their connections in traditional histories. With each set of data, the probability of chance decreases. How much? We cannot say, but the cumulative reduction must be substantial. From the null—that the alignment is pure chance—the probabilities become very small, approaching zero. In the face of the evidence, it is difficult to accept the null hypothesis.

I am frustrated by colleagues who follow my argument to this point, nod politely, and then ask, "Well, where's your proof?" What more proof could we realistically hope to find? All we have and all we will ever have is circumstantial evidence. Absent an ancient map showing Paquime and Chaco connected by a north-south line, or a hoard of surveying tools ornamented in Gallup and Ramos styles, or a line of identifiably Chaco or Paquime surveying monuments (copper "brass caps"? core-and-veneer cairns?), or some other fabulously unlikely discovery, it is difficult to envision proof more effective than the cumulative, independent circumstantial evidence.

There *always* remains a chance that the alignment was purely random, a fluke, a geographic freak, an accident. But the array of evidence for intentionality is strong, internally consistent, and—perhaps most importantly—independent. The architectural details have nothing to do with the meridian; the Acoma and Zuni stories were recorded without reference to these or any sites. The dating of the sites, by tree-rings, was accomplished by archaeologists with no interest vested in the matter: McKenna for Aztec, Dean and Ravesloot for Paquime, and a cast of thousands for Chaco. Indeed, most of the data were developed by other scholars; I've simply combined their arguments, old and new, in a novel way (a topic we will revisit, below).

The cumulative probability of coincidence seems infinitesimal. Layers of independent data—chronological, architectural, and contextual—progressively diminish the role of chance.

NOTES

1. One other very obvious line to the south beckoned, about 4 km east of Fritz's centerline: a meridian south from Una Vida (unaccountably translated, sometimes, as "One View") and/or Kin Nahasabas and/or Fajada Butte. From any (or all) of these features, a line due south runs through the tower kiva complex at Greenlee, and continues south to the remarkable Rams Pasture *herradura:*

    > The visibility from this location [Rams Pasture] is excellent. The structure is located on a line from Greenlee Ruin to Borrego Pass. From this position Huerfano Mesa is clearly visible on the far north horizon and appears to stand directly on top of Fajada Butte! When this feature [Rams Pasture] is viewed from Borrego Pass (20 miles to the south), the notch [setting of Rams Pasture], the cap of Fajada Butte, and Huerfano Mesa all roughly line up, again with Huerfano Mesa standing atop Fajada Butte. Because of the situation of the structure in a notch, visibility is restricted to the east and west. (Nials, Stein, and Roney 1987:182)

    Short north-south road segments were documented at Greenlee and Rams Pasture, but a continuous road (visible in aerial photos) could not be confirmed on the ground (Nials, Stein, and Roney 1987). I recommend this alignment to readers who are intrigued by my argument and who are looking for something interesting to do in the field.

2. Meridian surveys on this scale were not unprecedented in preindustrial history. About A.D. 725, a Chinese court astronomer named I Hsing created a "meridian line of 7973 *li* (just over 3500 km)," stretching from Mongolia to IndoChina (Needham 1959:292–293). (This happened at about the same time the first mosques were being aligned with Mecca.) The Chinese meridian stations were set for astronomical observations, not for geomantic symbolism; and 8th-century China was rather more complex than the 13th-century Southwest. More resources could be mobilized than were ever available to Chaco or Aztec or Paquime. But the tools and technical aspects of the work were similar: Finding north is pretty simple, and prolonging a line is pretty basic. (Needham notes that not all the points were exactly on a north-south line [1959:293n. c].) Even in Tang China, naked-eye surveying with simple instruments will necessarily encompass detectable error.

3. With a string for a compass, scribe a large circle on flat ground with open horizons. Hold a straight pole (a gnomon) on the center of the circle. A rock tied on the end of the string will keep everything plumb. The shadow of the head of gnomon will cross the circumference of the circle twice, once in the morning and once in the afternoon. A line connecting those two points defines east-west. Bisect the east-west line, using the string as a compass; a perpendicular through the mid-point and the center of the circle (i.e., the gnomon) defines north-south. Nothing more complicated needed for this operation than a piece of string, a pole, and a rock. This technique has been used to determine north, with considerable accuracy, at Chaco (Kim Malville, p. c. 1998).

4. Another technique to prolong a line, known in modern surveying as "wiggling in" or "balancing in" could also have been used (this has been suggested, independently, by William Calvin for the Chaco Meridian; Calvin 1997). (When the Zuni people were seeking their Middle Place, the water spider K'yan'asdebi stretched his legs in the four cardinal directions out to the surrounding ocean; with his belly he literally "wiggled in" on the center of the world, the heart of mother earth; Ferguson and Hart 1985:23. "Balancing in" involves a trial foresight station that is then aligned and realigned on the original "backsight" station through trial, error, and correction. A station on the line would be established on a high peak or ridge, chosen for its long view to the north. A trial foresight would be set approximately north on the horizon, and from that trial foresight north would be established astronomically. The alignment of north, "foresight" and "backsight" would establish the error in the trial station. The trial station would then be adjusted, north would be reestablished, the alignment rechecked, and the trial station again adjusted. The process would be repeated until the "foresight" was balanced in due north of the established station. Establishing each station would require several days, since north can be fixed only once a day, but this process could "jump" across big distances.

5. In addition to errors in the determination of north, the North Road's "as built" alignment reflects an opportunistic use of terrain features (hills, buttes, notches, etc.) that provided convenient visual fore- and backsights along the meridian. Sharply cone-shaped hills or pinnacles, such as the site of "El Faro" at the Pierre's site complex (about 20 km north of Chaco Canyon) are almost on the meridian.

Presumably, the North Road was laid out in part by referencing visually prominent features, such as "El Faro," which lay only a few meters off the meridian alignment.

6. Visual alignment of range-poles can be easy and accurate. The Scoutmaster stands on the line the Troop is trying to extend (or prolong), somewhere behind the last good point. Tenderfeet are sent out into the bushes and rocks, each with a tall pole or a truck flare. The Scout Master lines them up visually, sighting over the last good point on the line. In fact, the Scout Master can simply stick two poles or two flares in the ground, one at the last good point and another at a convenient distance back on the line, and go have a beer. The Tenderfeet backsight on the two poles or flares, and line themselves up. They repeat the process until they lose the backsight by crossing a ridge, falling into a hole, or tumbling off a cliff. (This is why you need a whole troop.) When the backsight disappears it is necessary to reestablish the direction of the line, and start all over again. It helps to keep foresights fairly short, and backsights long. Similar techniques are not unlikely in ancient Chaco, which had geometry and, perhaps, standard measures (Hudson 1972).

7. Consider the example of Pacific celestial navigation, remarkably accurate over voyages of up to 1,000 miles. Self-correction by multiple random errors in this kind of navigation has been proven in experimental voyages. "Navigational accuracy is not a function of the length of the voyage. If anything, longer passages provide a greater opportunity for random sea effects and errors of judgement to cancel each other out" (Lewis 1994:268). "while errors in dead-reckoning occur, these tend to cancel each other out over a long voyage rather than to accumulate, which is opposite to what was thought earlier" (Irwin 1992:46; see also citations under "navigation errors, tending to cancel each other out" in Goetzfridt 1992:291).

8. Dennis Doxtater, a professor of architecture, explored Chacoan regional geometries in a series of intriguing papers (the most accessible of which is Doxtater 1991; see also Doxtater 1984) His basic argument places various Chacoan buildings at the intersections of line connecting important peaks and landscape features—for example: Kin Bineola at the intersection of lines connecting Abajo Peak and Mount Taylor, and Chimney Rock and Dowa Yolanne. These regional geometries correspond, schematically, to Puebloan cosmologies. I am sympathetic to Doxtaters's interests and impressed with his argument that landscape maps cosmology; but (there's *always* "but") I doubt that his axes were technically possible with Chacoan techniques and knowledge. Abajo Peak is not visible from Mount Taylor, or Dowa Yolanne from Chimney Rock; while Chacoan surveying could accurately prolong a line over long distances, it had to have a visible target or direction. North was visible everywhere, so the meridian could cross broken terrain. The other long straight roads (or potential roads) were intra-Basin, and intra-visible: the "South" (really southwest) road to Hosta Butte, the West Road to the Chuskas, and the Coyote Canyon Road along the foreslopes of Lobo Mesa. They could see where they were going, where they *wanted to go*. To start at Chimney Rock, for example, and head off towards Dowa Yolanne requires spherical trig and an ability to determine latitude and longitude—and longitude, at least, was unknowable until the development of chronometers in the 18th century (Howse 1980; Sobel 1995).

9.   Alignments on the scale of Chaco-Aztec-Paquime hint of ley lines. Ley lines, according to aficionados, are "alignments of ancient sites stretching across the landscape" (Pennick and Devereux 1989:13)—a tame definition. There are such alignments in the Chacoan region, a fact which has been duly noted by the ley line crowd (e.g., Devereux 1992:42).

   Alignments are one thing, but ley lines are another. Ley lines, today, are identified with earth energy, UFOs, and all sorts of New Age mumbo-jumbo. Ley lines, today, are geomancy.

   Ley lines had a certain appeal in their original formulation, before the UFOs landed. It is hard not to like Alfred Watkins, the eccentric beer salesman who, in the 1920s, "discovered" (and named) ley lines. Watkins's Old Straight Track Club traced alignments of old churches, ancient megaliths, and modern motorways across England, Wales, and Scotland. Watkins may have been wrong, but his intentions were good and his methods were passable. He thought that ley lines represented ancient trails for clueless merchants and disoriented traders; their wayside monuments were overbuilt by later civilizations, not unlike the orientation of churches built on Aztec pyramids in Mexico City (Aveni, Calnek, and Hartung 1988). There may even be something in Watkin's leys. After Watkins, interest in ley lines waned for decades. Only in more recent, post-Roswell times have ley lines been appropriated by modern geomancers and flying saucer fanatics (Pennick 1979:80–83). Watkins (who died in 1935) should be spinning in his grave—creating, no doubt, a power rift in the cosmic vortex.

   Chaco is a magnet for modern nutcases; Chacoan roads, as noted above, have already been discovered by modern ley hunters and Chaco itself was an epicenter for the Harmonic Convergence. Flying saucer fanatics and harmonic convergers are not company I care to keep. Indeed, I am uncomfortable around the fringes of archaeoastronomy, although superb archaeoastronomical work has been done in Chaco and the Greater Southwest. Archaeoastronomy has a bum rap in the Southwest; there is some solid gold among the New Age dross.

10.   There are other approaches. A skeptical colleague, reviewing an earlier draft of this paper, asked: "What is the probability that ANY north-south line drawn through the Southwest would interest several important sites"? A good question, although the term "important" is problematic. Try it yourself, with a National Geographic or a AAA map and a ruler—and Olympian detachment for "important." Consider only the best and brightest, and eschew small scales: Look only for meridian alignments over 250 or 300 km in length. As a statistical procedure, it stinks; but as an experiment, it's illuminating.

   I find only three other north-south alignments of "important" sites, on this scale, in the Greater Southwest: Two come tantalizing close to defining the eastern and western boundaries of the Chacoan region, and the third marks a remarkable Arizona-Sonora connection. Chacoan Great Houses seem to be confined, along the whole 300 km length of the region, by longitude 107° 15' on the east (approximately the longitude of Chimney Rock and Guadalupe Ruin), and 110° on the west (approximately the longitude of the westernmost Great Houses on

Cedar Mesa, upper Polacca Wash, and the Little Colorado River). This Great House geography interests me strangely, of course; but it will probably explode as additional Great Houses are recognized in more distant parts of the Southwest. The third alignment lines Arizona and Sonora sites: Sunset Crater, Casa Grande, and Las Trincheras. Sunset Crater and Las Trincheras were either entirely or largely natural features; Casa Grande has, perhaps, connections to Paquime. They all *stick* (remarkably) *up*. Sunset Crater rose first; Casa Grande and Las Trincheras came a century or two later. Their meridian alignment is problematic, but interesting.

Map-and-ruler exercises are "ley hunting" (or "ley lying," to quote Simon Broadbent 1980). Map searches may demonstrate that the Chaco meridian was or was not unique in the greater Southwest, but they cannot assess statistical probability.

If we must be statistical, we could segment the latitude parallels of Chaco and Paquime into 1.5 km units and assume that Chaco and Paquime are each 1.5 km in their east-west dimensions ("width"), and free to fall within any segment of their respective parallels, anywhere around the great big world. Then we could calculate the absolute minimum probability that the two would fall by chance in the same 1.5-km-wide longitudinal zone: something less than 0.000000002. Of course, this model could place Chaco in Asia or Paquime in mid-Atlantic. If we limit the parallels of Chaco and Paquime to the Southwest (i.e., between longitudes 104° to 115°), the probability of the Chaco-Paquime alignment, by chance, increases to a whopping 0.0000026. But there is a temporal dimension to the problem. Chaco comes first, Paquime second; therefore the location of Chaco is fixed, and only Paquime is free to move. Recognizing this parameter increases the probability to 0.0016. Better, but not odds on which to wager your life's savings.

We could chip away at the problem, tightening this parameter and expanding that dimension, and develop a broad continuum of probabilities. But turn the argument on its pointy little head and go right for its pencil-necked throat: (1) assume that the position of Chaco was fixed as the boundaries of the modern park, i.e., between longitudes 107° 50' and 108° 2' 30", or about a 16 km "width"; (2) assume that Paquime is 1.5 km "wide" and free to vary, east-west and north-south— as long as it winds up on the banks of the Rio Casas Grandes above Ascension, a 120 km reach of the north-flowing river with a longitudinal "width" between 107° 53' 20" to 108° 3' 40", or about 15 km. Under these conditions and parameters, there would be about 0.90 chance that Paquime would fall in the same meridian corridor as some part of Chaco. It could hardly miss.

Stated one way, the chances for alignment are astoundingly small; stated another, the chances of alignment approach certainty. Intentional alignment equals certainty, too. Probabilities, in unique cases, depend entirely on how one formulates the case.

And I've left Aztec out of the mix; a three-part problem would be even more convoluted.

11. For those who cherish agency over environment, my argument might be happier if the chronology were reversed: Paquime fixed first in its bountiful river valley, followed by Aztec's arbitrary placement along a good creek, and finally Chaco

in its unlikely setting. The degree of arbitrariness would increase, pleasingly, through time. Instead, Chaco is problematic, Aztec is understandable, and Paquime makes great good sense. (I point this out because someone else is sure to do so.)

12. True geodesic positioning, eclipsing the Chaco-Aztec-Paquime meridian in scale and technical achievement, is spectacularly evident in the mosques of Islam. Either the mosque itself or the prayer niche (*mihrab*) in its walls are oriented by *qibla*, the direction from the point of prayer to the Kaaba in Mecca. The *Quran* requires that the *qibla* be an accurate alignment, but in some cases the *qibla* was conventional. The frequently realized ideal, however, is an accurate orientation of the mosque to Mecca. *Qibla*, a system of world-scale positional legitimation, structures religious architecture, city planning and daily life of 900 million Muslims, from Dakar to Sarawak, and has done so for more than a thousand years.

Positional legitimation developed in the earliest days of Islam. In 622 A.D., the *hegira* brought Mohammed north from Mecca to Medina; the *Quarn*, written in Medina, prescribed prayer in the direction of the Kaaba. (Coincidence places Medina and Mecca on almost the same meridian; it happens.) The subsequent conquest of Egypt and, particularly, the great intellectual center of Alexandria, introduced Arab scholars to Greek astronomy and geodesy by about 650. Arab astronomy, in particular, blossomed in large part through the development of Greek ideas to the challenge of accurate determination of *qibla* (King 1979). "Medieval Muslim scientists were able—within the limitations of medieval geography—to determine the direction to Mecca of any locality to within a few minutes of arc" (King 1995:253). Orientation to Mecca was a concrete representation of spiritual and political legitimation of the new regimes in lands conquered by Arab armies. Those lands were vast: By the early 12th century, *qibla* determined the orientation of mosques from Morroco to the Punjab, and from the Caucasus to the Gulf of Aden.

The determination of *qibla* was one of the principal practical challenges that led to the remarkable florescence of Arab astronomy. The critical role of Islamic learning in the history of European science is well known, and needs no elaboration here. Positional legitimation, in this case at least, was serious stuff: *Qibla* were a major link in the history of modern thought. The Chaco-Aztec-Paquime meridian is another, much simpler example of a basic domain of human cognition: geodesy, the measurement of the world on which we live—a subject to which we will return in chapter 5.

5

CONCLUSIONS?

> People don't realize what's really going on. They view life as
> a bunch of unconnected incidents and things. They don't
> realize that there's this, like, lattice of coincidence that lays on
> top of everything. . . . No explanation. No point in looking
> for one either. It's all part of the cosmic unconsciousness.
>
> Miller, *Repo Man*

A QUICK REVIEW, WITHOUT REFERENCES

In the 11th-century Southwest, the two major players were separated by the
Mogollon rim: Chaco on the Plateau and Hohokam in the Sonoran desert.
Mimbres, the third famous 11th-century tradition, emerged where Chacoan
lifestyles met Hohokam irrigation economies. Mimbres was, in some ways,
derivative; but the combination of Chaco and Hohokam produced a pattern
uniquely important in Southwestern prehistory: the first real pueblos and the
origins of kachina ceremony.

Chaco had begun about 900 as three villages competing, in a circumscribed
canyon, for agricultural land and labor. Those local energies spilled out of the
canyon, engaging and entangling allies from around the agriculturally rich rim
of the Chaco Basin. By 1020 Chaco had emerged as a small but important
central place. Variable rainfall meant that a good year in the north might be a
disaster in the south; Chaco's serendipitous middle place promoted its rise as a
kind of regional "capital"—a place to store and exchange commodities and a
"corn bank" to even out the agricultural variability of the Chaco Basin. Canyon
leaders administered redistribution and real political power, based on garnered
surpluses, developed within the canyon. Population centers around the Chaco
Basin became Chacoan "outliers."

The system found its form during climatically favorable decades in the mid-11th century. Elite power became institutional and probably hereditary. The elites could well be called "Lords of the Great House" (expanding on Zuni Pueblo traditions): a group of leaders, their kin, and retainers, who lived in Great Houses at the exact center of the world. The people supported the Lords of the Great House through levies and taxes; the Lords did not work. A proto-bureaucracy of administrators and officials took care of business. Leaders were buried in elaborate crypts in the oldest part of the oldest building, with rich offerings and, possibly, their retainers. Buildings and built environments were the principal expressions of power: Great Houses, ritual landscapes, regional sight-lines, earth-monuments (now called roads), and astronomical alignments that were rapidly evolving toward regional geomancy.

Other, more distant communities entered the regional system, attracted by Chaco's success. Beyond the Chaco Basin limits of commodity redistribution, those far-flung outliers were incorporated into a political prestige economy controlled by Chaco. Turquoise, shell, parrots, and copper served as badges of office, symbols of alliance, or rewards for service.

The regional system grew to incorporate most of the Pueblo world; Chaco was its primate center. The elite at Chaco numbered several hundred, perhaps a thousand—the residents of canyon Great Houses—with a thousand or more commoners in the canyon and its immediate surroundings. The ceremonial city grew around a north-south axis, the meridian manifest in two remarkable buildings, Pueblo Alto and Tsin Kletsin. Chaco, at its height, probably inspired "White House"—the legendary city remembered as a place of wonder and tragedy in many Pueblo origin stories.

As early as the 1080s, a shift began from the original capital to a new center, the north. Salmon Ruins was built on the San Juan River, the closest live water due north of Chaco. Elsewhere within the region, farming depended almost entirely on rainfall. A small but significant drought in the 1130s and 1140s threw regional subsistence into chaos which Chaco could not correct. At the same time, to the south in the Mimbres region, kachina ceremonialism had developed as a mechanism to integrate and sustain large towns. The earliest forms of this ritual reached the Chacoan world just as the rains failed. Something like a spiritual power struggle ensued at Chaco: The new kachina ceremonialism promised prosperity without government, but the Lords of the Great House were not ready to step aside. The Chacoan world split into northern and southern spheres. In the south, kachina ceremonialism spread east to the middle Rio Grande and west to Wupatki (where the spectacular eruption of Sunset Crater was a catalyst for cosmological experiment and ritual synthesis). New ritual patterns cemented both the southern region and the burgeoning towns within it, without hierarchies or governments. In the north, the San Juan and Mesa Verde regions perpetuated the older Chacoan patterns—stately, formal, rigid, even grim.

The end of Chaco was a major event over the entire Pueblo world. Far to the south, for example, the Mimbres achievement ended at the same time. Everywhere, major transformations appear in Southwestern archaeology between 1125 and 1150. Chaco was one of these changes, or one of their causes.

The capital moved from Chaco to the north. The San Juan River proved too large for effective management; Salmon Ruins was not the final place, and in 1100 another site was chosen due north, on the Chaco Meridan: Aztec. The New Chaco rose on the smaller, more managable Rio Animas. The political elite of Chaco directed construction of a major landscape monument to mark the Chaco meridian: the Great North Road. Between 1110 and 1275, Aztec rose as a new ceremonial city planned and built (like Chaco) around elaborate symmetries, manifested by tri-walled structures and Great Houses. Aztec never reached Chaco's size, but its architecture and scale perpetuated Chacoan models, with several important innovations. The tri- and bi-wall form was Aztec's particular formal signature. Aztec architecture continued Chacoan sandstone masonry methods, but Aztec North (one of the larger, later Aztec Great Houses) was built not of sandstone, but of massive puddled adobe, anticipating things to come. The central Aztec complex faced south-southeast, Aztec North faced south.

Aztec continued the traditions and forms of Chaco, but ruled a diminished realm, marked by "outlier" tri-wall and bi-wall buildings: the Mesa Verde region around the Four Corners. The flow of exotica (even trade pottery) diminished, an index of Aztec's isolation from the larger Southwest. While long-distance exchange decreased, control over subsistence production increased, at least at the center. Ditch irrigation supplied the fields at Aztec, but regional subsistence remained rainfall-based. The Great Drought, beginning about 1275, was disastrous for tens of thousands of rainfall farmers in Aztec's region and ended Aztec's domain. Aztec fell, like Chaco, because rainfall didn't. Aztec's end was probably the reason for the dramatically complete abandonment of the Four Corners. The totality of out-migration can only be understood as politically directed—proof (in the breach) of regional integration. Tens of thousands left Aztec's hinterlands. Most joined the western and eastern pueblos. Many continued beyond, into the Sonoran and Chihuahuan deserts.

The center itself—the several hundred elite residents of Aztec—reversed cosmological directions. They had moved north from Chaco, and no good had come of it. The governing principal moved south, seeking (among other things) a region whose economy could support the life-style. The Chaco-

Aztec elite marched down the Chaco meridian, presumably with much pomp and ceremony. The process was a ritual drama of the highest interest. Where would the progress end? The elite knew the country to which they were headed but could not have known the exact place that they would stop, to reestablish Chaco and Aztec in a third ceremonial city, until they reached it.

The Plateau had twice frustrated Chacoan power: Vagaries of rainfall undermined Chaco in 1125 and destroyed Aztec in 1275. The elite moved completely off the Plateau, through the vacant despoiled Mimbres country and into an empty niche, ripe for major canal irrigation. They built their new city, Paquime, on the Rio Casas Grandes. Small ditches supported Aztec; major canals supported Paquime and its many outliers, providing a more stable economic base than was ever possible with Plateau rainfall.

Paquime was the most wonderful city ever built in the Pueblo Southwest: Mexican ballcourts, effigy mounds, and "pyramids" surrounded a huge, poured-adobe Great House pueblo. Local populations who built the city and supported its elite were not, in the main, Plateau peoples. They were, instead, desert-dwelling descendants of the Mimbres, and they carried Mimbres memories and traditions. Chaco, to them, was not a vague fable about a mythical city, but the principal political center of their great-great-grandparents' world; Aztec was a more distant place, where Chaco lived on in their own lifetimes. However they presented themselves, the Chaco-Aztec elite would not be strangers—historical or cosmological—in the desert. The meridian alignment validated the new city and its governors.

That city was filled with exotic goods that eclipsed the riches of Chaco or Aztec. The political prestige economy of Chaco and Aztec exploded into a mercantile economy at Paquime. Hundreds of macaws were raised to supply the demands created by the rapid spread of kachina ceremonialism among the many towns that Paquime had left behind, to the north. Shell, copper, and other tradable exotic goods flowed through Paquime in quantities never seen, before or after, at other Pueblos. Much of that commerce fed the evolving popular religions of the north; at Paquime, a more authoritarian cosmology was commemorated by structures adopted from distant, more hierarchical regions: ballcourts and "pyramid" mounds. Something like the grim old Chaco cosmology, perpetuated through manipulation of symbols and forms from the South.

The people of the Hopi Mesas, Zuni, Acoma, and the Rio Grande were content in their place. They knew Paquime only as a distant city, far to the south, the source of fabulous goods and ritual necessities, and the even greater cities south of Paquime only as rumors. The stories of the northern Pueblos diverged from the political history of Chaco-Aztec-Paquime, and they developed strong internal controls to prevent the rise of any new elites. White House—Chaco and Aztec—was remembered a wonderful place, but also a place where things had happened that did not belong in the Pueblo world.

A pretty yarn, a just-so story, a tale told by an idiot . . . no, stop. The story contains little that is really new. It is almost all other peoples' archaeology and other peoples' traditions, assembled in a novel way. The parts are mainstream: the time is dendro, the myths Pueblo, the mode retro. The narrative conforms to the facts, and they are *really big* facts. Chaco, Aztec, and Paquime were the three most important sites in Pueblo prehistory. Other archaeologists pair them in dyads: Stein and Fowler (and others) link Chaco and Aztec, Di Peso and Kelley (and others) link Chaco and Paquime. I take the next step and link all three in meridian nexus, a historic sequence that meshes archaeological facts and Pueblo traditions.

Who knows?—my story may even be right. But if it is right, so what? What larger interests are being served? I mount this shaky soap box to address three themes of broader notice: emergent order, cognitive evolution, and (last, least?) archaeological methods. This Chaco-Aztec-Paquime business has implications for all three. What follows are not conclusions but, rather, predictions or forecasts of how Southwestern teapot-tempests might rain on other, grander parades.

EMERGENT ORDER

More than once, the Pueblo world shifted from order to disorder and back again. Chaco brought order, a Pax Chaco over most of the Plateau. Aztec attempted to maintain that order, within a diminished area and without great success; its region and others in the 13th century were fragmented by balkanization (Lekson 1997) and violence, even warfare (LeBlanc 1997). Paquime restored order, at least within its region. The following proto-historic period, both south and north, was remarkable for an archaeological opacity that almost certainly represents social disarray—many small clusters of sites, with no evident center or panregional political system (Upham 1982). Kachina ceremonialism and new social orders militated against the reemergence of polities on the Chaco-Aztec-Paquime scale.

Cycles of order and disorder reach farther afield, beyond garden-variety Southwestern "strong patterns" to theoretical "complexity"—the study of complex adaptive systems—recently and experimentally applied to archaeological problems (Gumerman and Gell-Mann 1994; Kohler 1993; Lekson 1994; McGlade 1995). The bundled ideas behind "complexity" are well summarized by Roger Lewin (1992—who begins his account with Chaco) and, more technically, by Stuart Kauffman (1993, 1995).

Pueblo history was marked by three major cycles of order: Chaco, Aztec, and Paquime. Each dominated large regions, beyond which there were no clear settlement hierarchies or large regional entities (ignoring, for the moment, Hohokam). Three is not a strong sample for defining periodic phenomenon. The Southwestern story reads like an abbreviated version of more epic Mississippian political "cycling," recently explored by David Anderson:

> Cycling [is the] recurrent process of the emergence, expansion, and fragmentation of complex chiefdoms amid a regional backdrop of simple chiefdoms. The adoption of a regional perspective is critical to the investigation of this process, since changes in the number of decision-making levels in the chiefdoms within a given region are rarely concurrent. That is, chiefdoms rarely form or collapse in precisely the same location or with the same periodicity; instead, these societies typically expand or contract at the expense of or because of the actions of other chiefdoms. Centers of power shift or rotate over the landscape. (Anderson 1994:9–10)

Mississippian cycling provides an intriguing contrast to Chaco-Aztec-Paquime. In the Southeast, Mississippian chiefdoms appear and disappear like bubbles on the surface of a slow-boiling cauldron. The metaphor (mine, not Anderson's) of a bubbling surface is appropriate: Complex adaptive systems learn (adapt) and self-organize in regimes between chaos and order—that thin, interesting skin, the edge of chaos, where order and history originate. Chiefdoms bubbled and burst, dissolving back into the primordial chaotic soup. The Southeastern pot boiled longer and harder than the Southwestern. Cycles of order-disorder bubbled simultaneously through scores of Mississippian chiefdoms; at any one time, there were dozens of chiefdoms-in-process. Cycles in the Southwest were larger in geographic scope but much slower in frequency. In Pueblo prehistory, there were three, and each lasted about two centuries.

The differences between Southeast and Southwest in the tempo and distribution of complexity (both Santa Fe Institute complexity and more conventional sociopolitical complexity) must have been related to dramatically differing environments: the arid Southwest versus the lush Southeast. There was more fuel for the fire in the Southeast: The pot boiled longer and harder. The Southwest—famously marginal—could only support one of these operations at a time.

But the Southwest had something that the Southeast did not: the incredible stability of Hohokam, with its deep infrastructure of canals (Crown and Judge 1991; Lekson 1993).[1] Like a spoon in the kettle, Hohokam absorbed energy from the low heat of Southwestern cycling without ever allowing the pot to boil over. While Pueblos seethed and frothed, Hohokam set and jelled. The Pueblo past was remarkably dynamic: *contra* stereotype, pueblos (prior to the Spanish) typically lasted only a generation or so, and then moved to recreate themselves in the next valley, over the next ridge (Lekson 1996c). Some movements were long; many more were short (e.g., Adler 1990; Varien 1997). But movement was a constant.

Unit pueblos and whole towns bounced around like corn in a popper. (Against that agitated background, the movements of Chaco, Aztec, and Paquime seem almost stately.) Hohokam sites, tethered to their huge canals, begin early and end late. It is not unusual for big Hohokam sites to span six or seven centuries; Pueblo Bonito, constructed over two and a half centuries, was a legitimate phenomenon, nearly unique on the Plateau. Hohokam's stability, and the productivity of its canal systems, was unmatched by any other agricultural society north of Mexico. The irrigated desert basins could absorb populations spun off the Plateau (for example, the once and future Salado; and see Berry 1982—a study ahead of its time). That kind of a heat sink could, perhaps, counterbalance the political peregrinations of Plateau elites.

"Cycling" reflects a human urge to order. Anderson's chiefdoms form and collapse with dogged persistence. Indeed, "chiefdom" itself is a category that recognizes the universality of emergent order: Time and again, in place after place, political leadership emerged in human communities. Details differ, but somebody always wants to be the boss. Recent dissatisfactions with "chiefdom" as a term and an evolutionary stage rise from the anthropological fact that each emergence of leadership has its own historical, contingent context; no two are really alike. Yet modal ends belie disparate means: There is a shape to political power that early anthropologists recognized repeatedly at different times, places, environments, and societies. How is it that so many separate historical strands all led to similar knots? Are there common conditions that obviate historical differences, leading to chiefly leadership?

One critical dimension, common to societies with or without power structures, is population size. Political power is power over a group, and scalar stresses within groups may in fact lead to the emergence of political structure. Increasing community size creates far more potential dyads, triads, and other multipartner relationships. At some point, the density of potential interactions exceeds our capacities to categorize the players, to know the rules of engagement.

An old saw in business administration, introduced to archaeology by Gregory Johnson (1978), is the rule of seven: Seven is the maximum for effective group action; seven is the top number of tasks a single administrator can juggle. Whether or not this magic number has survived the recent explosion of cognitive research, it points in a likely direction: Some simple rules or limits of human cognition reach a scalar limit, beyond which direction is necessary. At some size, you can't know everybody in town. Communities of strangers are no longer communities. They need rulers to provide rules and the need for rulers arises from the ruled. In complexity parlance, the agents themselves create the circumstance of their suppression. Simple, agent-based rules, creating "order for free" is what complexity is all about. Hardwired agent-based rules could create bosses in the widest variety of physical and social environments.

Several researchers have independently discovered, through cross-cultural analyses, a key population threshold at about 2,500 (citations in Kosse 1990, 1994, 1996; Lekson 1985, 1990b): communities that exceed that size almost invariably have chiefs, kings, queens, bosses, police, people-in-power. (A town can exceed that limit if it is part of larger political structure, where the boss resides elsewhere.) That empirical pattern strongly suggests an underlying complexity: agent-based rules that perk along in a variety of historical and environmental settings, but which create a uniform phase shift when the key dimension—population size—exceeds a threshold. It's an interesting model, because it is simultaneously agent-based and processual. Research on settlement scalar thresholds, stalled for about a decade, continues in a brilliant, recently published study by Roland Fletcher (1995).

Cushing's "Masters of the Great House" at Zuni may be a case in point. Pueblos typically fission into mother and daughter villages when they approach 2,000 to 2,500 people (Bernardini 1996; Rohn 1983, 1996). Zuni, historically and today, is much larger, and Zuni's traditional government is much more complex—so complex that I invoked Cushing's reconstruction as a model for Chaco (chap. 2). Recall that Edmund Ladd (1979) suggested that Zuni's centralized elite was a response to colonial situations, specifically the combination of the separate "cites of Cibola" into the mega-Pueblo of Zuni, aggregated for defense against conquistadors. Previously separate small settlements were suddenly merged into one very large community, of perhaps 5,000 people. The scale threshold was exceeded, almost overnight, and a government was required. Was Zuni government invented or revived? Something like the Masters of the Great House had ruled Chaco and Aztec; at risk of circularity, I would like to think that histories of Chaco influenced the form of Zuni government.

I believe, with Carneiro (1981), that the emergence of the political structure we conventionally call "chiefdom" was a key transition in human social history. There were many roads to that transition, and many results; but the uniform competence of the few to decide for the many is conceptually and historically critical. Once political power appears, it can go in many directions: up, down, nowhere, somewhere. But the "state" (and the state we're in) is inconceivable without something earlier, like the chiefdom. When we understand how "chiefdoms"—simple political power—emerged, we might begin to unravel the Gordian knots of states.

I would not claim that Chaco was a state—long ago, that kind of provocation was evil fun. But, no: I'm older now and (if not wiser) more cautious. States were a limited, exclusive Old Boys' Club. Norman Yoffee (arbiter *de luxe* in these matters) decrees that if you have to argue about it, it's not a state. Despite some nagging teleological difficulties, Yoffee's dictum keeps out the riff-raff, like Chaco. Compared with Cuzco, Chaco *was* small potatoes; but Cuzco was once small potatoes, too. Even in an anthropology beset by particularizing and contingency, we may still learn something about the world's Cuzcos by looking at the world's Chacos.

Chaco was a remarkably clean example of "cycling"—a chiefdom failing to become a state. In this cycling metaphor, empty bubbles reach their physical limits and burst. The stew's surface might be seen as a threshold, the 2,500 person scalar limit. Inchoate gasses reach that limit, form perfect spheres, maintain a microsecond, and then fail. For statehood, my boiling cauldron figure fails, as well: What trope fits those chiefdom-bubbles that passed the threshold and elevated to Yoffee's club, to states? A local scumming of the stew, a temporary increase in viscosity allowing a bubble to expand hugely, ominously beyond the size of its evanescent neighbors.

Big bubbles blow, eventually (leaving a mess), but one consensus criterion of statehood is persistence—states last longer than chiefdoms before they collapse and go back under. Archaeologically, states leave deeper holes and higher piles. Chiefly "cycling" had a kind of transitory permanence: The urge to order surfaced and collapsed, but then reappeared claiming connection to preceding formations (Anderson 1994). Those connections could last a long time. Consider Chaco, Aztec, and Paquime. If Paquime was the result of a political history which began at Chaco, then there was political continuity for almost five centuries, a respectable state-length run. But it didn't happen in one spot, Chaco, Aztec, and Paquime stretched over a 720 km line. Yoffee's states are solidly permanent, situated *in situ*.

We value sedentism and spatial persistence perhaps because, since the Age of Expansion, we have become ourselves so rootless; but not all societies favored fixity. How would we know, archaeologically, peregrinating polities—states in space, not states in time? Great things were done on the hoof (Alexander and Genghis Kahn come to mind). And this brings me to my second theme: cognitive evolution and, specifically, the invention of space.

COGNITION

I can say (with a certainty and confidence unique in these pages), that I don't think the same way people of Chaco, Aztec, or Paquime thought. And the people of Chaco, Aztec, and Paquime would, I'm sure, be very glad to hear it.

We were differently trained. I began learning geometry before they dragged me off to kindergarten; we all were spoon-fed the concepts and then force-fed the formulae of a Euclidian world. Chacoans were making it up as they went along, and it was an impressive performance. First in building design (Lekson 1981), then in landscape production (Stein and Lekson 1992), and finally in geodesic space—demonstrably with the North Road and inferentially with the Chaco-Paquime meridian. Chaco, Aztec, and Paquime thinkers moved beyond the immediate landscape: They invented space.

Abstract space, absolute space, geometric space is important to us, in the very late 20th century; I literally cannot imagine a world without it. As an archaeologist, I want to watch space being invented (and forgotten), because I can learn from what I can't imagine. The unimaginable is a critical point-of-entry for thinking about cognition, particularly cognitions different from our own. Our familiar spatial thinking is dichotomized: experiential (such as wayfinding) or abstract (such as maps) (e.g., volumes such as Downs and Stea 1977 or Mark and Frank 1991). We are missing something in the middle, something archaeology alone can provide: the critical transition from experiential to abstract spatial thinking. Histories of cartography customarily nod at this topic but, by the time we have maps, it's far too late; spatial thinking predates cartography by aeons.

Spatial thinking was critical to the evolution of human thought and society (e.g., Clarke 1992: chaps. 2, 4). Susan Kus, following the lead of geographer David Harvey, makes the distinction between "effective" and "created" space. Effective space is experienced, quotidian, pragmatic, space-as-lived; created space is space manipulated to serve political or ideological ends, like the GLO grids overlying the western United States. "With increasing differentiation in social formations created space replaces effective space as the overriding principle of geographic organization" (Kus 1983:287)—the Chacoan situation. Evolving sociopolitical complexity provided the context for cognitive developments on the architectural and landscape scales, and for the explosion of spatial scales. Leaders must think big. Projections of power over distance make distance itself important.

In the New World, power was projected over remarkable distances. Teotihuacan was a notable, perhaps seminal, example: Teotihuacan "enclaves" were built at Kaminaljuyu and Tikal, each about 1,000 km distant. Aztatlan, an on-again-off-again Cahokia colony, was 500 km from the great Mississippian city. The nature of power relations between Teotihuacan and Tikal, and Cahokia and Aztatlan are matters of continuing research; but the scales of those long-standing questions are easily comparable to that of the Chaco-Aztec-Paquime meridian. Questions of political power in the New World are framed on scales of 500 or 1,000 km. Chaco, Aztec, and Paquime's 720 km fits in that range.

Chaco, Aztec, and Paquime gained the power of distances through prestige political economies, brokering turquoise, macaws, and shell within and beyond their regions. They partook of symbol systems founded in Mexico: Colonnades, for example, were elite symbols to be understood only through reference to the architectural cannons of Mesoamerica. Chaco, Aztec, and Paquime used Mary Helms's "authority of distant knowledge" as a primary political tool. Ultimately, Paquime was established and legitimated by the tangible mastery of space itself: physical alignment, over great distance, with the older centers at Chaco and Aztec. This was hot stuff—an altogether new way to use space and distance for political power.

Space isn't just out there, the final frontier; space must be projected and defined. "It was long after geometrical devices had been used for laying out and dividing land that the notion ever suggested itself of abstracting and studying these for their own sake.... We think space before we think *of* it" (Blanshard, cited in Robinson and Petchenik 1976:87). Spatial cognition moved through a series of scales, abstractions, and viewpoints, as we see at Chaco (Lekson 1981).

They thought about space. How should we think about thinking about space? Space itself changes when we shift from looking up at the stars to looking down from the Space Shuttle. Christopher Tilley (1994) and many others argue that an observer-defined, human-scale "landscape" is the proper space for Mesolithic and Neolithic societies—that is, how we should think of *them* thinking about *their* landscapes. Modern regional, continental or global scales—the geometries of our scholarly lives—are, they argue, inappropriate for thinking about thinking about past landscapes. Neolithic people, in this view, only knew what they could see from their front porch. In contrast, Lewis Binford, Robert Kelley, and many others have shown us the surprising scales of hunter-gatherer and early agricultural economic territories. However small and home-scale their thoughts, prehistoric peoples actually *used* stunningly large slabs of space.

So do geese. Tilley may be right: For cognitive issues, "landscape" may be as appropriate to early societies as "space" is appropriate for later societies, like ours (see Tuan 1990, among many others). That's an interesting if simple model, and a place to start: People thought about what they could see—effective, experienced space. The Chaco Meridian signaled a shift—a point-of-change, a transition—from a landscape world to a spatial world: thinking beyond the seeable. Not thinking *about*—any primate can think about what's over the next hill—but thinking *with*: abstract geometry in that term's very literal translation. The meridian is a peculiarly human, *spatial* interest. It is both fixed and arbitrary: fixed as the only real direction, yet arbitrary in its economic uselessness. The Chaco-Aztec-Paquime alignment imposed a remarkable spatial geometry, referenced to that fixed direction, over a series of unrelated landscapes—

regions so large and diverse that today we label them the Colorado Plateau, the Mogollon Uplands, and the Chihuahuan desert; and we consider their archaeologies to represent altogether different cultures.

The imposition of a large-scale global geometric—created, abstract—grid, was a major step in understanding and thinking about the world. "What the clock did for time, the rectangular grid did for space" (Boorstin 1983:111). At about the same time as the Chaco meridian, geodetic grids were being developed in China (the astonishing *Yu ju tu* map, dating about 1100; Needham 1959:533 ff). Medieval Arabic astronomy, contemporary with Chaco, Aztec, and Paquime, developed to align mosques with Mecca kept space alive while Europe retreated back to Dark Age landscape scales. That kind of space was pretty important in Old World intellectual history. Alfred Crosby makes a strong case that arbitrary, absolute space formed "a new model of reality" in the later Middle Ages and Renaissance: "These people were thinking of reality in quantitative terms with greater consistency than any other members of their species" (Crosby 1997:xi). Today, we can't imagine thought without space.[2]

The Chaco-Aztec-Paquime meridian was fraught with cultural symbolism, but it escaped the confines of landscape. The shift from landscape to abstract space was a major cognitive development. How and why did that shift of scale take place? Space was not a universal cognitive sensibility; it arose from the analytical interplay of thought-rules, context, and necessity. Spatial cognition arose at Chaco, Aztec, and Paquime reflected and supported increasingly centralized political power.

Mary Helms, in *Craft and the Kingly Ideal,* identifies a key role of kings (and other preindustrial leaders) as builders and world-makers:

> He transforms, through culture hero-like acts of creativity that constantly create (or impose) sociopolitical order out of (or on to) the constantly threatening potential chaos of group living. . . . He legitimates his use of power and his authority, his transformative, constructive, and exemplative efforts, by invoking liminal associations with the culture-hero crafters who originally initiated these marks of cultured existence. By constantly performing these activities anew, the ideal ruler collapses time/space dimensions that separate the here-and-now from the there-and-then and relates himself to ancestral places and acts of origin on one or the other axis or dimension of the outside realm. (Helms 1993:87)

Kings and chiefly leaders emerge from agent-based, scalar thresholds that demand order over chaos. They create worlds that define and confine their people. Power is manifest by controlling actions over distance; rulers invent space and then invest space to consolidate that power. Chacoan leaders could not look down from above, but they could use the firmament to fix the space beneath their feet; archaeoastronomy is a window to ancient political power as valid as mortuary analysis and monumental architecture. Chacoan space was profoundly astronomical. "Astronomical knowledge confers power" (Krupp 1997:13). Chacoan leaders unquestionably looked *north* to design their world, and they built the first great Southwestern ceremonial city around the meridian. The North Road projected Chaco's power across distance—but within the old Chaco region—to a new locus, Aztec. To legitimate a new political economy in the far desert, the architects of Paquime transferred power over even greater distances beyond Chaco/Aztec to a new regional center. Their tools of power were profoundly spatial: exotica and meridian. Cognitive evolution followed political development.

Space was invented and reinvented many different times and places, early and often. It did not always persist; most probably, it seldom persisted, disappearing like bubbles. "An invention may appear to meet the edge of possibility, but if it exceeds the penumbra [between actuality and the future], it remains a curious toy or it disappears into fantasy" (Kubler 1962:65). Space is good to think, perhaps, but it need not stick (Crosby 1997:17).

The Chaco-Aztec-Paquime invention of space was dramatically evident in the North Road and, I argue, the meridian alignment. And that sense of space had a persistent, pervasive effect on subsequent Southwestern societies. Contexts changed when the political economy of the Pueblo Southwest fell apart, sometime in the 15th century. New cognitions replaced Chaco-Paquime spatial geometries with more localized senses of place, but vestiges of Chacoan spatial precision and orientation remain. The cardinals are critical to all Pueblo world-making (Dozier 1970:203–207; Ortiz 1970:204–207, except at Hopi, which until recently relied on solar directions, Hieb 1979:577–578; Parsons 1996:365n). They define Pueblo place, ceremony, and world view with particular accuracy. "All peoples try to bring their definitions of group space somehow into line with their cosmologies, but the Pueblos are unusually precise about it" (Ortiz 1972:142). The Chaco meridian is still in place.

Alfonso Ortiz contrasts the dry-painting techniques of Pueblo and Navajo. A Navajo singer works from the inside of his design out to its circumference. The Pueblo priest, however, begins by framing the space of his design and then in-fills toward the center (Ortiz 1972:143). For Pueblo people, space is socially known, defined by points visible and invisible, real and abstract. Self is *not* the central axis of the social world. "World view notions take on a group character ...one cannot discuss the person apart from the group nor, indeed, from all else in the Pueblo world" (Ortiz 1972:154). Pueblo space is not experiential, but profoundly social, cosmological. (Tilley's personal, phenomonological approaches will not work for Pueblo spatial cognition today; they almost certainly would not work for the even larger spatial scales of Chaco, Aztec, and Paquime in the ancient past.)

Spatial cognition evolved from the personal to social to political through the development of Chacoan architecture from rigidly geometric buildings, to ritual landscapes, to spatial worlds. The shift from landscape to space is an event of signal importance in human cognition. It happened not in later days, with Euclid or Descartes, but in Mesolithic and Neolithic milieus. Its data are archaeological; how do we find and study them? If, by fiat, we decree that "pre-capitalist, nonwestern, small-scale traditional" societies can't imagine space—lived only in landscapes—we will never learn how they invented space. We may have to invent new methods to escape the small spatial structures of our archaeological thinking; which leads us to . . .

New Methods Needed: Apply Within

The fundamental importance of north in Chacoan cosmology and polity marks an empirical pattern—meridian alignment of the three great Southwestern cities—of obvious interest. The high likelihood, through mostly circumstantial evidence, that the meridian alignment was *not* coincidence should move my argument to *quod erat demonstradum.* For me, it's QED; but for most of my colleagues, Chaco-Aztec-Paquime is DOA.

Friends and critics toe-tag and body-bag the Chaco-Aztec-Paquime hypothesis because the two ends of the sequence *don't look alike* (front., 3.1). I have tried to show that there were fundamental parallels between those two great centers, beauties more than skin deep (chap. 3). But, it's true: Chaco does *not* look like Paquime.

That's a real problem because the tactics of southwestern prehistory are based on similarity, even (and especially) across punctuations like the Great Drought. We are all, at heart, local gradualists. And our happiest evidence is identity: If A resembles B, then A = B. We can encompass (moderate) change—dissimilarity—through time: Shared similarities in the sequential phases of a local sequence overshadow the differences that define the phases themselves. We have much more trouble with dissimilarity across space. Local identity shows most clearly in the putative absence of identity relationships: Each archaeologist's valley or site is "a little different" than the one over the next hill. Curiously, dissimilarities between Phases A and B within one local sequence are almost always greater than the dissimilarity between Phase B and Phase Wanna-B in two different valleys. Implicit and (largely) unstated models of prehistoric dynamics give us different standards for similarity across time and space. Chaco-Aztec-Paquime tracks change through time *and* space—dissimilar ties in both dimensions—and, consequently, it is a really hard sell.

Similarity and dissimilarity are the very basis of our logic, and structure our temporal and spatial thinking. Basic similarities mark basal structures:

"Index wares" define "cultures" over which disembodied ideas and ideologies float in ethereal osmosis. Anasazi "influences," for example, might reach brown-ware culture areas, but those ideas were adopted or rejected, passed or strained by the variable permeability of the cultural bedrock, the pottery and masonry substrate. Even when small groups are seen to move, they are almost invariably transformed and absorbed by the spirit of the country, the *genius loci.* Families flee Mesa Verde and merge imperceptibly into distant host villages. The archaeological exceptions are truly exceptional: smoking-gun enclaves of Mesa Verde in the Rio Grande, or Patayan in the Phoenix Basin. Rare birds, indeed.

But . . . what if? What if Pueblo histories are true, and sites we classify as archaeologically different were, in fact, historically linked? One of the interesting outcomes of NAGPRA is the contrast of archaeological logic and Native history. There is, of course, significant congruence. It is my experience that Pueblo historians appreciate and use similarity of physical remains much like archaeologists, but—unlike archaeologists—they are not limited by it. Similarity may be overruled by history. If history says A *became* B then A = B, whether or not they are superficially similar. If we take traditional history seriously, we may have to develop new methods to encompass those unlooked-for possibilities. The issue goes far beyond Chaco, Aztec, and Paquime; it cuts to the heart of any claim of cultural affiliation to any ancient site.[3]

People change clothes, architectonics, and pantheons; we know this from documented societies. We embrace those sea-changes as phenomena of great interest. Without documents, however, archaeology cannot cope with sea-change. Our methods, founded in similarity and identity, fight against it. We demand extremely high standards of evidence—smoking guns—to establish continuity across dissimilarity. "Extremely high standards" sound good and even noble; but unreasonably high standards can deny us insights of real interest.

What are reasonable standards for similarity and dissimilarity? Similarity (other than identity) is always a statistical judgment, and statistical judgments depend on the parameters of the comparison and the criteria for rejection. Both are necessarily arbitrary: We do not have a global sample against which to calibrate our tests and our thinking. In the end, we fall back on our preconceptions about past dynamics: As noted above, similarity through time is judged differently than similarity over space.

How different is too different? How similar is sufficiently similar? For Chaco-Aztec-Paquime, I can only answer those questions by argument and not by test. To evaluate continuity across dissimilarity—for matters of more moment than ceramic production or house size or irrigation techniques—we must build a new comparative archaeology for larger scales—a comparative archaeology of polities and their residual landscapes, of the archaeologically-knowable empirical patterns of architecture, settlement, and region (Lekson, Cordell, and Gumerman 1994). This does not currently exist[4]; we have only typologies (bands, tribes, chiefdoms, states; heterachies and hierarchies; simple and complex) into which sites and regions may be summarily docketed. Unsatisfactory—but without those typologies we are bereft and adrift. There are no other material bases for comparison, for calibration, for judgement. Textbooks, atlases, and other compendia are notorious for not even trying to represent those data systematically. Trial syntheses exist of house form (Blanton 1994) and city size (Fletcher 1995). But we look in vain for any sustained program on the shape and scale of polities. The data are there, in thousands of reports and monographs, but we lack a structure—a method—to bring together the fruits of a century's labor.[5]

So, what are we to make of Native histories and archaeological data that link dissimilar sites? Our customary evidential protocols make ceramics and architecture preponderant: For example, grayware cultures are dissimilar to brownware cultures, thus Chaco and Paquime are significantly different; Chaco is sandstone and Paquime is puddled mud, thus they are significantly different. And those parallels presented in chapter 3? Ideas, filtered from one to the other and down-the-line trade might have moved exotica from desert to plateau. But the preponderance of the *basic* evidence—pottery, wall form, that sort of thing—demonstrates differences that are fundamental and fatal to my argument.

Basic evidence reflects base populations, presumably. I do not argue that tens of thousands of people moved from Chaco to Aztec to Paquime. Rather, I propose that an evolving ideology—an ideology of hierarchy and control—links those three places. The ruling principals and principles moved, not the base of the pyramid. Ideas may percolate through populations, but ideologies are carried by people with attitudes—particularly, attitudes about asymmetric power relations. Ideologies moved, and not by vague "influences." Aztec was no knock-off, some rube's lame copy of Chaco's bright lights. Nor was Paquime.

The people who benefited most from the ideology carried it into new territories. Those people may not have been marked by sherds, axe hafts, or masonry styles. They didn't make their own pottery. They didn't build their own houses. They probably didn't even cook their own meals. They directed those activities, but the actions and their embedded technologies were the work of others. So, what *should* we expect to see, if governing power moved from Chaco to Aztec to Paquime?

It's hard to say, really: The problem outpaces our methods. We are not incapable of jumping gaps, but usually by argument rather than method: Our methods balk at gaps. We bridged the Basketmaker to Pueblo disjuncture—at one point, different peoples—through argument and persuasion more than through data. Today, decades later, we see continuity across some rather remarkable material changes, where our intellectual forefathers read replacement. We can, for example, posit continuity across previously conclusive and categorical changes from Mimbres to post-Mimbres sites (chap. 2). But, still, major changes in architecture and pottery conventionally signal either new kids on the block, or a fundamental rift in the man-land relationship. Arguments for continuity across gaps are necessarily circumstantial, anecdotal, juristic. Nagging small similarities; contrasting larger shifts in pottery and building form; formal or structural translations that seem, in context, telling; scenarios that make narrative sense of an otherwise confused record—these things nudge us off center, from linear to non- (or at least less-) linear prehistories. Phase shifts—in other peoples' pasts and in our present thinking—are really interesting.

Southwestern archaeologists are predisposed to explain that change as evolutionary or perambulatory: adaptation or replacement. That sort of thinking has served us well, for most purposes. Political or ideological change is a tough one; we've only begun to think about it (e.g., Crown 1994). Things do change, and centers fall apart; but new centers gain power through reference, real or fictive, to the past. In the Southwest, we have an extraordinarily visible, knowable example of political continuity across time and tide, if we allow ourselves to see it.

NOTES

1. What to do with Hohokam? I reserve Hohokam for future treatment; it is too big for this book. By a simple accident of career, I visited Casas Grandes before I saw Casa Grande, and I have always been struck by their similarities (see also Wilcox and Shenk 1977:128). I admire Casa Grande's tin roof, but the building itself is Paquime writ small. Hohokam archaeologists are quick to deny the connection, but perhaps they protest too much (Lekson in press c). As McGuire (e.g., 1993b) and others have noted, the Phoenix Basin and Paquime form two ends of a densely settled, 14th band or zone across the Sonoran and Chihuahua deserts, where those deserts lap up against the Colorado Plateau (Lekson in press c). Peer polities? Chaco and Aztec lacked rivals. Nothing on the Colorado Plateau challenged either of those great centers. Chaco and the sedentary period Hohokam ignored each other (Crown and Judge 1991); Aztec was even farther north, even more remote. The lack of peer interactions may have contributed to the ultimate collapse of the first two capitals. Paquime, however, was not alone in the desert.

2. I'd like to cite Ernst Cassirer here, because he annoys po-mos. Cassirer made a big point about the importance of Cartesian geometric space in the history of European, scientific thought—and he didn't apologize for either Europe or science. See *An Essay on Man*, especially the first half of chapter 4, "The Human World of Space and Time" (Cassirer 1944:42–49).

3.   The problem has deep roots, of course. The conflation of archaeological "culture" (a taxonomic unit) with wider anthropological usages of that term has plagued us for a century. Boas disassembled "culture" as an essential aggregate of people, language, and things. Post-modern emphases on agency and the individual further atomizes "culture" into populations, distributions, polythetic sets (that one's not really po-mo)—a thing of shreds and patches. There's not much left of anthropological or archaeological "culture." For example: "anthropologists would do well to throw out the concept of culture, except that we have nothing with which to replace it . . . first step in this direction would be the recognition of each person as a unique individual carrying a unique repertoire of cultural understandings and beliefs" (Rodseth 1998:55, 57). We might answer that biography is not a genre available to archaeology—to say nothing of the uniformitarian cognitive assumptions of post-modern programs (a problem far beyond the scope of a footnote). Archaeology confronts things, organized analytically as alike or not-alike. Similarity and identity are our base logics. The society in which we work operates as if culture (and race) are real, which makes our internal debate moot: we are asked to do history—NAGPRA insists—and we must work with what we have. What we have are assemblages of alike and not-alike things, and what we lack is a logic that transcends identity. We would do well to throw out the concept of similarity, except that we have nothing with which to replace it. David Wilcox's relational logic might work.

4.   Attempts to disentangle typologies of low-end complexity (e.g., Feinman and Neitzell 1984; McGuire 1983; Upham 1987) or to build new multivariate social models (Jorgensen 1980, 1983) typically focus on social characteristics and exclude their material correlates, particularly for larger scales, like landscapes and regions. We still appeal to hoary hierarchies of settlement tiers, or crude rules-of-thumb from theoretical models or ethnological data ("chiefdoms should look like . . ."). I want comparative measures appropriate to archaeological contexts. How do we meaningfully compare the material residues—landscapes, built environments—of Chaco and Cahokia? Energetics (Lekson 1986a; Nelson 1995) may be a start; spatial syntax seems less promising, but these are approaches that we are only beginning to develop. Only when we systematize those archaeological data can we usefully engage the ethnographic record.

5.   There are useful treatments, which are necessarily selective and anecdotal. For example, Kent Flannery's (1998) essay on "Ground Plans of Archaic States" and Gary Feinman's (1998) review of scale in early states are a good beginning. But these are only beginnings. As Feinman notes:

> When I first conceptualized the topic of scale, settlement pattern and the ancient state, I envisioned a rather straightforward comparative discussion. . . . Now I recognize that such preliminary thoughts were rather optimistic (Feinman 1998).

Data exist for shape and size of pre-state and early state polities, but systematic compilation of those data will require an HRAF-scale effort.

Appendix A

T-Shaped Doors

"The T- or Tau-shaped door is an enigma," mused Neil Judd (1964:28); he found thirty-two at Pueblo Bonito (fig. A.1). Charles Di Peso listed T-shaped doors as one of 23 specific architectural details linking Casas Grandes and Chaco Canyon (Di Peso, Rinaldo, and Fenner 1974a:211); he found 335 at Paquime.

The T shape was also spectacularly manifest on two remarkable altar stones from Paquime. The better preserved example was a finely finished rectangle of felsite, 58 cm by 55 cm and 15 cm thick, with a perfectly proportioned T-shaped opening cut through its center (Di Peso 1974:558)—a miniature T-door in a remarkable, ceremonial context.

Di Peso was ambivalent and even uncertain about the T shape's provenance. The Mexican connection for the T shape was not particularly strong: "Below the Tropic of Cancer, it was used both on the Chichen Itza friezes and as a window design, but apparently never as an entry [door] form" (Di Peso 1974:446). The T altar, in contrast, was seen as "vaguely analagous to those of the *kachinki* and the altar screens of the water serpent ceremonies of the modern Pueblo groups" (Di Peso 1974d:324); elsewhere he alludes to the T representing a rattlesnake's tail (Di Peso 1974:694: n. 44) or even Tlaloc (Di Peso, Rinaldo, and Fenner 1974a:236). Whatever its ultimate iconography, the T-door seemed, to Di Peso, to be a particularly

A.1a.

A.1b.

A.1c.

Figure A.1. T-Shaped doors: a, Chaco; b, Aztec; c, Paquime.

potent symbol of Paquime: "This was one of the diagnostic Casas Grandes architectural features which, like the raised hearth, helped to give identity to the Paquime cultural tradition" (Di Peso, Rinaldo, and Fenner 1974a:236)—except that, as Di Peso noted, T-doors also appeared at Chaco and other Anasazi sites.

Four years after Di Peso's *Casas Grandes* report, Robert Lister (then director of the NPS Chaco Project) published a list of "traits noted in Chaco Canyon that are identified as, or presumed to be, Mesoamerican"; among these traits were T-shaped doorways (Lister 1978:236). This went a step beyond Di Peso, who could not finger a Mesoamerican source for Paquime's T-doors. Lister was probably thinking of Paquime itself as a "Meso-american" source for Chaco (for Lister, Paquime was early and Mexican). He wrote long before Dean and Ravesloot's (1993) redating and the Puebloan-Paquime revanche (Lekson in press e).

Randy McGuire responded to this suggestion, negatively, with a journal article in 1980, and I added a conference paper in 1981 (Lekson 1983b). We reclaimed T-doors for the Southwest. McGuire (citing Love's 1975 survey of T-doors) noted that the "T-shaped doorway originated in the SW; not Mesoamerica" (McGuire 1980:Table 1); and I couldn't have agreed more (Lekson 1983b:185). The T-door was an Anasazi leitmotiv: We see T-openings on Mesa Verde mugs, and the doors themselves at ruins from Navajo Mountain on the west to the La Plata Valley on the east, from nameless tiny cliff-dwellings near Moab on the north to . . . how far south, exactly? Far south of Paquime, in cliff-dwellings in the Sierra Madres (Lister 1958:58ff).

That ubiquity seemed to void entirely Di Peso's claims for T-doors. If T-doors were everywhere, they could not support Di Peso's arguments for a unique linkage between Paquime and Chaco. Case closed.

What a difference a decade makes. T-doors encapsulate my changed thinking on Chaco, Aztec, and Paquime. And T-doors are an especially good talking point, because they are a visual bromide in the contemporary Southwest. Only bandanna-wearing coyotes and promiscuous flute players are more obnoxiously popular, more quintessentially Santa-Fe retail. The T form is inescapable: in hotel lobbies and red-tiled kitchens, as posters and fine-art photographs, on questionably Indian-made jewelry—but not for actual, functional doorways: it's too hard to hang a T-shaped door.

T-doors are pervasive in contemporary Southwestern style in part because they were (and are) so obvious in their original, ancient use: T-doors were generally exterior, ground-floor entries, open to the outside world. Not all T-doors were exterior but, at Chaco, most at least *began* as exterior doors; an informal analysis of other Anasazi T-doors suggests that they were predominately exterior features (Lekson 1986a). The situation at Paquime is not so clear:

There were many interior T-doors that never saw the light of day (Di Peso 1974). But T-doors were conspicuous as exterior "public" doors at Paquime and at cliff-dwellings in the Sierra Madre and greater Southwest. The T-door is popular in contemporary Southwestern design precisely because so many people have seen these doors, dramatically, at Cliff Palace or Keet Seel or Gila Cliff Dwellings. They catch our eye because they were *meant to be seen.*

T-doors at cliff-dwellings look, today, much as they would have looked in antiquity. We can safely assume that exterior T-doors were intended to be visible, to friend and stranger. Clothes, coiffure, pottery, arrow fletching, and other "stylistic" media carry messages; buildings did too. If houses told a story (Lekson 1990b:142–145; Rapoport 1969), buildings like Chaco, Aztec, Paquime spoke volumes. Given the fact that T-doors were generally exterior—visible to the world— the message may well have been one of membership or inclusion. A T- door proclaimed that its building was part of a larger, similarly marked set of buildings.

Other visual keys and clues undoubtedly marked building exteriors. We don't really know how ancient pueblos actually *looked.* By the time archaeologists see them, their exteriors have survived centuries of wind and weather. Or rather, they have *not* survived: Mud plaster is gone, roofs have collapsed, transitory embellishments, hangings, and furniture have long since vanished. Cliff-dwellings are best preserved, and they seldom turn very decorative faces to the world; the appeal of cliff-dwellings is in their massing—facets of their component cubes— and not their ornament.

Pueblo forms seem basic: flat roofs, rectangular elevations. The homogeneity implied by those simple forms leads to archaeological and anthropological abstractions—probably false—like "Anasazi" or "Pueblo." What we group together, by shared rectangular building units, represents a wide diversity of linguistic and social entities; but it all looks the same, to us. A Pueblo person of the 11th century probably could read differences in wall proportions or beam spacings or other visible building keys from one boxy little "pueblo" to the next, but those things are too subtle for archaeological eyes, centuries later. We need more obvious signs; emblems, in fact.

There is no evidence for exterior mural painting (what that might suggest for Pueblo Bonito!) but we can be sure that the outward form of the great buildings at Chaco, Aztec, and Paquime was carefully composed and skillfully realized. They, too, were meant to be seen. In considering these buildings, our archaeological energies have gone into the analysis of masonry styles, perhaps the most basic but certainly most banal of "architectural" clues. (Exterior walls were, more often than not, plastered over.) We need new ways of analyzing buildings that avoid the pitfalls of critical subjectivity, but that acknowledge *design*: buildings were designed to be seen, and some buildings (like Pueblo

Bonito) were designed to send an active and specific message (Keivit 1997). We can at least detect the signal, even if we cannot decode it.

I submit that T-doors are an archaeologically obvious architectural message design, too long overlooked. We focus on masonry styles because wall technology can be analyzed like pottery or other artifacts, but the architectural clues were principally formal: shapes, dimensions, proportions. The T-door is most accessible of these formal indicators: For that very reason, T-doors capture and hold our attention, and the attention of Santa Fe retailers. The Santa Fe people make money off T-doors; archaeologists make too little of them. We don't know what they mean, and that makes us uncomfortable; so flinching from a strong iconic pattern, we reduce T-doors by trivial, functional attributions.

Archaeological explanations of this very unusual shape can be found in any textbook or National Park signage. The T shape allowed burdens to be carried through the door, diminished winter draughts, and other simple solutions: pragmatic conjectures about portage and ambient temperatures. I will not summarize the archaeological treatments—rudimentary or cosmological—here; what they routinely miss is that evident role of T-shaped doors as highly visible clues to the nature of the building itself. T-shaped doors were emblems. The Paquime altars demonstrate that the shape was not merely practical. And we know, from interior doors, that other shapes were known and used to penetrate walls; the T shape on an exterior wall was a very conscious choice to send a very particular message.

T-doors begin with Chaco. There are, apparently, no T-doors in the preceding Pueblo I era (Richard Wilshusen, personal communication 1997; contra Love's 1975:296 report of a T-shaped door at Mesa Verde dated to 831).[1] T-doors at Chaco all postdate 1020; that is, they were not part of Chaco's early days, but rather a feature of the Chaco florescence (Judd 1964:28; Lekson 1986a). They appear at many of the excavated outliers (e.g., Lowry, Guadalupe, Escalante)—but not, conspicuously, at smaller 11th-century sites (Love 1975 and anecdotal queries of colleagues). T-doors were seminal in the Chacoan canon.

During Aztec's era, T-doors were a major feature at Aztec itself, and they were found at sites throughout the Pueblo world, within and beyond the putative Aztec domain. T doors show up in the Kayenta district, at Salado ruins, in the Gila Cliff Dwellings, and other 13th-century sites. They are, of course, particularly conspicuous in the Northern San Juan—Aztec's would-be region. If some enterprising graduate student were to cross the eyes and dot the Ts onto a regional map, there would (I am reasonably sure) be far more north than south of the San Juan and its immediate tributaries. Like tri-wall structures, T-shaped doors get around, but hung mostly to the north, around Aztec.

Most telling is the distribution in the 14th century, and beyond. Di Peso considered the T-shaped door a defining element of Paquime and its region (as noted above). With Paquime's rise, T-doors all but disappear from the northern Southwest. A few 14th- and 15th-century examples are known from later sites on the Rio Grande (for example, Gran Quivira [Hayes 1981:39]) and at Hopi ruins (Mindeleff 1891:190), but they are rare, compared with Paquime and its region. More than half of the doors at that great 14th-century city were T-shaped (Di Peso, Rinaldo, and Fenner 1974a:236; Di Peso 1974:684 n. 43).

T-doors in the post-Chaco, post-Aztec northern southwest have the feel of cultural detritus, remnants of an earlier symbolic system (but see Luxan's 1582 account of the Piro Pueblos: Hammond and Rey 1929:74). Intriguingly, the T-shaped door may have been particularly prominent at Acoma Pueblo (Love 1975:300). Acoma's history seems closely linked to Chaco, Aztec, and Paquime (chap. 4). But the distribution of T-shaped doors clearly shifted south about 1300. Marian Love, in the most complete survey of the subject concludes:

> That such a distinctive shape as the T-shaped doorway should have been concentrated in the Mesa Verde-Chaco and Casas Grandes regions, and thinly spread in other areas suggests that the original idea diffused from a center through trade and/or via parties of migrants. At present, the few dates we have suggest such diffusion from north to south. Should this, in fact, be the case, the T-shaped doorway will be the only feature known to have diffused southward from the Southwest into Mexico. (Love 1975:303)

One thinks of the bow and arrow, of course; but the point here is not the conclusions but the pattern behind Love's age-area rhetoric: we now have the dates, and we can say with some confidence that T-shaped doors began with Chaco, proliferated during the Aztec era, all but disappeared from the northern Southwest to reappear, in the south, at Paquime and in its region. T-doors are, indeed, everywhere on the map; but in focus and sequence, T-doors follow the Chaco-Aztec-Paquime meridian.

T-shaped doors do not show the remarkable specificity of colonnades, room-wide platforms, and sandstone disks (chap. 3); instead, they were widespread architectural emblems that could operate at Great House and small, at the capital and in the villages. The worlds of Chaco, Aztec, and Paquime were constructed worlds, architectural and geodesic. It beggars the imagination to think that something as prominent and conspicuous as exterior T-doors were not powerfully meaningful architectural messages. The symbolism of the T may have related to direction, like the Great North Road and the Mound of the Cross, but I will leave those speculations unpursued.

Whatever their meaning, T-doors were signals and icons. They began at Chaco, and appear to have been used mainly at Great Houses in the larger Chacoan region. The use of T-doors at Aztec and Paquime (and, more rarely, at Pueblos left behind in that epic of location and relocation) undoubtedly altered the content of their message but the *fact* of the signal remained strong—so strong, that the form still calls us, centuries removed from its proper cultural context.

Notes

1. Preservation is a problem in the distribution of T-doors. Any wall reduced below the level of the T would show no clear evidence of the door's original shape. At Pueblo I sites, for example, walls are rarely preserved any higher than about 75 cm, which could eliminate the T shape. Sites where walls could be expected to preserve T-doors would include Great Houses and Cliff Dwellings. Great House walls introduce a circularity into the argument, and the most famous Cliff Dwellings are mostly post-Chaco. But some caves and cliffs contain Basketmaker, Pueblo I, and Pueblo II remains, and these do not offer examples of pre-Chaco T-shaped doors. The thin record supports the statements made here, but preservation is always a problem.

Appendix B

Culiacán

What's south of Paquime? Some of the most spectacularly rugged country in the world (fig. B.1): the Barranca del Cobre of the Sierra Madre. And south of that? The colonial center of Batopilas, and beyond that, in Sinaloa, the site of Culiacán. Culiacán was a very late Native regional capital, which conquistadors considered the northwesternmost extension of civilized Mexico (and archaeologists; beginning with Kelly 1945; Sauer and Brand 1932). Culiacán is the same distance from Paquime, as Paquime was from Chaco Canyon.

I am reasonably familiar with Chaco, Aztec, and Paquime, but I have never traveled over the Sierra Madre to the Culiacán Valley. I should not, perhaps, boldly extend an overextended argument where I have never gone before. But, as Dr. John says, if I don't do it, somebody else will. This footnote registers some geographic relationships and reports some things found in a review of the literature; and, of course, I toss in a few gratuitously provocative observations.

The Barranca del Cobre is a formidable barrier for horses, carts, cars, tour buses, and trucks. It seems an hazardous feature for any route or line to cross. We shy away from deep canyons. Carl Sauer assumed that pre- and protohistoric paths shared the characteristics of later horse and wagon road in *The Road to Cibola* (1932:1). Anthropologists and archaeologists follow Sauer's lead and reconstruct major prehistoric routes along or beneath modern roads, usually along rivers and almost never over ridges or ranges (e.g., Riley and Manson 1991; Kelley 1986). But people crossed the barrancas on foot; Carl Lumholtz did, a century ago, following ancient trails (Lumholtz 1973,

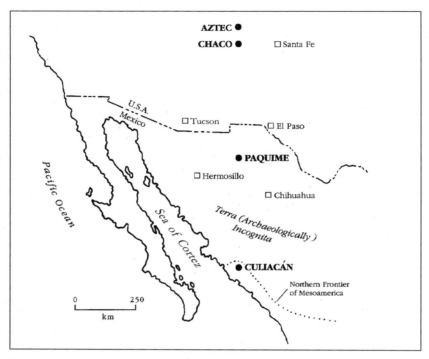

Figure B.1. The Southwest and West Mexico.

vol. I: 179; Riley and Manson 1991:140). His guides called the rough tracks across the mountains *"el camino de los antiguos"* (Lumholtz 1973:108); he (and his horse) rebelled against "the Mexican method of going uphill as straight as possible" and cut new trails "zigzag" (Lumholtz 1973:33).

Native routes were seldom suited for horses. Why should they be? Pueblo trails and Chacoan roads, whether symbolic or functional, were not bridle paths. We guard against the tyranny of ethnography; in matters of cross-country movement, we must also beware the pervasive authority of the AAA "Indian Country" map. Why should native routes prefigure design characteristics of colonial *caminos?* Native societies did not have *caballos y caretas.* Some ancient trails were perpetuated in later roads; many more were not. Wagon roads, developed for new transportation technologies, may not represent the most important ancient routes.

Kelley (1986) routes ancient trade from the Sinaloa coast across the mountains through the "Topia gate," a valley pass that makes sense for horse and foot travel (although the actual location of historically documented Topia is, apparently, unknown; Kelley 1986). Road-ready valleys undoubtedly contained trails, but cross-country routes were probably equally important. Riley and Kelley are quite correct to insist that we connect the Southwest with Mexico, but—following Sauer—they tend to overlook possibilities open to foot traffic, but closed to horsemen or carts. Among potential routes possible for foot traffic and impossible for horsemen, was the extension of the Chaco-Aztec-Paquime meridian across the sierras to Culiacán. The earliest historical accounts approach this matter from the south, from the Culiacán end.

When Nuno de Guzman led his armies into Sinaloa in 1530 (several years before Cabeza de Vaca), he was seeking the Seven Cities of Cibola. The Seven Cities were a medieval Spanish myth translated to the American Southwest, presumably on information gathered from Indians familiar with Chaco, Aztec, and Paquime—or, less likely, pueblos like those at Zuni. Guzman's goal were these fabulous cities, and he thought he knew where they were. "Guzman had this information from an Indian whose father traded into the back country, exchanging fine feathers for ornaments, by a forty days journey north, and one which involved passage of a wilderness" (Sauer 1932:9). Native guides led him from Guadalajara along the west coast route, pioneered by Guzman's rival Cortes, to the city of Culiacán. The current Culiacán is located about 24° 47' latitude, 107° 23' longitude, or approximately 55 km east of the Chaco-Aztec-Paquime meridian. Culiacán was relocated along river-side several times (Sauer 1932:8n). Culiacán Viejo, the prehistoric and historic site (Kelley 1945), was many kilometers downstream to the west, and much closer to the Chaco meridian.

Culiacán Viejo was the last great city on the precolonial west coast, and it became the jumping-off point for early Spanish explorations into the trackless north. Prehistorically, it was the center of the Aztatlan tradition (Sauer and Brand 1932), an archaeological entity with Mesoamerican pottery but lacking, apparently, ballcourts and pyramids (Kelly 1945). "Although Culiacán survived into the Spanish Contact period, it reached its height and thereafter declined after A.D. 1450. Culiacán was entirely Postclassic," according to J. Charles Kelley (personal communication 1997). The archaeological nature of Aztatlan is a matter of debate (Carpenter 1996, 1997), but we can be reasonably certain that Culiacán itself was a big deal. Even in decline, the Culiacán of Guzman's time was a city—"of urban extensiveness" (Sauer and Brand 1932:29), "a ceremonial-administrative-market center of urban proportions" (Gerhard 1993:257). It was a political capital, whose "king" ruled large territory, extending as far south as Chametla (Gerhard 1993:257, citing colonial accounts, with some reservations).

Guzman reached Culiacán over routes later identified by Sauer (1932) as the coastal "Road to Cibola"—a putatively ancient route that prefigured modern Highway 15. Sauer was genuinely distressed when Guzman (a thug, but no fool) ignored the future Highway 15 and, at Culiacán, turned north directly into the mountains.

It is curious, therefore, that, being at Culiacán, about halfway on the direct road to Cibola, Guzman should have altered the direction of his march, away from the supposed objective. At Culiacán he began a series of attempts to scale the mountain barrier (Sauer 1932:9)

The conquistador had native guides who claimed to know the way to the Seven Cities. From Culiacán, those guides did not follow the coast, but instead pushed directly north, into the Sierra Madre Occidental. The first and most sustained of these attempts was up the Humaya Valley, which runs north-south above Culiacán. Two divisions of Guzman's army marched north for three weeks before "being stopped by the sierra rampart" at the present Chihuahua line (Sauer 1932:9). "This route might have led to Cibola, but it was not possible for a party on horse" (Sauer 1932:9). While several subsequent attempts were made to scale the mountains to the north, only a single party was sent up the coast, to bring unconquered villages and towns into the new Spanish dominion. Guzman directed his assets to the north, through the mountains. Ultimately, he failed and returned to the *Mesa Central.*

Sauer is correct: a northern route straight over the mountains would have reached fabled Cibola—Paquime (or Zuni or whatever it might have been). The northern route was more "direct" but more difficult than the coast. Guzman presumably knew what he was doing when he left the coastal flats and turned north from Culiacán to reach the Seven Cities.

Paquime was only a century gone—maybe less—when Guzman marched to Culiacán. Its memory was fresh, certainly to Guzman's guide's father's generation (and, we may assume, to the rulers of Culiacán). Guzman's guide's father had travelled forty days through the wilderness to reach cities of great wealth. As an exercise, divide 630 km—the distance between Culiacán and Paquime—by 40 days: about 16 km a day. Wilcox (e.g., 1996a) has codified 35 km/day (22 miles/day) as the preferred pace of prehistory, but the miles between Culiacán and Paquime were not a cake-walk. They crossed canyons and mountains, and the Barranca del Cobre. That kind of terrain, although passable on foot, slows one down. Trekking over the Sierra Madre north from Culiacán or south from Paquime might well result in a reduced pace (and an error of 50-odd km from the straight and narrow!); forty days might be about right.

What should we make of all this? Is it yet another coincidence that the capital of the northeastern frontier of Mesoamerica lies practically due south of Chaco, Aztec, Paquime? I have difficulties dismissing *grosso modo* the alignment of Culiacán with Chaco, Aztec, and Paquime as pure coincidence. Like those three centers, Culiacán was the primate center of its region and heavily engaged in long-distance trade and all the related hanky-panky. The history of Guzman's campaign suggests that his native guides knew that great cities lay due north of Culiacán, and that a northern route over the mountains was the established line for communication. Culiacán was a going concern when the Spanish arrived; Paquime was a century gone; Aztec two and half centuries; and Chaco four. Was Culiacán the last hurrah? Or was it, in an earlier form, the source of Southwestern political geopolitics? Or is Culiacán another beautiful fact, killed by an ugly theory? Sing the benediction: More research is necessary.

References

Adams, E. Charles

1991   *The Origin and Development of the Pueblo Katsina Cult.* University of
         Arizona Press, Tucson.

Adler, Michael A.

1990   Communities of Soil and Stone: An Archaeological Investigation of
         Population Aggregation Among the Mesa Verde Anasazi, A.D. 900–1300.
         Ph.D. dissertation, University of Michigan, Ann Arbor.

Adler, Michael A., editor

1996   *The Prehistoric Pueblo World, A.D. 1150–1350.* University of Arizona
         Press, Tucson.

Akins, Nancy J.

1985   Prehistoric Faunal Utilization in Chaco Canyon Basketmaker III
         Through Pueblo III. In *Environment and Subsistence of Chaco Canyon,
         New Mexico*, edited by Frances Joan Mathien, pp. 305–445. Publications
         in Archaeology 18E, National Park Service, Albuquerque.

1986   *A Biocultural Approach to Human Burials from Chaco Canyon, New Mexico.*
         Reports of the Chaco Center 9. National Park Service, Santa Fe.

Akins, Nancy J. and John D. Schelberg

1984   Evidence for Organizational Complexity as Seen from the Mortuary
         Practices at Chaco Canyon. In *Recent Research on Chaco Prehistory*, edited
         by W. James Judge and John D. Schelberg, pp. 89–102. Reports of the
         Chaco Center 8. National Park Service, Albuquerque.

Anderson, David G.

1994   *The Savannah River Chiefdoms, Political Change in the Late Prehistoric
         Southwest.* University of Alabama Press, Tuscaloosa.

Anyon, Roger and Steven A. LeBlanc

1980   The Architectural Evolution of Mogollon-Mimbres Communal
         Structures. *The Kiva* 45(3):253–277.

1984   *The Galaz Ruin, A Prehistoric Mimbres Village in Southwestern New
         Mexico.* University of New Mexico Press, Albuquerque.

Anyon, Roger, T. J. Ferguson, Loretta Jackson, Lillie Lane, and Philip Vicenti

1997   Native American Oral Tradition and Archaeology: Issues of Structure,
         Relevance, and Respect. In *Native Americans and Archaeologists: Stepping
         Stones to Common Ground*, edited by Nina Swidler, Kurt E. Dongoske,
         Roger Anyon, and Alan S. Downer, pp. 77–87. AltaMira Press, Walnut
         Creek, California.

Ashmore, Wendy

1991   Site-Planning and Concepts of Directionality Among the Ancient Maya. *Latin American Antiquity* 2(3):199–226.

Aveni, Anthony F.

1977   Concepts of Positional Astronomy Employed in Ancient Mesoamerican Architecture. In *Native American Astronomy*, edited by Anthony F. Aveni, pp. 3–19. University of Texas Press, Austin.

Aveni, Anthony F., E. E. Calnek, and H. Hartung

1988   Myth, Environment, and the Orientation of the Templo Mayor of Tenochtitlan. *American Antiquity* 53(2):287–309.

Bandelier, A. F.

1892   *Final Report of Investigation Among Indians of the Southwestern United States, Carried on Mainly in the Years from 1880 to 1885, Part II.* Paper of the Archaeological Institute of America, American Series IV. Archaeological Institute of America, Cambridge.

Bernardini, Wesley

1996   Transitions in Social Organization: A Predictive Model from Southwestern Archaeology. *Journal of Anthropological Archaeology* 15:372–402.

Berry, Michael S.

1982   *Time, Space and Transition in Anasazi Prehistory.* University of Utah Press, Salt Lake City.

Blake, Michael, Steven A. LeBlanc, and Paul E. Minnis

1986   Changing Settlement and Population in the Mimbres Valley, SW New Mexico. *Journal of Field Archaeology* 13:449–464.

Blanton, Richard E.

1994   *Houses and Households: A Comparative Study.* Plenum Press, New York.

Boorstin, Daniel J.

1983   *The Discoverers.* Random House, New York.

Borson, Nancy, Frances Berdan, Edward Stark, Jack States, and Peter J. Wettstein

1998   Origins of an Anasazi Macaw Feather Artifact. *American Antiquity* 63(1):131–142.

Bradley, Bruce A.

1996   Pitchers to Mugs: Chacoan Revival at Sand Canyon Pueblo. *The Kiva* 61(3):241–255.

Bradley, Richard

1993   *Altering the Earth.* Monograph Series 8. Society of Antiquaries of Scotland, Edinburgh.

Bradley, Rona J.

1993   Marine Shell Exchange in Northwest Mexico and the Southwest. In *The American Southwest and Mesoamerica: Systems of Prehistoric Exchange*, edited by Jonathan E. Ericson and Timothy G. Baugh, pp. 121–152. Plenum Press, New York.

Brandt, Elizabeth A.

1994   Egalitarianism, Hierarchy, and Centralization in the Pueblos. In *The Ancient Southwestern Community*, edited by W.H. Wills and Robert D. Leonard, pp. 9–23.

Breternitz, Cory D., David E. Doyel, and Michael Marshall, editors

1982   *Bis sa'ani: A Late Bonito Phase Community on Escavada Wash, Northwest New Mexico.* Navajo Nation Papers in Anthropology 14. Navajo Nation Cultural Resources Management Program, Window Rock, Arizona.

Broadbent, Simon

1980   Simulating the Ley Hunter. *Journal of the Royal Statistical Society Series A* 143(2):109–140.

Brody, J. J.

1977   *Mimbres Painted Pottery.* University of New Mexico Press, Albuquerque.

Brumfiel, Elizabeth M. and Timothy K. Earle, editors

1997   *Specialization, Exchange, and Complex Societies.* Cambridge University Press, Cambridge.

Bunzel, Ruth L.

1932   Zuni Origin Myths. *Forty-Seventh Annual Report of the Bureau of American Ethnology, 1929–1930,* pp. 545–609. Government Printing Office, Washington.

Calvin, William H.

1997   Leapfrogging Gnomons: A Method for Surveying a Very Long North-South Without Modern Instruments. Website: *The Calvin Bookshelf* (3 Jan 1997); wever.u.washington.edu/~wcalvin/gnomon.htm.

Cameron, Catherine M.

1998   Coursed Adobe Architecture, Style, and Social Boundaries in the American Southwest. In *The Archaeology of Social Boundaries*, edited by Miriam T. Stark, pp. 183–207, Smithsonian Institution Press, Washington.

Cameron, Catherine M., William E. Davis, and Stephen H. Lekson

1997   *1996 Excavations at the Bluff Great House.* Department of Anthropology, University of Colorado, Boulder.

Carlson, Roy

1966   Twin Angles Pueblo. *American Antiquity* 31:676–682.

Carneiro, Robert L.

1981   The Chiefdom: Precursor of the State. In *The Transition to Statehood in the New World*, edited by Grant D. Jones and Robert R. Kautz, pp. 37–79. Cambridge University Press, Cambridge.

Carpenter, John P.

1996   Rethinking Mesomarican Meddling: External Influences and Indigenous Developments at Guasave, Sinaloa. Paper presented at the 61st Annual Meeting of the Society for American Archaeology, New Orleans.

1997   Passing Through the Netherworld: New Insights from the American Museum of Natural History's Sonora-Sinaloa Archaeological Project (1937–1940). In *Prehistory of the Borderlands*, edited by John Carpenter and Guadalupe Sanchez, pp. 113–127. Arizona State Museum Anthropological Series 186, Tucson.

Cassirer, Ernst

1944   *An Essay on Man: An Introduction to a Philosophy of Human Culture.* Yale University Press, New Haven.

Churchill, Melissa J., Kristin A. Kuckleman, and Mark D. Varien

1998   Public Architecture in the Mesa Verde Region A.D. 900 to 1300. Paper presented at the 63rd Annual Meeting, Society for American Archaeology, Seattle.

Clarke, Grahame

1986   *Symbols of Excellence: Precious Materials as Expressions of Status.* Cambridge University Press, Cambridge.

1992   *Space, Time, and Man.* Cambridge University Press, Cambridge.

Cobb, Charles R.

1993   Archaeological Approaches to the Political Economies of Nonstratified Societies. In *Archaeological Method and Theory* Vol. 5, edited by Michael B. Schiffer, pp. 43–100.

Connerton, Paul

1989   *How Societies Remember.* Cambridge University Press, Cambridge.

Cordell, Linda S.

1984   *Prehistory of the Southwest.* Academic Press, Orlando.

1994   *Ancient Pueblo Peoples.* St. Remy Press, Montreal.

1997   *Archaeology of the Southwest.* Academic Press, San Diego. Second edition, retitled, of *Prehistory of the Southwest.*

Cosgrove, H.S. and C.B. Cosgrove

1932   *The Swarts Ruin, A Typical Mimbres Site in Southwestern New Mexico.* Papers of the Peabody Museum of American Archaeology and Ethnology 15(1). Peabody Museum, Cambridge.

Creel, Darrell

1989   A Primary Cremation at the NAN Ranch Ruin, with Comparative
            Data on the Other Cremations in the Mimbres Area, New Mexico.
            Journal of Field Archaeology 16:309–329.

1997   Interpreting the End of the Mimbres Classic. In *Prehistory of the Border-
            lands: Recent Research in the Archaeology of Northern Mexico and the
            Southern Southwest,* edited by John Carpenter and Guadalupe Sanchez,
            pp. 25–31. Arizona State Museum Archaeological Series 186. University
            of Arizona Press, Tucson.

1998   Status Report on Excavations at the Old Town Site (LA 1113), Luna
            County, New Mexico, Summer 1997. Report submitted to the Bureau
            of Land Management, New Mexico State Office, Santa Fe.

Creel, Darrell and Charmion McKusick

1994   Prehistoric Macaws and Parrots in the Mimbres Area, New Mexico.
            American Antiquity 59(3):510–524.

Crosby, Alfred W.

1997   *The Measure of Reality: Quantification and Western Society, 1250–1600.*
            Oxford University Press, Oxford.

Crown, Patricia

1994   *Ceramics and Ideology: Salado Polychrome Pottery.* University of New
            Mexico Press, Albuquerque.

Crown, Patricia and W. James Judge

1991   *Chaco and Hohokam: Prehistoric Regional Systems in the American
            Southwest.* School of American Research Press, Santa Fe.

Cushing, Frank Hamilton

1896   Outlines of Zuni Creation Myths. In *Thirteenth Annual Report of the
            Bureau of American Ethnology, 1891–92,* pp. 321–447. Government
            Printing Office, Washington.

Dean, Jeffrey S.

1996   Demography, Environment, and Subsistence Stress. In *Evolving
            Complexity and Environmental Risk in the Prehistoric Southwest,* edited
            by Joseph A. Tainter and Bonnie Bagley Tainter, pp. 25–56. Santa Fe
            Institute Studies in the Sciences of Complexity Proceedings Vol. 24.
            Addison-Wesley Publishing Company, Reading.

Dean, Jeffrey S. and John C. Ravesloot

1993   The Chronology of Cultural Interaction in the Gran Chichimeca. In
            Culture and Contact: Charles C. Di Peso's Gran Chichimeca, edited by
            Anne I. Woosley and John C. Ravesloot, pp. 83–103. Amerind
            Foundation New World Studies Series 2. University of New Mexico
            Press, Albuquerque.

Deloria, Vine, Jr.

    1995   *Red Earth, White Lies: Native Americans and the Myth of Scientific Fact.*
                Scribner, New York.

Devereux, Paul

    1992   *Secrets of Ancient and Sacred Places.* Blandford, London.

Di Peso, Charles C.

    1974   *Casas Grandes: A Fallen Trading Center of the Grand Chichimeca Volumes
                1–3.* Amerind Foundation, Dragoon.

Di Peso, Charles C., John B. Rinaldo, and Gloria Fenner

    1974a   *Casas Grandes : A Fallen Trading Center of the Grand Chichimeca Volume
                4 (Dating and Architecture).* Amerind Foundation, Dragoon.

    1974b   *Casas Grandes : A Fallen Trading Center of the Grand Chichimeca Volume
                5 (Architecture).* Amerind Foundation, Dragoon.

    1974c   *Casas Grandes : A Fallen Trading Center of the Grand Chichimeca Volume
                6 (Ceramics and Shell).* Amerind Foundation, Dragoon.

    1974d   *Casas Grandes : A Fallen Trading Center of the Grand Chichimeca Volume
                7 (Stone and Metal).* Amerind Foundation, Dragoon.

    1974e   *Casas Grandes : A Fallen Trading Center of the Grand Chichimeca Volume
                8 (Bone-Economy-Burials).* Amerind Foundation, Dragoon.

Dongoske, Kurt E., Michael Yeatts, Roger Anyon, and T.J. Ferguson

    1997   Archaeological Cultures and Cultural Affiliation: Hopi and Zuni Per-spectives
                in the American Southwest. *American Antiquity* 62(4): 600–608.

Doolittle, William E.

    1990   *Canal Irrigation in Prehistoric Mexico.* University of Texas Press, Austin.

    1993   Canal Irrigation at Casas Grandes: A Technological and Developmental
                Assessment of Its Origins. In *Culture and Contact: Charles C. Di Peso's
                Gran Chichimeca*, edited by Anne I. Woosley and John C. Ravesloot,
                pp. 133–151. Amerind Foundation New World Studies Series 2.
                University of New Mexico Press, Albuquerque.

Douglas, Amy

    1990   *Prehistoric Exchange and Sociopolitical Development in the Plateau
                Southwest.* Garland Press, New York.

Douglas, John E.

    1995   Autonomy and Regional Systems in the Late Prehistoric Southwest.
                American Antiquity 60:240–257

    1992   Distant Sources, Local Contexts. *Journal of Anthropological Research*
                48(1):1–24.

Downs, Roger M. and David Stea

    1977   *Maps in Minds.* Harper and Row, New York.

Doxtater, Dennis

1984   Spatial Opposition in Non-Discursive Expression: Architecture as Ritual Process. *Canadian Journal of Anthropology* 4(1):1–17.

1991   Reflections of the Anasazi Cosmos. In *Social Space: Human Spatial Behavior in Dwellings and Settlements*, edited by Ole Gron, Ericka Engelstad, and Inge Lindblom, pp. 155–184. Odense University Press, Odense.

Doyel, David E.

1991   Hohokam Exchange and Interaction. In *Chaco and Hohokam*, edited by Patricia L. Crown and W. James Judge, pp. 225–252. School of American Research Press, Santa Fe.

Doyel, David E. and Stephen H. Lekson

1992   Regional Organization in the American Southwest. In *Anasazi Regional Organization and the Chaco System*, edited by David E. Doyel, pp. 15–21. Papers of the Maxwell Museum of Anthropology 5. Maxwell Museum of Anthropology, University of New Mexico, Albuquerque.

Doyel, David E., Cory D. Breternitz, and Michael P. Marshall

1984   Chacoan Community Structure: Bis Sa'ani Pueblo and the Chaco Halo. In *Recent Research on Chaco Prehistory*, edited by W. James Judge and John D. Schelberg, pp. 37–54. Reports of the Chaco Center 8. National Park Service, Albuquerque.

Dozier, Edward P.

1970   *The Pueblo Indians of North America.* Holt, Rinehart and Winston, New York.

Drennan, Robert D.

1984   Long-distance Transport Costs in Prehispanic Mesoamerica. *American Anthropologist* 86:105–112.

Dutton, Bertha P.

1963   *Sun Father's Way: The Kiva Murals of Kuaua.* University of New Mexico Press, Albuquerque.

Earle, Timothy

1997   *How Chiefs Come to Power: The Political Economy in Prehistory.* Stanford University Press, Stanford.

Ebert, James I. and Robert K. Hitchcock

1980   Locational Modelling in the Analysis of the Prehistoric Roadway System At and Around Chaco Canyon, New Mexico. In *Cultural Resources Remote Sensing*, edited by T. R. Lyons and F. J. Mathien, pp. 157–172. Reports of the Chaco Center 1. National Park Service, Albuquerque.

Echo-Hawk, Roger C.

1993   Exploring Ancient Worlds. *SAA Bulletin* 11(4):5–6.

1997   Forging a New Ancient History for Native America. In *Native Americans and Archaeologists: Stepping Stones to Common Ground,* edited by Nina Swidler, Kurt E. Dongoske, Roger Anyon, and Alan S. Downer, pp. 88–102. AltaMira Press, Walnut Creek, California.

Eddy, Frank W.

1977   *Archaeological Investigations at Chimney Rock Mesa: 1970–1972.* Memoirs of the Colorado Archaeological Society 1. Boulder.

Eggan, Fred

1983   Comparative Social Organization. In *Handbook of North American Indians Volume 10: Southwest,* edited by Alphonse Ortiz, pp. 723–742. Smithsonian Institution Press, Washington.

Ellis, Florence H.

1967   Where Did the Pueblo People Come From? *El Palacio* 74(3):35–43.

Elson, Mark D.

1998   *Expanding the View of Hohokam Platform Mounds: An Ethnographic Perspective.* Anthropological Papers of the University of Arizona 63. University of Arizona Press, Tucson.

Evans, Roy H., R. Evelyn Ross, and Lyle Ross

1985   *Mimbres Indian Treasure.* The Lowell Press, Kansas City.

Feinman, Gary M.

1998   Scale and Social Organization: Perspectives on the Archaic State. In *Archaic States,* edited by Gary M. Feinman and Joyce Marcus, pp. 95–133. School of American Research Press, Santa Fe.

Feinman, Gary and Jill Neitzel

1984   Too Many Types: An Overview of Sedentary Prestate Societies in the Americas. In *Advances in Archaeological Theory and Method* 7, edited by Michael B. Schiffer, pp. 39–102. Academic Press, Orlando.

Ferdon, Edwin N., Jr.

1955   A Trial Survey of Mexican-Southwestern Architectural Parallels. *School of American Research Monograph 21.* Santa Fe.

Ferguson, T. J. and E. Richard Hart

1985   *A Zuni Atlas.* University of Oklahoma Press, Norman.

Ferguson, William M. and Arthur H. Rohn

1986   *Anasazi Ruins of the Southwest in Color.* University of New Mexico Press, Albuquerque.

Fernandez-Armesto, Felipe

1987   *Before Columbus: Exploration and Colonization from the Mediterranean to the Atlantic, 1229–1492.* University of Pennsylvania Press, Philadelphia.

Fish, Suzanne K. and Paul R. Fish

1994   Prehistoric Desert Farmers of the Southwest. In *Annual Review of Anthropology* 21:83–108.

Flannery, Kent V.

1998   The Ground Plans of Archaic States. In *Archaic States*, edited by Gary M. Feinman and Joyce Marcus, pp. 15–57. School of American Research Press, Santa Fe.

Fletcher, Roland

1995   *The Limits of Settlement Growth: A Theoretical Outline.* Cambridge University Press, Cambridge.

Fowler, Andrew P. and John R. Stein

1992   The Anasazi Great House in Space, Time, and Paradigm. In *Anasazi Regional Organization and the Chaco System*, edited by David E. Doyel, pp. 101–122. Papers of the Maxwell Museum of Anthropology 5. Maxwell Museum of Anthropology, University of New Mexico, Albuquerque.

Fowler, Andrew P., John R. Stein, and Roger Anyon

1987   *An Archaeological Reconnaissance of West-Central New Mexico: The Anasazi Monuments Project.* Office of Cultural Affairs, Santa Fe.

Frisbie, Theodore R.

1978   High Status Burials in the Greater Southwest: An Interpretive Synthesis. In *Across the Chichimec Sea*, edited by Carroll L. Riley and Basil C. Hedrick, pp. 202–227. Southern Illinois University Press, Carbondale.

Fritz, John M.

1978   Paleopsychology Today: Ideational Systems and Human Adaptation in Prehistory. In *Social Archaeology: Beyond Subsistence and Dating*, edited by Charles L. Redman et al., pp. 37–59. Academic Press, New York.

1987   Chaco Canyon and Vijayanagra: Proposing Spatial Meaning in Two Societies. In *Mirror and Metaphor: Material and Social Constructions of Reality*, edited by D. W. Ingersoll and G. Bronitsky, pp. 313–348. University Press of America, Lanham.

Fuller, Steven L.

1988   Cultural Resource Inventories for the Animas-La Plata Project: The Wheeler and Koshak Borrow Sources. *Four Corners Archaeological Project Report* 12. CASA, Cortez.

Gabriel, Kathryn

1991   *Roads to Center Place: A Cultural Atlas of Chaco Canyon and the Anasazi.* Johnson Books, Boulder.

Garcia-Mason, Velma

1979   Acoma Pueblo. In *Handbook of North American Indians Volume 9: Southwest*, edited by Alfonso Ortiz, pp. 450–466. Smithsonian Institution Press, Washington.

Gerhard, Peter

1993   *The North Frontier of New Spain.* Revised edition, University of Oklahoma Press, Norman.

Germick, Stephen

1985   *An Archaeological Reconnaissance Along the San Juan and Lower Mancos Rivers, Northwestern New Mexico.* Northern Arizona University Archaeological Reports 748. Flagstaff.

Gladwin, Harold Sterling

1957   *A History of the Ancient Southwest.* Bond Wheelright, Portland.

Goetzfridt, Nicholas J., compiler

1992   *Indigenous Navigation and Voyaging in the Pacific, A Reference Guide.* Greenwood Press, New York.

Green, Jesse, editor

1990   *Cushing at Zuni: The Correspondence and Journals of Frank Hamilton Cushing 1879–1884.* University of New Mexico Press, Albuquerque.

Greiser, Sally T. and James L. Moore

1995   The Case for Prehistoric Irrigation in the Northern Southwest. In *Soil, Water, Biology, and Belief in Prehistoric and Traditional Southwestern Agriculture*, edited by H. Wolcott Toll, pp. 189–195. New Mexico Archaeological Council Special Publication 2. Albuquerque.

Gumerman, George J., editor

1988   *The Anasazi in a Changing Environment.* Cambridge University Press, Cambridge.

Gumerman, George J. and Murray Gell-Mann, editors

1994   *Understanding Complexity in the Prehistoric Southwest.* Addison-Wesley Publishing Company, Reading.

Gumerman, George J. and Alan P. Olson

1968   Prehistory in the Puerco Valley, Eastern Arizona. *Plateau* 40(4):113–127.

Hammond, G.P. and Agapito Rey, editors

1929   *Journal, Expedition into New Mexico made by Antonio de Espejo, 1582–1583.* Quivira Society, Los Angeles.

Harbottle, Garman and Phil C. Weigand

1992   Turquoise in Pre-Columbian America. *Scientific American* 266(2):78–85.

Hargrave, Lyndon L.

1970   *Mexican Macaws, Comparative Osteology and Survey of Remains from the Southwest.* Anthropological Papers of the University of Arizona 20. University of Arizona Press, Tucson.

1979   A Macaw Feather Artifact from Southeastern Utah. *Southwestern Lore* 45(4):1–6.

Haury, Emil W.

1936   *The Mogollon Culture of Southwestern New Mexico.* Medallion Paper 20. Globe, Arizona.

1950   A Sequence of Great Kivas in the Forestdale Valley, Arizona. In *For the Dean,* edited by Erik K. Reed and Dale S. King: 29–39. Southwestern Monuments Association, Santa Fe.

1958   Evidence at Point of Pines for a Prehistoric Migration from Northern Arizona. In *Migrations in New World Culture History,* edited by Raymond H. Thompson. University of Arizona Bulletin 29(2) Social Science Bulletin 27:1–8.

1986   Thoughts After Sixty Years as a Southwestern Archaeologist. In *Emil W. Haury's Prehistory of the American Southwest,* edited by J. Jefferson Reid and David E. Doyel, pp. 435–464. University of Arizona Press, Tucson.

1988   Recent Thoughts on the Mogollon. *The Kiva* 53(2):195–196.

Hawthorn, Geoffrey

1991   *Plausible Worlds: Possibility and Understanding in History and the Social Sciences.* Cambridge University Press, Cambridge.

Hayes, Alden C.

1981   A Survey of Chaco Canyon Archaeology. In *Archaeological Surveys of Chaco Canyon, New Mexico,* edited by Alden C. Hayes, David M. Brugge, and W. James Judge, pp. 1–68. Publications in Archaeology 18A. National Park Service, Washington.

Hayes, Alden C. and Clifford C. Chappell

1962   A Copper Bell from Southwest Colorado. *Plateau* 35(2):53–56.

Hayes, Alden C., Jan Nathan Young, and A.H. Warren

1981   *Excavation of Mound 7, Gran Quivira National Monument, New Mexico.* Publications in Archaeology 16. National Park Service, Washington.

Hegmon, Michelle, Margaret C. Nelson, and Susan M. Ruth

1998   Abandonment and Reorganization in the Mimbres Region of the American Southwest. *American Anthropologist* 100(1):148–162.

Helms, Mary W.

1988   *Ulysses' Sail: An Ethnographic Odyssey of Power, Knowledge, and Geographical Distance.* Princeton University Press, Princeton.

1992   Long-Distance Contacts, Elite Aspirations, and the Age of Discovery in
            Cosmological Context. In *Resources, Power, and Interregional Interaction*,
            edited by Edward M. Schortman and Patricia A. Urban, pp. 157–174.
            Plenum Press, New York.

1993   *Craft and the Kingly Ideal: Art, Trade, and Power.* University of Texas
            Press, Austin.

Herr, Sarah Alice

1994   Great Kivas as Integrative Architecture in the Silver Creek Community,
            Arizona. M.A. Thesis, Department of Anthropology, University of
            Arizona, Tucson.

Herrington, Selma Laverne

1982   Water Control Systems of the Mimbres Classic Phase. In *Mogollon
            Archaeology: Proceedings of the 1980 Mogollon Conference*, edited by Patrick
            H. Beckett, pp. 75–90. Acoma Books, Ramona, California.

Hibben, Frank C.

1966   A Possible Pyramidal Structure and Other Mexican Influences at Pottery
            Mound, New Mexico. *American Antiquity* 31(4):522–529.

1975   *Kiva Art of the Anasazi at Pottery Mound.* KC Publications, Las Vegas.

Hieb, Louis A.

1979   Hopi World View. In *Handbook of North American Indians Volume 9:
            Southwest*, edited by Alfonso Ortiz, pp. 577–580. Smithsonian Institution
            Press, Washington.

Hirth, Kenneth G.

1996   Political Economy and Archaeology: Perspectives on Exchange and
            Production. *Journal of Archaeological Research* 4(3):203–239.

Hoebel, E. Adamson

1979   Zia Pueblo. In *Handbook of North American Indians Volume 9: Southwest*,
            edited by Alfonso Ortiz, pp. 407–417. Smithsonian Institution Press,
            Washington.

Hosler, Dorothy

1994   *The Sounds and Color of Power: The Sacred Metallurgical Technology of
            Ancient West Mexico.* MIT Press, Cambridge.

Hough, Walter

1907   *Antiquities of the Upper Gila and Salt River Valleys in Arizona and New
            Mexico.* Bulletin 35. Bureau of American Ethnology, Washington.

Howe, Sherman S.

1947   *My Story of the Aztec Ruins.* Times Hustler Press, Farmington.

Howse, Derek

1980   *Greenwich Time and the Discovery of Longitude.* Oxford University Press,
            Oxford.

Hudson, Dee T.

1972   Anasazi Measurement Systems at Chaco Canyon, New Mexico. *The Kiva* 38(1):27–42.

Hudson, L. B.

1978   A Quantitative Analysis of Prehistoric Exchange in the Southwestern United States. Ph.D. dissertation, Department of Anthropology, University of California, Los Angeles.

Hurst, Winston

1998   Chaco Outlier or Wannabe? Comments and Observations on a Provincial Chacoesque Great House at Edge of the Cedars Ruin, Utah. Paper presented at the 63rd Annual Meeting of the Society for American Archaeology, Seattle.

Irwin, Geoffrey

1992   *The Prehistoric Exploration and Colonisation of the Pacific.* Cambridge University Press, Cambridge.

Irwin-Williams, Cynthia, editor

1972   *The Structure of Chacoan Society in the Northern Southwest, Investigations at the Salmon Site—1972.* Contributions in Anthropology 4(3). Eastern New Mexico University, Portales.

Jett, Stephen C. and Peter B. Moyle

1986   The Exotic Origins of Fishes Depicted on Prehistoric Mimbres Pottery from New Mexico. *American Antiquity* 51(4):688–720.

Johnson, Gregory A.

1978   Information Sources and the Development of Decision-Making Organizations. In *Social Archaeology*, edited by C. L. Redman, J. Berman, E. V. Curtin, W. T. Langhorne, Jr., N. M. Versaggi, and J. C. Wanser, pp. 87–112. Academic Press, New York.

1989   Dynamics of Southwest Prehistory: Far Outside—Looking In. In *Dynamics of Southwest Prehistory*, edited by Linda S. Cordell and George J. Gumerman, pp. 371–389. Smithsonian Institution Press, Washington.

Jorgensen, Joseph G.

1980   *Western Indians: Comparative Environments, Languages, and Cultures of 172 Western American Indian Tribes.* W. H. Freeman and Company, San Francisco.

1983   Comparative Traditional Economies and Adaptations. In *Handbook of North American Indians Volume 10: Southwest*, edited by Alfonso Ortiz pp. 684–710. Smithsonian Institution, Washington.

Judd, Neil M.

1954   *The Material Culture of Pueblo Bonito.* Smithsonian Miscellaneous Collections 124 (whole volume). Smithsonian Institution, Washington.

1959   *Pueblo Del Arroyo, Chaco Canyon, New Mexico.* Smithsonian
                Miscellaneous Collections 138(1). Smithsonian Institution, Washington.

1964   *The Architecture of Pueblo Bonito.* Smithsonian Miscellaneous Collections
                147(1). Smithsonian Institution, Washington.

Judge, W. James

1979   The Development of a Complex Cultural Ecosystem in the Chaco Basin,
                New Mexico. In *Proceedings of the First Conference on Scientific Research
                in the National Parks, Part 3,* edited by R. M. Linn, pp. 901–906. National
                Park Service, Washington.

1984   New Light on Chaco Canyon. In *New Light on Chaco Canyon,* edited
                by David Grant Noble, pp. 1–12. School of American Research Press,
                Santa Fe.

1989   Chaco Canyon—San Juan Basin. In *Dynamics of Southwest Prehistory,*
                edited by Linda S. Cordell and George J. Gumerman, pp. 209–261.
                Smithsonian Institution Press, Washington.

1991   Chaco: Current Views of Prehistory and the Regional System. In *Chaco
                and Hohokam,* edited by Patricia L. Crown and W. James Judge, pp. 11–
                30. School of American Research Press, Santa Fe.

1993   Resource Distribution and the Chaco Phenomenon. In *The Chimney Rock
                Archaeological Symposium,* edited J. McKim Malville and Gary Matlock, pp.
                35–36. General Technical Report RM–227. USDA Forest Service, Rocky
                Mountain Forest and Range Experiment Station, Fort Collins.

Judge, W. James and J. McKim Malville

1993   The Uses of Esoteric Astronomical Knowledge in the Chaco Regional
                System. Paper presented at the Fourth Oxford International Conference
                on Archaeoastronomy, Stara Zagora.

Judge, W. James, William B. Gillespie, Stephen H. Lekson, and H. Wollcott Toll

1981   Tenth-Century Developments in Chaco Canyon. In *Collected Papers in
                Honor of Erik Kellerman Reed,* edited by Albert H. Schroeder. Papers of
                the Archaeological Society of New Mexico 6:65–98. Archaeological
                Society of New Mexico, Albuquerque.

Kauffman, Stuart A.

1993   *The Origins of Order: Self-Organization and Selection in Evolution.* Oxford
                University Press, Oxford.

1995   *At Home in the Universe.* Oxford University Press, New York.

Keivit, Karen A.

1997   Seeing and Reading the Architecture of the Chaco Anasazi at A.D. 1100.
                Ph.D. dissertation, University of Colorado, Boulder.

Kelley, J. Charles

1986   The Mobile Merchants of Molino. In *Ripples in the Chichimec Sea: New
                Considerations of Southwestern-Mesoamerican Interactions,* edited by

Frances Joan Mathien and Randall H. McGuire, pp. 81–104. Southern Illinois University Press, Carbondale.

1993   Zenith Passage: The View From Chalchihuites. In *Culture and Contact: Charles C. Di Peso's Gran Chichimeca*, edited by Anne I. Woosley and John C. Ravesloot, pp. 227–250. Amerind Foundation New World Studies Series 2. University of New Mexico Press, Albuquerque.

1995   Trade Goods, Traders, and Status in Northwestern Greater Mesoamerica. In *The Gran Chichimeca: Essays on the Archaeology and Ethnohistory of Northern Mesoamerica*, edited by Jonathan E. Reyman, pp. 102–145. Avebury, Aldershot.

Kelley, Jane H. and Maria Elisa Villalpando C.

1996   An Overview of the Mexican Northwest. In *Interpreting Southwestern Diversity: Underlying Principles and Overarching Patterns*, edited by Paul R. Fish and J. Jefferson Reid, pp. 69–77. Anthropological Research Papers 48. Arizona State University, Tempe.

Kelley, Klara Bonsack and Harris Francis

1994   *Navajo Sacred Places.* Indiana University Press, Bloomington.

Kelly, Isabel

1945   Excavations at Culiacán, Sinaloa. *Ibero-Americana* 25. University of California Press, Berkeley.

Kendall, David G. and Wilfrid S. Kendall

1980   Alignments in Two-Dimensional Random Sets of Points. *Advances in Applied Probability* 12(2):380–424.

Kincaid, Chris, editor

1983   *Chaco Roads Project Phase I: A Reappraisal of Prehistoric Roads in the San Juan Basin.* Bureau of Land Management, Albuquerque.

King, David A.

1979   Kibla. *Encyclopedia of Islam* 5:82–88.

1995   The Orientation of Medieval Islamic Religious Architecture and Cities. *Journal for the History of Astronomy* 26:253–274.

Kintigh, Keith W.

1985   *Settlement, Subsistence and Society in Late Zuni Prehistory.* Anthropological Papers of the University of Arizona 44. University of Arizona Press, Tucson.

1996   The Cibola Region in the Post-Chacoan Era. In *The Prehistoric Pueblo World, A.D. 1150–1350*, edited by Michael A. Adler, pp. 131–144. University of Arizona Press, Tucson.

Kintigh, Keith W., Todd L. Howell, and Andrew I. Duff

1996   Post-Chacoan Social Integration at the Hinkson Site, New Mexico. *The Kiva* 61(3)257–274.

Kohler, Timothy A.

1993   News from the Northern American Southwest: Prehistory on the Edge of Chaos. *Journal of Archaeological Research* 1(4):267–321.

Kosse, Krisztina

1990   Group Size and Societal Complexity: Thresholds in the Long-Term Memory. *Journal of Anthropological Archaeology* 9:275–303.

1994   The Evolution of Large, Complex Groups: A Hypothesis. *Journal of Anthropological Archaeology* 13:35–50.

1996   Middle Range Societies from A Scalar Perspective. In *Interpreting Southwestern Diversity: Underlying Principles and Overarching Patterns*, edited by Paul R. Fish and J. Jefferson Reid, pp. 87–96. Anthropological Research Papers 48. Arizona State University, Tempe.

Krupp, E. C.

1997   *Skywatchers, Shamans, and Kings: Astronomy and the Archaeology of Power.* John Wiley and Sons, New York.

Kubler, George

1962   *The Shape of Time: Remarks on the History of Things.* Yale University Press, New Haven.

Kus, Susan M.

1983   The Social Representation of Space: Dimensioning the Cosmological and the Quotidian. In *Archaeological Hammers and Theories*, edited by James A. Moore and Arthur S. Keene, pp. 277–298. Academic Press, New York.

Ladd, Edmund J.

1979   Zuni Social and Political Organization. In *Handbook of North American Indians, Volume 9: Southwest*, edited by Alfonso Ortiz, pp. 482–491. Smithsonian Institution Press, Washington.

Laumbach, Karl W.

1992   *Reconnaissance Survey of the National Park Service Ojo Caliente Study Area, Socorro County, New Mexico.* Human Systems Research, Las Cruces.

Laumbach, Karl W. and James L. Wakeman

in press   Rebuilding an Ancient Pueblo: The Victorio Site in Regional Perspective. In *Proceedings of the Mogollon Conference*, edited by Stephanie Whittlesey.

LeBlanc, Steven A.

1983   *The Mimbres People, Ancient Pueblo Painters of the American Southwest.* Thames and Hudson, London.

1986a   Development of Archaeological Thought on the Mimbres Mogollon. In *Emil W. Haury's Prehistory of the American Southwest*, edited by J. Jefferson Reid and David E. Doyel, pp. 297–304. University of Arizona Press, Tucson.

1986b   Aspects of Southwestern Prehistory: A.D. 900–1400. In *Ripples in the Chichimec Sea, New Considerations of Southwestern-Mesoamerican Interactions*, edited by Frances Joan Mathien and Randall H. McGuire, pp. 105–134. Southern Illinois University Press, Carbondale.

1989   Cultural Dynamics in the Southern Mogollon Area. In *Dynamics of Southwest Prehistory*, edited by Linda S. Cordell and George J. Gumerman, pp. 179–207. Smithsonian Institution Press, Washington.

1997   Modeling Warfare in Southwestern Prehistory. *North American Archaeologist* 18(3):235–276.

Lekson, Stephen H.

1981   Cognitive Frameworks and Chacoan Architecture. *New Mexico Journal of Science* 21(1):27–36.

1983a   Dating the Hubbard Tri-Wall and Other Tri-Wall Structures. *Southwestern Lore* 49(4):15–23.

1983b   Chacoan Architecture in Continental Context. In *Proceedings of the Anasazi Symposium 1981*, edited by Jack E. Smith, pp. 183–194. Mesa Verde Museum Association, Mesa Verde.

1984a   Standing Architecture at Chaco Canyon and the Interpretation of Local and Regional Organization. In *Recent Research on Chaco Prehistory*, edited by W. James Judge and John D. Schelberg, pp. 55–73. Reports of the Chaco Center 8. National Park Service, Albuquerque.

1984b   Mimbres Settlement Size in Southwestern New Mexico. In *Recent Research in Mogollon Archaeology*, edited by Steadman Upham, Fred Plog, David G. Batcho, and Barbara E. Kauffman, pp. 68–74. Occasional Papers 10. University Museum, New Mexico State University, Las Cruces.

1985   Largest Settlement Size and Socio-political Complexity at Chaco Canyon, New Mexico. *Haliksa'i: UNM Contributions to Anthropology* 4:68–75. Department of Anthropology, University of New Mexico, Albuquerque.

1986a   *Great Pueblo Architecture of Chaco Canyon, New Mexico.* University of New Mexico Press.

1986b   The Mimbres Region. In *Mogollon Variability*, edited by Charlotte Benson and Steadman Upham, pp. 147–155. Occasional Papers 15. University Museum, New Mexico State University, Las Cruces.

1986c   Mimbres Riverine Adaptations. In *Mogollon Variability*, edited by Charlotte Benson and Steadman Upham, pp. 147–155. Occasional Papers 15. University Museum, New Mexico State University, Las Cruces.

1988a   The Mangas Phase in Mimbres Archaeology. *The Kiva* 53(2):129–145.

1988b   The Idea of Kivas in Anasazi Archaeology. *The Kiva* 53:213–234.

1988c   Socio-political Complexity at Chaco Canyon, New Mexico. Unpublished Ph.D. dissertation, University of New Mexico, Albuquerque.

1989a   Kivas? In *The Architecture of Social Integration in Prehistoric Pueblos*, edited by William D. Lipe and Michelle Hegmon. Occasional Papers of the Crow Canyon Archaeological Center 1. Crow Canyon Archaeological Center, Cortez.

1989b   Sedentism and Aggregation in Anasazi Archaeology. In *The Sociopolitical Structure of Prehistoric Southwestern Societies*, edited by Steadman Upham, Kent G. Lightfoot, and Roberta A. Jewett, pp. 333–340. Westview Press, Boulder.

1989c   The Community in Anasazi Archaeology. In *Households and Communities*, edited by Scott MacEachern, David J.W. Archer, and Richard D. Garvin, pp. 181–183. The Archaeological Association of the University of Calgary, Calgary.

1989d   Regional Systematics in the Later Prehistory of Southern New Mexico. In *Fourth Jornada Conference: Collected Papers*, edited by Meli Duran and Karl W. Laumbach, pp. 1–37. Human Systems Research, Las Cruces.

1990a   The Great Pueblo Period in Southwestern Archaeology. In *Pueblo Style and Regional Architecture*, edited by Nicolas C. Markovich, Wolfgang F. E. Preiser, and Fred G. Sturm, pp. 64–77. Van Nostrand Reinhold, New York.

1990b   Cross-cultural Perspectives on the Community. In *Vernacular Architecture: Paradigms of Environmental Response*, edited by Mete Turan, pp.122–145. Avebury, Aldershot.

1990c   *Mimbres Archaeology of the Upper Gila, New Mexico.* Anthropological Papers of the University of Arizona 33. University of Arizona Press, Tucson.

1991   Settlement Pattern and the Chaco Region. In *Chaco and Hohokam*, edited by Patricia L. Crown and W. James Judge, pp. 31–55. School of American Research Press, Santa Fe.

1992a   Mimbres Art and Archaeology. In *Archaeology, Art, and Anthropology: Papers in Honor of J. J. Brody*, edited by Meliha Duran and David T. Kirkpatrick, pp. 111–122. Archaeological Society of New Mexico, Albuquerque.

1992b   *Archaeological Overview of Southwestern New Mexico.* Human System Research, Las Cruces.

1992c   The Surface Archaeology of Southwestern New Mexico. *The Artifact* 30(3):1–36.

1992d   Para-Salado, *Perro Salado*, or Salado Peril? In *Proceedings of the Second Salado Conference*, edited by Richard C. Lange and Stephen Germick, pp. 334–336. Arizona Archaeological Society, Phoenix.

1993   Chaco, Mimbres, and Hohokam: The 11th and 12th Centuries in the American Southwest. *Expedition* 35(1):44–52.

1994   Chaco, Cahokia, and Complexity. Paper presented at the 59th Annual Meeting of the Society for American Archaeology, Anaheim.

1996a   Scale and Process in the American Southwest. In *Interpreting Southwestern Diversity: Underlying Principles and Overarching Patterns*, edited by Paul R. Fish and J. Jefferson Reid, pp. 81–86. Anthropological Research Papers 48. Arizona State University, Tempe.

1996b   Southwestern New Mexico and Southeastern Arizona. In *The Prehistoric Pueblo World*, A.D. *1150–1350*, edited by Michael A. Adler, pp. 170–176. University of Arizona Press, Tucson.

1996c   The Pueblo Southwest After A.D. 1150. In *Interpreting Southwestern Diversity: Underlying Principles and Overarching Patterns*, edited by Paul R. Fish and J. Jefferson Reid, pp. 41–44. Anthropological Research Papers 48, Arizona State University, Tempe.

in press a Unit Pueblos and the Mimbres Problem. In *Papers in Honor of Patrick Beckett*, edited by David Kirkpatrick and Meliha Duran, Archaeological Society of New Mexico.

in press b Great Towns in the American Southwest. In *Great Towns and Polities, in the American Southwest*, edited by Jill Neitzel. University of New Mexico Press, Albuquerque.

in press c Salado in Chihuahua. In *The Salado Culture of Southern Arizona*, edited by Jeffrey S. Dean. University of New Mexico Press, Albuquerque.

in press d Southeastern Arizona from Southwestern New Mexico. In *The Land Between*, edited by Henry Wallace. University of New Mexico Press, Albuquerque.

in press e Was Casas a Pueblo? In *Casas Grandes*, edited by Curtis Schaafsma and Carroll Riley. University of Utah Press, Odgen.

Lekson, Stephen H. and Catherine M. Cameron

1995   The Abandonment of Chaco Canyon, the Mesa Verde Migrations, and the Reorganization of the Pueblo World. *Journal of Anthropological Archaeology* 14:184–202.

Lekson, Stephen H., Linda Cordell, and George J. Gumerman

1994   Approaches to Understanding Southwestern Prehistory. In *Understanding Complexity in the Prehistoric Southwest*, edited by George J. Gumerman and Murray Gell-Mann, pp. 15–24. Addison-Wesley Publishing Company, Reading.

Lekson, Stephen H., John R. Stein, Thomas Windes, and W. James Judge

1988   The Chaco Canyon Community. *Scientific American* 259(1):100–109.

Lewin, Roger

1992   *Complexity: Life at the Edge of Chaos*. Macmillan Publishing Company, New York.

Lewis, David

1994   *We, The Navigators: The Ancient Art of Landfinding in the Pacific*. 2d ed. University of Hawaii Press, Honolulu.

Lightfoot, Kent G.

1979   Food Redistribution Among Prehistoric Pueblo Groups. *The Kiva* 44(4):319–339.

Lister, Florence C.

1993   *In the Shadow of the Rocks: Archaeology of the Chimney Rock District in Southern Colorado.* University Press of Colorado, Niwot.

Lister, Robert C.

1958   *Archaeological Excavations in the Northern Sierra Madre Occidental, Chihuahua and Sonora, Mexico.* University of Colorado Studies, Series in Anthropology 7. University of Colorado Press, Boulder.

1978   Mesoamerican Influence at Chaco Canyon, New Mexico. In *Across the Chichimec Sea: Papers in Honor of J. Charles Kelley,* edited by Carroll L. Riley and Basil C. Hedrick, pp. 233–241. Southern Illinois University Press, Carbondale.

Lister, Robert C. and Florence C. Lister

1987   *Aztec Ruins on the Animas.* University of New Mexico Press, Albuquerque.

Love, Marian F.

1975   A Survey of the Distribution of T-Shaped Doorways in the Greater Southwest. In *Collected Papers in Honor of Florence Hawley Ellis,* edited by Theodore R. Frisbie, pp. 296–311. Papers of the Archaeological Society of New Mexico 2. Santa Fe.

Lumholtz, Carl

1973   *Unknown Mexico.* Rio Grande Press, Glorieta. [reprint of 1902 edition]

Malotki, Ekkehart and Michael Lomatuway'ma

1987   *Earth Fire: A Hopi Legend of the Sunset Crater Eruption.* Northland Press, Flagstaff.

Malville, J. McKim and W. James Judge

1993   The Uses of Esoteric Astronomical Knowledge in the Chaco Regional System. Paper presented at the Fourth Oxford International Conference on Archaeoastronomy, Stara Zagora.

Malville, J. McKim and Nancy J. Malville

1995   Pilgrimage and Astronomy at Chaco Canyon, New Mexico. Paper presented at the National Seminar on Pilgrimage, Tourism, and Conservation of Cultural Heritage, Allahabad.

Mark, David M. and Andrew U. Frank

1991   *Cognitive and Linguistic Aspects of Geographic Space.* Kluwer Academic Publishers, Dordrecht.

Marshall, Michael P.

1997   The Chacoan Roads—A Cosmological Interpretation. In *Anasazi*

Architecture and American Design, edited by Baker H. Morrow and V.B. Price, pp. 62–74. University of New Mexico Press, Albuquerque.

Marshall, Michael P., John R. Stein, Richard W. Loose, and Judith E. Novotny

1979   *Anasazi Communities of the San Juan Basin.* Historic Preservation Bureau, Santa Fe.

Mathien, Frances Joan

1983   The Mobile Trader and the Chacoan Anasazi. In *Proceedings of the Anasazi Symposium 1981*, edited by Jack E. Smith, pp. 197–206. Mesa Verde Museum Association, Mesa Verde.

1986   External Contact and the Chaco Anasazi. In *Ripples in the Chichimec Sea: New Considerations of Southwestern-Mesoamerican Interactions*, edited by Frances Joan Mathien and Randall H. McGuire, pp. 220–242. Southern Illinois University Press, Carbondale.

1993   Exchange Systems and Social Stratification Among the Chaco Anasazi. In *The American Southwest and Mesoamerica: Systems of Prehistoric Exchange*, edited by Jonathan E. Ericson and Timothy G. Baugh, pp. 27–63. Plenum Press, New York.

McCluney, Eugene B.

1962   *Clanton Draw and Box Canyon.* Monograph 26. School of American Research, Santa Fe.

1968   A Mimbres Shrine at the West Baker Site. *Archaeology* 21(3):196–205.

n.d.   The Excavation at the Joyce Well Site, Hidaldo County, New Mexico. Ms. on file, School of American Research, Santa Fe.

McGlade, James

1995   Archaeology and the Ecodynamics of Human-Modified Landscapes. *Antiquity* 69(262):113–132.

McGuire, Randall H.

1980   The Mesoamerican Connection in the Southwest. *The Kiva* 46(1–2):3–38.

1983   Breaking Down Cultural Complexity: Inequality and Heterogeneity. In *Advances in Archaeological Theory and Method* 6, edited by Michael B. Schiffer, pp. 91–142. Academic Press, Orlando.

1989   The Greater Southwest as a Periphery of Mesoamerica. In *Center and Periphery, Comparative Studies in Archaeology*, edited by Timothy C. Champion, pp. 40–66. Unwin Hyman, London.

1993a   Charles Di Peso and the Mesoamerican Connection. In *Culture and Contact, Charles C. Di Peso's Gran Chichimeca*, edited by Anne I. Woosley and John C. Ravesloot, pp. 23–38. University of New Mexico Press, Albuquerque.

1993b   The Structure and Organization of Hohokam Exchange. In *The American Southwest and Mesoamerica: Systems of Prehistoric Exchange*, edited by Jonathan E. Ericson and Timothy G. Baugh, pp. 95–119. Plenum Press, New York.

McKenna, Peter J.

1998   The Cultural Landscape of Aztec Ruins, New Mexico. Paper presented at
            the 63rd Annual Meeting of the Society for American Archaeology, Seattle.

McKenna, Peter J. and James E. Bradford

1989   *The TJ Ruin, Gila Cliff Dwellings National Monument.* Southwest Cultural
            Resources Center Professional Paper 21. National Park Service, Santa Fe.

McKenna, Peter J. and H. Wolcott Toll

1992   Regional Patters of Great House Development Among the Totah
            Anasazi, New Mexico. In *Anasazi Regional Organization and the Chaco
            System,* edited by David E. Doyel, pp. 133–143. Papers of the Maxwell
            Museum of Anthropology 5. Maxwell Museum of Anthropology,
            University of New Mexico, Albuquerque.

McPherson, Robert

1992   *Sacred Land, Sacred View: Navajo Perceptions of the Four Corners Region.*
            Charles Redd Center for Western Studies. Bringham Young University
            Press, Provo.

Meyer, Jeffrey F.

1991   *The Dragons of Tiananmen: Beijing as a Sacred City.* University of South
            Carolina Press, Columbia.

Michell, J.

1974   *The Old Stones of Land's End.* Garnstone Press, London.

1977   Statistical Leyhunting. *The Ley Hunter* 74:11–12.

Mindeleff, Victor

1891   A Study of Pueblo Architecture: Tusayan and Cibola. *In Eighth Annual
            Report of the Bureau of Amercian Ethnology, 1886–87.* Government
            Printing Office, Washington.

Minnis, Paul E.

1984   Regional Interaction and Integration on the Northeastern Periphery of
            Casas Grandes. *American Archaeology* 4(3):181–193.

1985   *Social Adaptations to Food Stress: A Prehistoric Southwestern Example.*
            University of Chicago Press, Chicago.

1988   Four Examples of Specialized Production at Casas Grandes, North-
            western Chihuahua. *The Kiva* 53:181–193.

1989   The Casas Grandes Polity in the International Four Corners. In *The
            Sociopolitical Structure of Prehistoric Southwest Societies,* edited by
            Steadman Upham, Kent G. Lightfoot, and Roberta A. Jewett, pp. 269–
            305. Westview Press, Boulder.

Morgan, William N.

1994   *Ancient Architecture of the Southwest.* University of Texas Press, Austin.

Morris, Earl H.

1919   *The Aztec Ruin.* Anthropological Papers of the American Museum of Natural History 26(1). New York.

1921   *The House of the Great Kiva at the Aztec Ruin.* Anthropological Papers of the American Museum of Natural History 26(2). New York.

1924a   *Burials in the Aztec Ruin.* Anthropological Papers of the American Museum of Natural History 26(3). New York.

1924b   *The Aztec Ruin Annex.* Anthropological Papers of the American Museum of Natural History 26(4). New York.

1928   *Notes on Excavtions in the Aztec Ruin.* Anthropological Papers of the American Museum of Natural History 26(5). New York.

Motsinger, Thomas N.

1998   Hohokam Roads at Snaketown, Arizona. *Journal of Field Archaeology* 25:89–96.

Multhauf, Robert P.

1985   Early Instruments in the History of Surveying: Their Use and Their Invention. In *Plotter and Patterns of American Land Surveying: A Collection of Articles from the Archives of the American Congress on Surveying and Mapping,* edited by Roy Minnick, pp. 57–70. Landmark Enterprises, Rancho Cordova, Ca.

Nabokov, Peter

1996   Native Views of History. In *The Cambridge History of the Native Peoples of the Americas,* edited by Bruce G. Trigger and Wilcomb E. Washburn, pp. 1–59. Cambridge University Press, Cambridge.

Naranjo, Tessie

1995   Thoughts on Migration by Santa Clara Pueblo. *Journal of Anthropological Archaeology* 14(2):247–250.

Naylor, Thomas H.

1995   Casas Grandes Outlier Ballcourts in Northwest New Mexico. In *The Gran Chichimeca: Essays on the Archaeology and Ethnohistory of Northern Mesoamerica,* edited by Jonathan E. Reyman, pp. 224–239. Avebury, Aldershot.

Needham, Joseph

1959   *Science and Civilization in China.* Volume 3, *Mathematics and the Sciences of the Heavens and Earth.* Cambridge University Press, Cambridge.

Neitzel, Jill E.

1989a   Regional Exchange Networks in the American Southwest: A Comparative Analysis of Long-Distance Trade. In *The Sociopolitical Structure of Prehistoric Southwestern Societies,* edited by Steadman Upham, Kent G. Lightfoot, and Roberta A. Jewett, pp. 149–195. Westview Press, Boulder.

1989b   The Chacoan Regional System: Interperting the Evidence for Socio-
         political Complexity.   In *The Sociopolitical Structure of Prehistoric
         Southwestern Societies*, edited by Steadman Upham, Kent G. Lightfoot,
         and Roberta A. Jewett, pp. 509–556. Westview Press, Boulder.

Nelson, Ben A.

1995   Complexity, Hierarchy, and Scale: A Controlled Comparison Between
         Chaco Canyon, New Mexico and La Quemada, Zacatecas. *American
         Antiquity* 60(4):597–618.

1996   Southwestern Sedentism and the Spread of the Mesoamerican Tradition.
         Paper presented at the Southwest Symposium, Tempe.

Nelson, Ben A. and Roger Anyon

1996   Fallow Valleys: Asynchronous Occupations in Southwestern New
         Mexico. *The Kiva* 61(3):275–294.

Nelson, Richard S.

1981   The Role of a Pochteca System in Hohokam Exchange. Unpublished
         Ph.D. dissertation, Department of Anthropology, University of Arizona,
         Tucson.

1986   Poctecas and Prestige: Mesoamerican Artifacts in Hohokam Sites. In *Ripples
         in the Chichimec Sea: New Considerations of Southwestern-Mesoamerican
         Interactions*, edited by Frances Joan Mathien and Randall H. McGuire, pp.
         155–182. Southern Illinois University Press, Carbondale.

Nials, Fred, John Stein, and John Roney

1987   *Chacoan Roads in the Southern Periphery: Results of Phase II of the BLM
         Chaco Roads Project.* Cultural Resource Series 1. Bureau of Land
         Management, Albuquerque.

Ortiz, Alfonzo

1972   Ritual Drama and the Pueblo World View. In *New Perspectives on the
         Pueblos,* edited by Alfonso Ortiz, pp. 135-161. University of New Mexico
         Press, Albuquerque.

Parsons, Elsie Clews

1996   *Pueblo Indian Religion.* Bison Books, Boulder. Originally published by
         University of Chicago Press, 1939.

Pennick, Nigel

1979   *The Ancient Science of Geomancy.* Thames and Hudson, London.

Pennick, Nigel and Paul Devereux

1989   *Lines on the Landscape: Leys and Other Linear Enigmas.* Robert Hale, London.

Pepper, George H.

1920   *Pueblo Bonito.* Anthropological Papers of the American Museum of
         Natural History 27. New York.

Phillips, David A., Jr.

1989   Prehistory of Chihuahua and Sonora, Mexico. *Journal of World Prehistory*
            3(4):373–401.

Pippin, Lonnie C.

1987   *Prehistory and Paleoecology of Guadelupe Ruin, New Mexico.*
            University of Utah Anthropological Papers 107. University of Utah
            Press, Salt Lake City.

Plog, Stephen

1997   *Ancient Peoples of the American Southwest.* Thames and Hudson, London.

Powers, Robert P., William B. Gillespie, and Stephen H. Lekson

1983   *The Outlier Survey: A Regional View of Settlement in the San Juan Basin.*
            Reports of the Chaco Center 3. National Park Service, Albuquerque.

Rapoport, Amos

1969   *House Form and Culture.* Prentice-Hall, Englewood Cliffs.

1977   *Human Aspects of Urban Form.* Pergamon Press, Oxford.

1993   On the Nature of Capitals and Their Physical Expression. In *Capital
            Cities*, edited by John Taylor, Jean G. Lengelle, and Caroline Andrew,
            pp. 31–67. Carlton University Press, Ottawa.

Ravesloot, John C.

1988   *Mortuary Practices and Social Differentiation at Casas Grandes, Chihuahua,
            Mexico.* Anthropological Papers of the University of Arizona 49. Tucson.

Reyman, Jonathan E.

1985   A Reevaluation of Bi-wall and Tri-wall Structures in the Anasazi Area.
            In *Contributions to the Archaeology and Ethnohistory of Greater
            Mesoamerica*, edited by William J. Folan, pp. 293–333. Center for
            Archaeological Investigations, Southern Illinois University, Carbondale.

1987   Priests, Power, and Politics: Some Implications of Socioceremonial
            Control. In *Astronomy and Ceremony in the Prehistoric Southwest,* edited
            by John B. Carlson and W. James Judge, pp. 121–147. Papers of the
            Maxwell Museum of Anthropology 2. Maxwell Museum of Anthro-
            pology, University of New Mexico, Albuquerque.

Richert, Roland

1964   *Excavations of a Portion of the East Ruin, Aztec Ruin National Monument,
            New Mexico.* Southwestern Monuments Association Technical Series 4.
            Globe, Arizona.

Riley, Carroll L.

1976   *Sixteenth Century Trade in the Greater Southwest.* Mesoamerican Studies
            10, Research Records of the University Museum, Southern Illinois
            University, Carbondale.

Riley, Carroll and Joni L. Manson

1991   The Sonoran Connection: Road and Trail Networks in the Protohistoric
            Period. In *Ancient Road Networks and Settlement Hierarchies in the New
            World*, edited by Charles D. Trombold, pp. 132–144. Cambridge
            University Press, Cambridge.

Roberts, David

1996   The Old Ones of the Southwest. *National Geographic* 189(4):86–109.

Robinson, Arthur H. and Barbara Bartz Petchenik

1976   *The Nature of Maps, Essays Toward Understanding Maps and Mapping.*
            University of Chicago Press, Chicago.

Rodseth, Lars

1998   Distributive Models of Culture. *American Anthropologist* 100(1):55–69.

Rohn, Arthur H.

1983   Budding Urban Settlements in the Northern San Juan. In *Proceedings of
            the Anasazi Symposium 1981*, edited by Jack E. Smith, pp. 175–180. Mesa
            Verde Museum Association, Mesa Verde.

1996   Anasazi Culture at the Threshold of Complexity. In *Debating Complexity*,
            edited by Daniel A. Meyer, Peter C. Dawson, and Donald T. Hanna, pp. 1–
            9. The Archaeological Association of the University of Calgary, Calgary.

Roney, John R.

1992   Prehistoric Roads and Regional Integration in the Chacoan System. In *Anasazi
            Regional Organization and the Chaco System*, edited by David E. Doyel,
            pp. 123–131. Papers of the Maxwell Museum of Anthropology 5. Maxwell
            Museum of Anthropology, University of New Mexico, Albuquerque.

1995   Mesa Verdean Manifestations South of the San Juan River. *Journal of
            Anthropological Archaeology* 14(2):170–183.

1996   The Pubelo III Period in the Eastern San Juan Basin and the Acoma-
            Laguna Areas. In *The Prehistoric Pueblo World, A.D. 1150–1350*, edited
            by Michael A. Adler, pp. 145–169. University of Arizona Press, Tucson.

Ruppe, Reynold J., Jr.

1953   The Acoma Culture Province. Ph.D. dissertation, Harvard University,
            Cambridge.

Saitta, Dean J.

1997   Power, Labor, and the Dynamics of Change in Chacoan Political
            Economy. *American Antiquity* 62(1):7–26.

Sando, Joe S.

1992   *Pueblo Nations: Eight Centuries of Pueblo Indian History.* Clear Light
            Publishers, Santa Fe.

Sauer, Carl

1932   *The Road to Cibola.* Ibero-Americana 3. University of California Press, Berkeley.

Sauer, Carl and Donald Brand

1932   *Aztatlan: Prehistoric Mexican Frontier on the Pacific Coast.* Ibero-Americana 1. University of California Press, Berkeley.

Schaafsma, Curtis F.

1979   The "El Paso Phase" and its Relationship to the "Casas Grandes Phenomenon." In *Jornada Mogollon Archaeology,* edited by Patrick H. Beckett and Regge N. Wiseman, pp. 383–388. New Mexico State University, Las Cruces.

Schaafsma, Polly, editor

1994   *Kachinas in the Pueblo World.* University of New Mexico Press, Albuqueruqe.

Schelberg, John D.

1984   Analogy, Complexity, and Regionally-Based Perspectives. In *Recent Research on Chaco Prehistory,* edited by W. James Judge and John D. Schelberg, pp. 5–21. Reports of the Chaco Center 8. National Park Service, Albuquerque.

1992   Hierarchical Organization as a Short-term Buffering Strategy in Chaco Canyon. In *Anasazi Regional Organization and Chaco System,* edited by David E. Doyel, pp. 59–74. Papers of the Maxwell Museum of Anthropology 5. Maxwell Museum of Anthropology, University of New Mexico, Albuquerque.

Schmidt, Robert H., Jr. and Rex E. Gerald

1988   The Distribution of Conservation-Type Water-Control Systems in the Semi-Arid Northern Sierra Madre Occidental. *The Kiva* 53:165–179.

Sebastian, Lynne

1991   Sociopolitical Complexity and the Chaco System. In *Chaco and Hohokam: Prehistoric Regional Systems in the American Southwest,* edited by Patricia L. Crown and W. James Judge, pp. 109–134. School of American Research Press, Santa Fe.

1992   *The Chaco Anasazi: Sociopolitical Evolution in the Prehistoric Southwest.* Cambridge University Press, Cambridge.

Shafer, Harry J.

1995   Architecture and Symbolism in Transitional Pueblo Development in the Mimbres Valley, SW New Mexico. *Journal of Field Archaeology* 22(1):23–47.

Shafer, Harry J. and Anna J. Judkins

1996   Archaeology at the NAN Ruin, 1996 Season. *The Artifact* 34(3–4):1–62.

1997   *Archaeology at the NAN Ranch Ruin, 1996 Season.* Special Report 11,

Anthropology Laboratory, Department of Anthropology, Texas A&M University, College Station.

Silko, Leslie Marmon

1995   Interior and Exterior Landscapes: The Pueblo Migration Stories. In *Landscape in America*, edited by George F. Thompson, pp. 155–169. University of Texas Press, Austin.

Smith, Bardwell and Holly Baker Reynolds, editors

1987   *The City as a Sacred Center.* Brill, Leiden.

Smith, Watson

1952   *Kiva Mural Decoration at Awatovi and Kawaika-a.* Papers of the Peabody Museum of American Archaeology and Ethnology, Harvard University 37. Peabody Museum, Cambridge.

Snygg, John and Tom Windes

1998   Long, Wide Roads and Great Kiva Roofs. *The Kiva* 64(1):7–25.

Sobel, Dava

1995   *Longitude.* Walker and Company, New York.

Sofaer, Anna

1997   The Primary Architecture of the Chacoan Culture: A Cosmological Expression. In *Anasazi Architecture and American Design*, edited by Baker H. Morrow and V. B. Price, pp. 88–132. University of New Mexico Press, Albuquerque.

Sofaer, Anna P. and Rolf M. Sinclair

1987   Astronomical Markings a Three Sites on Fajada Butte. In *Astronomy and Ceremony in the Prehistoric Southwest*, edited by John B. Carlson and W. James Judge, pp. 43–70. Papers of the Maxwell Museum of Anthropology 2. Maxwell Museum of Anthropology, University of New Mexico, Albuquerque.

Sofaer, Anna, Michael P. Marshall, and Rolf M. Sinclair

1989   The Great North Road: A Cosmographic Expression of the Chaco Culture of New Mexico. In *World Archaeoastronomy: Selected Papers from the 2nd Oxford International Conference of Archaeoastronomy*, edited by Anthony F. Aveni. Cambridge University Press, Cambridge.

Stanislawski, Michael

1963   Wupatki Pueblo: A Study in Cultural Fusion and Change in Sinagua and Hopi Prehistory. Ph.D. dissertation, University of Arizona, Tucson.

Stein, John R.

1987   An Archaeological Reconnaissance in the Vicinity of Aztec Ruins National Monument, New Mexico. National Park Service, Santa Fe.

1989   The Chaco Roads. *El Palacio* 94(3):5–17.

Stein, John R. and Andrew Fowler

1996   Looking Beyond Chaco in the San Juan Basin and Its Peripheries. In *The Prehistoric Pueblo World*, A.D. 1150–1350, edited by Michael A. Adler, pp. 114–130. University of Arizona Press, Tucson.

Stein, John R. and Stephen H. Lekson

1992   Anasazi Ritual Landscapes. In *Anasazi Regional Organization and the Chaco System*, edited by David E. Doyel, pp. 87–100. Papers of the Maxwell Museum of Anthropology 5. Maxwell Museum of Anthropology, University of New Mexico, Albuquerque.

Stein, John R. and Peter J. McKenna

1988   *An Archaeological Reconnaissance of A Late Bonito Phase Occupation Near Aztec Ruins National Monument, New Mexico.* National Park Service, Santa Fe.

Stein, John R., Judith E. Suiter, and Dabney Ford

1997   High Noon at Old Bonito: Sun, Shadow, and Geometry in the Chaco Complex. In *Anasazi Architecture and American Design*, edited by Baker H. Morrow and V. B. Price, pp. 133–148. University of New Mexico Press, Albuquerque.

Stirling, Matthew W.

1942   Origin Myths of the Acoma and Other Records. *Bureau of American Ethnology Bulletin* 135. Washington.

Sullivan, Mary and J. McKim Malville

1993   Clay Sourcing at Chimney Rock: The Chemistry and Mineralogy of Feather Holders and Other Ceramics. In *The Chimney Rock Symposium*, edited by J. McKim Malville and Gary Matlock, pp. 29–34. USDA Forest Service Rocky Mountain Forest and Range Experiment Station General Technical Report RM–227. Fort Collins.

Swanson, Steven John

1997   Atalayas of Paquime: A GIS Analysis of Prehistoric Communication Features. M.A. Thesis, Anthropology, University of Oklahoma.

Tainter, Joseph A.

1988   *The Collapse of Complex Societies.* Cambridge University Press, Cambridge.

Tainter, Joseph A., and Bonnie Bagley Tainter

1996   Evolving Complexity and Environmental Risk in the Prehistoric Southwest. *Santa Fe Institute Studies in the Sciences of Complexity Proceedings* Vol. 24. Addison-Wesley Publishing Company, Reading.

Tainter, Joseph A., and Fred Plog

1994   Strong and Weak Patterning in Southwestern Prehistory: The Formation of Pueblo Archaeology. In *Themes in Southwestern Prehistory*, edited by George Gumerman, pp. 109–134. School of American Research Press, Santa Fe.

Taylor, John R.

    1982   *An Introduction to Error Analysis: The Study of Uncertainties in Physical Measurements.* Oxford University Press, Oxford.

Teague, Lynn S.

    1993   Prehistory and the Traditions of the O'Odham and Hopi. *The Kiva* 58(4):435–454.

Tedlock, Dennis, translator

    1972   *Finding the Center: Narrative Poetry of the Zuni Indians.* The Dial Press, New York.

Tilley, Christopher

    1994   *A Phenomenology of Landscape: Places, Paths, and Monuments.* Berg Publishers, Oxford.

Toll, H. Wolcott

    1990   A Reassessment of Chaco Cylinder Jars. In *Clues to the Past,* edited by Meliha S. Duran and David T. Kirkpatrick, pp. 273–305. Archaeological Society of New Mexico, Albuquerque.

    1991   Material Distributions and Exchange in the Chaco System. In *Chaco and Hohokam: Prehistoric Regional Systems in the American Southwest,* edited by Patricia L. Crown and W. James Judge, pp. 77–107. School of American Research Press, Santa Fe.

Tuan, Yi-Fu

    1990   *Topophilia: A Study of Environmental Perception, Attitudes, and Values.* Second Edition. Columbia University Press, New York.

Turner, Christy G., II

    1993   Southwest Indian Teeth. *National Geographic Research and Exploration* 9(1):32–53.

Tyler, Hamilton A.

    1991   *Pueblo Birds and Myths.* Northland Publishing, Flagstaff. Originally published by University of Oklahoma Press, 1979.

Upham, Steadman

    1982   *Polities and Power: An Economic and Political History of the Western Pueblos.* Academic Press, New York.

    1987   A Theoretical Consideration of Middle Range Societies. In *Chiefdoms in the Americas,* edited by Robert D. Drennan and Carlos A. Uribe, pp. 345–367. University Press of America, Lanham.

Van West, Carla

    1994   *Modeling Prehistoric Agricultural Productivity in Southwestern Colorado: A GIS Approach.* Reports of Investigations 67. Department of Anthropology, Washington State University, Pullman.

1996   Agricultural Potential and Carrying Capacity in Southwestern Colorado,
               A.D. 901 to 1300. In *The Prehistoric Pueblo World A.D. 1150-1350,* edited
               by Michael A. Adler, pp. 214–227. University of Arizona Press, Tucson.

Vansina, Jan

1985   *Oral Tradition as History.* University of Wisconsin Press, Madison.

1996   Agricultural Potential and Carrying Capacity in Southwestern Colorado,
               A.D. 901 to 1300. In *The Prehistoric Pueblo World A.D. 1150–1350,* edited
               by Michael A. Adler, pp. 214–227. The University of Arizona Press,
               Tucson.

Vargas, Victoria D.

1995   *Copper Bell Trade Patterns in the Prehispanic U.S. Southwest and Northwest
               Mexico.* Archaeological Series 187. Arizona State Museum, Tucson.

Varien, Mark D.

1997   New Perspectives on Settlement Patterns: Sedentism and Mobility in a
               Social Landscape. Ph.D. dissertation, Arizona State University, Tempe.

Varien, Mark D., William D. Lipe, Michael A. Adler, Ian M. Thompson, and
Bruce A. Bradley

1996   Southwestern Colorado and Southeastern Utah Settlement Patterns: A.D.
               1100 to 1300. In *The Prehistoric Pueblo World A.D. 1150–1350,* edited by
               Michael A. Adler, pp. 86–113. The University of Arizona Press, Tucson.

Vivian, Gordon R.

1959   *The Hubbard Site and Other Tri-wall Structures in New Mexico and Colorado.*
               Archaeological Research Series 5. National Park Service, Washington.

1960   *The Great Kivas of Chaco Canyon.* School of American Research Monographs
               22. School of American Research, Santa Fe.

Vivian, Gordon R. and Tom W. Mathews

1964   *Kin Kletso: A Pueblo III Community in Chaco Canyon, New Mexico.*
               Technical Series 6(1). Southwest Parks and Monuments Association.
               Globe, Arizona.

Vivian, Gordon R. and Paul Reiter

1960   *The Great Kivas of Chaco Canyon.* School of American Research Monographs
               22. School of American Research, Santa Fe.

Vivian, R. Gwinn

1990   *The Chacoan Prehistory of the San Juan Basin.* Academic Press, San Diego.

1991   Chacoan Subsistence. In *Chaco and Hohokam: Prehistoric Regional Sytems
               in the American Southwest,* edited by Patricia L. Crown and W. James
               Judge, pp. 57–75. School of American Research Press, Santa Fe.

1997a   Chacoan Roads: Morphology. *The Kiva* 63(1):7–34.

1997b   Chacoan Roads: Function. *The Kiva* 63(1):35–67.

Watts, Linda K.

1997   Zuni Family Ties and Household Group Values: A Revisionist Cultural Model of Zuni Social Organization. *Journal of Anthropological Research* 53:17–29

Weigand, Phil C. and Garman Harbottle

1993   The Role of Turquoises in the Ancient Mesoamerican Trade Structure. In *The American Southwest and Mesoamerica: Systems of Prehistoric Exchange*, edited by Jonathan E. Ericson and Timothy G. Baugh, pp. 159–177. Plenum Press, New York.

Whalen, Michael E. and Paul E. Minnis

1996a   Ball Courts and Political Centralization in the Casas Grandes Region. *American Antiquity* 61(4):732–746.

1996b   Studying Complexity in Northern Mexico: The Paquime Regional System. In *Debating Complexity*, edited by Daniel A. Meyer, Peter C. Dawson, and Donald T. Hanna, pp. 282–289. The Archaeological Association of the University of Calgary, Calgary.

1996c   The Context of Production in and Around Paquime, Chihuahua, Mexico. In *Interpreting Southwestern Diversity*, edited by Paul R. Fish and J. Jefferson Reid, pp. 173–182. Anthropological Research Papers 84. Arizona State University, Tempe.

Wheatley, Paul

1971   *The Pivot of the Four Corners: A Preliminary Inquiry into the Origins and Character of the Ancient Chinese City.* Aldine Publishing Company, Chicago.

White, Leslie A.

1932   The Acoma Indians. *47th Annual Report of the Bureau of American Ethnology for the Years 1929–1930*, pp. 17–192. Washington.

Whitecotton, Joseph W. and Richard A. Pailes

1986   New World Precolumbian World Systems. In *Ripples in the Chichimec Sea: New Considerations of Southwestern-Mesoamerican Interactions*, edited by Frances Joan Mathien and Randall H. McGuire, pp. 183–204. Southern Illinois University Press, Carbondale.

Whiteley, Peter M.

1988   *Deliberate Acts: Changing Hopi Culture Through the Oriabi Split.* University of Arizona Press, Tucson.

Wiget, Andrew O.

1982   Truth and the Hopi: An Historiographic Study of Documented Oral Tradition Concerning the Coming of the Spanish. *Ethnohistory* 29(3):181–199.

Wilcox, David R.

1993   The Evolution of the Chacoan Polity. In *The Chimney Rock Archaeological Symposium*, edited by J. McKim Malville and Gary Matlock, pp.

76–90. USDA Forest Service Rocky Mountain Forest and Range Experiment Station General Technical Report RM–227. Fort Collins.

1996a The Diversity of Regional and Macroregional Systems in the American Southwest. In *Debating Complexity*, edited by Daniel A. Meyer, Peter C. Dawson, and Donald T. Hanna, pp. 375–390. The Archaeological Association of the University of Calgary, Calgary.

1996b Pueblo III People and Polity in Relational Context. In *The Prehistoric Pueblo World A.D. 1150–1350*, edited by Michael A. Adler, pp. 241–254. The University of Arizona Press, Tucson.

in press a Macroregional Systems in the Prehistoric Southwest. In *Great Towns and Regional Polities in the American Southwest*, edited by Jill Neitzel. University of New Mexico Press, Albuquerque.

in press b The Wupatki Nexus: Chaco-Hohokam-Chumash Connectivity, A.D. 1150–1225. In *The Archaeology of Contact: Proceedings of the 25th Annual Chacmool Conference*, edited by Kurtis Lesick. Archaeological Association of the University of Calgary, Calgary.

Wilcox, David R., T. Randall McGuire, and Charles Sternberg

1981 *Snaketown Revisited.* Arizona State Museum Archaeological Series 155. Tucson.

Wilcox, David R. and Lynette O. Shenk

1977 *The Architecture of the Casa Grande and Its Interpretation.* Archaeological Series 115. Arizona State Museum, Tucson.

Wilcox, David R. and Phil C. Weigand

1993 Chacoan Capitals: Centers of Competing Polities. Paper presented at the 58th Annual Meeting of the Society for American Archaeology, St. Louis.

Wilshusen, Richard

1991 Early Villages in the American Southwest: Cross-cultural Perspectives. Ph.D. dissertation, University of Colorado, Boulder.

Wilson, Angela Cavender

1997 Power of the Spoken Word: Native Oral Traditions in American Indian History. In *Rethinking American Indian History*, edited by Donald L. Fixico, pp. 101–116. University of New Mexico Press, Albuquerque.

Windes, Thomas C.

1984 A New Look at Population in Chaco Canyon. In *Recent Research on Chaco Prehistory*, edited by W. James Judge and John D. Schelberg, pp. 75–87. Reports of the Chaco Center 8. National Park Service, Albuquerque.

1987a *Investigations at the Pueblo Alto Complex, Chaco Canyon, New Mexico, Vol I: Summary of Tests and Excavations at the Pueblo Alto Complex.* Publications in Archaeology 18F. National Park Service, Santa Fe.

1987b   *Investigations at the Pueblo Alto Complex, Chaco Canyon, New Mexico, Vol II: Architecture and Stratigraphy.* Publications in Archaeology 18F. National Park Service, Santa Fe.

Windes, Thomas C. and Rachel Anderson

1998   Sunrise, Sunset: Sedentism and Mobility in the Chaco East Community. Paper presented at the 63rd Annual Meeting, Society for American Archaeology, Seattle.

Windes, Thomas C. and Dabney Ford

1996   The Chaco Wood Project: The Chronometric Reappraisal of Pueblo Bonito. *American Antiquity* 61(2):295–310.

Wiseman, Regge N. and J. Andrew Darling

1986   The Bronze Trail Site Group: More Evidence for a Cerrillos-Chaco Turquoise Connection. In *By Hands Unknown: Papers on Rock Art and Archaeology*, edited by Anne Poore, pp. 115–143. Papers of the Archaeological Society of New Mexico 12. Ancient City Press, Santa Fe.

Woodson, Michael Kyle

1995   The Goat Hill Site: A Western Anasazi Pueblo in the Safford Valley of Southeastern Arizona. M.A. Thesis, University of Texas at Austin.

Woosley, Anne I. and John C. Ravesloot, editors

1993   *Culture and Contact: Charles C. Di Peso's Gran Chichmeca.* Amerind Foundation New World Studies Series 2. University of New Mexico Press, Albuquerque.

Young, M. Jane

1987   Issues in the Archaeoastronomical Endeavor in the American Southwest. In *Astronomy and Ceremony in the Prehistoric Southwest*, edited by John B. Carlson and W. James Judge, pp. 219–232. Papers of the Maxwell Museum of Anthropology 2. Maxwell Museum of Anthropology, University of New Mexico, Albuquerque.

Zeilik, Michael

1987   Anticipation in Ceremony: The Readiness is All. In *Astronomy and Ceremony in the Prehistoric Southwest*, edited by John B. Carlson and W. James Judge, pp. 25–41. Papers of the Maxwell Museum of Anthropology 2. Maxwell Museum of Anthropology, University of New Mexico, Albuquerque.

Zuidema, R. Tom

1982   Bureaucracy and Systematic Knowledge in Andean Civilization. In *The Inca and Aztec States 1400–1800: Anthropology and History*, edited by George A. Collier, Renato I. Rosaldo, and John D. Wirth, pp. 419–458. Academic Press, New York.

Author Index

The following typographical conventions used in this index are: *f* identifies a figure; *n* identifies a note.

SUBJECT INDEX

The following typographical conventions used in this index are: *f* identifies a figure; *n* identifies a note.

ABOUT THE AUTHOR

STEPHEN H. LEKSON received his B.A. from Case Western Reserve University and Ph.D. in Anthropology from the University of New Mexico in 1988. His principal mentors were David Brose at the former and Lewis Binford at the latter, although both were happily unaware of their roles. James Fitting, Linda Cordell, George Gumerman, Alden Hayes, and Jim Judge were highly influential in his training. Lekson's obstinate independence renders them all blameless.

His archaeological field work focuses on the 9th- to 15th-century Southwest: Mimbres, Chaco, Mesa Verde, Tucson Basin Hohokam, Salado, Casas Grandes, and Rio Grande Abajo. This research has been reported in a dozen books and monographs, sixty book chapters and articles, several popular books and museum exhibits.

Lekson was born at West Point, New York, to a military family. Movement was constant; his formative years were spent, one or two years at a time, in Austria, Italy, Korea and various southeastern United States. He still considers himself Southern, sans prejudices (and now sadly sans "y'all"). His father, John S. Lekson, retired as a Major General; his mother, Gladys M. (Pecsok) Lekson had an equally successful career in military society; his brother, J. Michael Lekson, is a diplomat. Lekson is married to Catherine M. Cameron, a Southwestern archaeologist of impeccable reputation—not responsible for the intellectual foibles and debits of her husband. They live in Boulder and work at the University of Colorado. Cameron drinks herbal tea; Lekson does not.